A Lawyer's Guide to Estate Planning

FUNDAMENTALS FOR THE LEGAL PRACTITIONER

Fourth Edition

L. RUSH HUNT
LARA RAE HUNT

Cover design by Jill Tedhams/ABA Design

The materials contained herein represent the opinions of the authors and/or the editors, and should not be construed to be the views or opinions of the law firms or companies with whom such persons are in partnership with, associated with, or employed by, nor of the American Bar Association or the Solo, Small Firm and General Practice Division, unless adopted pursuant to the bylaws of the Association.

Nothing contained in this book is to be considered as the rendering of legal advice for specific cases, and readers are responsible for obtaining such advice from their own legal counsel. This book is intended for educational and informational purposes only.

© 2018 American Bar Association. All rights reserved.

No part of this publication may be reproduced, stored in a retrieval system, or transmitted in any form or by any means, electronic, mechanical, photocopying, recording, or otherwise, without the prior written permission of the publisher. For permission contact the ABA Copyrights & Contracts Department, copyright@americanbar.org, or complete the online form at http://www.americanbar.org/utility/reprint.html.

Printed in the United States of America.

26 25 24   7 6

Library of Congress Cataloging-in-Publication Data

Names: Hunt, L. Rush., author. | Hunt, Lara Rae, 1970- author. | American Bar
   Association. Solo, Small Firm and General Practice Division, sponsoring
   body.
Title: A Lawyer's guide to estate planning : fundamentals for the legal
   practitioner / L. Rush Hunt, Lara Rae Hunt.
Description: [4] | Chicago, Illinois : American Bar Association, [2018] |
   Includes bibliographical references and index.
Identifiers: LCCN 2018001806 (print) | LCCN 2018003097 (ebook) | ISBN
   9781641050296 (ebook) | ISBN 9781641050289 (alk. paper) | ISBN 9781641050296
   (e-ISBN)
Subjects: LCSH: Estate planning—United States.
Classification: LCC KF750 (ebook) | LCC KF750 .H85 2018 (print) | DDC
   346.7305/2—dc23
LC record available at https://lccn.loc.gov/2018001806

ISBN: 978-1-64105-028-9
e-ISBN: 978-1-64105-029-6

Discounts are available for books ordered in bulk. Special consideration is given to state bars, CLE programs, and other bar-related organizations. Inquire at Book Publishing, ABA Publishing, American Bar Association, 321 N. Clark Street, Chicago, Illinois 60654-7598.

www.shopABA.org

Dedication

Rush would like to dedicate this book to:
My parents, L.R. and Medibeth
for their never-ending confidence and encouragement.

Lara would like to dedicate this book to:
My wonderful father for your unending love, support, and generosity.
I am so thankful for the opportunity to come home and work with you again.

Contents

Preface xiii
About the Authors xv
Acknowledgments xvii

1 Beginning the Process 1

1.1 Initial Client Contact 1
1.2 Initial Conference 2
    1.21 Client's Side of the Desk 2
    1.22 Lawyer's Side of the Desk 3
1.3 Formulating the Estate Plan 5

Appendix A
  Family Questionnaire 6
  Asset Questionnaire 11

Appendix B
  Engagement Letter for Individual 15
  Engagement Letter for Couple 17
  Additional Terms and Conditions of Client Employment 20
  Privacy Notice 22

Appendix C
  Estate Tax Worksheet 23

Appendix D
  Dispositive Checklist 24

Appendix E
  Letter of Instructions 28

2 Estate Tax Overview 29

2.1 Introduction 29
2.2 Gross Estate 30
    2.21 Gifts 30
    2.22 Transfers with Control Retained by Decedent 32
    2.23 Annuities and Retirement Benefits 33

    2.24 Joint Interests   35
    2.25 Powers of Appointment   36
    2.26 Life Insurance   37
 2.3 Adjusted Gross Estate   38
 2.4 Taxable Estate   39
 2.5 Net Estate Tax   40
 2.6 Filing and Payment   41
Appendix A
 Unified Transfer Tax Rate Schedule   44

3 Gift Tax Overview   45

 3.1 Background   46
    3.11 Gift Tax Overview   46
    3.12 Advantages of Gift Giving   46
    3.13 General Requirements   47
    3.14 Special Considerations   48
       3.141 Gifts of Services   48
       3.142 Disclaimers   49
       3.143 Assignment of Income   49
       3.144 Delivery of the Gift   49
 3.2 Annual Exclusion and Split Gifts   50
    3.21 Annual Exclusion   50
    3.22 Gift-Splitting   51
 3.3 Income Tax Basis in Gift Property   51
 3.4 Transfers Not Subject to Gift Tax   53
    3.41 Marital Deduction   53
    3.42 Charitable Deduction   54
    3.43 Tuition and Medical Expenses   54
 3.5 Gifts for the Benefit of Children   54
 3.6 Special Situations   56
    3.61 Net Gifts   56
    3.62 Gift Subject to an Indebtedness   58
Appendix A
 2018 Individual Income Tax Rate Schedules   60

APPENDIX B
2018 Income Tax Rate Schedules for Use by Estate and Nongrantor Trusts   62

4 Generation-Skipping Transfer Tax   63

4.1 Background   63
4.2 Overview   64
    4.21 Skip Person   64
    4.22 Transferor   64
    4.23 Taxable Distribution   65
    4.24 Taxable Termination   66
    4.25 Direct Skip   66
4.3 Additional Cautions   67
    4.31 Pot Trusts   67
    4.32 Tax Apportionment Clauses   67
    4.33 Disclaimer   69
    4.34 Double Taxation   69
    4.35 Portability   69

5 Trusts and Their Uses   73

5.1 Background   73
5.2 Types of Trusts   74
    5.21 A-B Trust   74
    5.22 QTIP Trust   76
    5.23 Premarital Trust   77
    5.24 Charitable Remainder Trusts   77
    5.25 Special Needs Trust   78
    5.26 Income-Only Trust   79
    5.27 Crummey Trust   80
    5.28 Disclaimer Trust   80
    5.29 Generation-Skipping Trust   81
        5.210 Living Trust   81
        5.211 Minor's or 2503(c) Trust   82
        5.212 Pot Trust   82
        5.213 Spendthrift Trust   83
        5.214 Standby Trust   84

6 Powers of Appointment 85

6.1 Background 85
6.2 Estate and Gift Tax Provisions 87
6.3 Effective Uses of Powers 88
    6.31 Limited Power of Appointment 88
    6.32 Power Limited to Ascertainable Standard 89
    6.33 5 or 5 Power 90
6.4 Interpretation and Drafting Considerations 91
    6.41 Miscellaneous Forms 92

7 Marital Deduction Planning 95

7.1 Background 95
7.2 Basic Requirements 96
    7.21 Survived by a Spouse 97
    7.22 Property Must Pass to Survivor 98
    7.23 Includable in Gross Estate 99
    7.24 Terminable Interest Rule 99
        7.241 General Requirements 99
        7.242 Exceptions 101
7.3 Marital Deduction and Portability 102

8 Life Insurance Planning 105

8.1 Basic Types of Life Insurance 105
    8.11 Term Life Insurance 106
    8.12 Whole Life Insurance 106
    8.13 Universal Life Insurance 106
    8.14 Variable Life Insurance 107
8.2 Taxation of Life Insurance Benefits 108
    8.21 Benefits Received during Lifetime 108
    8.22 Benefits Received following Death 108
8.3 Special Types of Life Insurance 110
    8.31 Split-Dollar Insurance 110
    8.32 Key-Man Insurance 110
    8.33 Group Life Insurance 111

8.4 Life Insurance Trusts   111
    8.41 Revocable Life Insurance Trusts   111
    8.42 Irrevocable Life Insurance Trusts   113

Appendix A
Uniform Premiums for $1,000 of Group Term Life Insurance Protection   117

9 Charitable Giving   119

9.1 Background   119
9.2 Estate and Gift Tax Requirements   120
9.3 Income Tax Requirements   120
    9.31 Cash and Ordinary Income Property   120
    9.32 Long-Term Capital Gain Property   121
    9.33 Tangible Personal Property   121
    9.34 Future-Interest Property   122
    9.35 Tax-Exempt Organizations   122
9.4 Special Types of Charitable Gifts   123
    9.41 Remainder Interest in Farm or Personal Residence   123
    9.42 Qualified Conservation Contributions   123
    9.43 Gift Annuities   124
    9.44 Gift of Undivided Interest   125
    9.45 Pooled Income Fund   125
9.5 Charitable Remainder Trusts   125
9.6 Charitable Lead Trust   129
9.7 IRA Distribution   130

10 Business Buy-Sell Agreements   133

10.1 Background   133
10.2 Redemption and Cross-Purchase Agreements   134
    10.21 General Considerations   134
    10.22 Establishing the Sales Price   135
10.3 Specific Considerations   136
    10.31 Insurance   136
    10.32 Income Tax Basis   139
    10.33 Dividend Problems with Redemption Agreements   140

                10.331 General Considerations 140
                10.332 Attribution Rules 140
        10.34 AMT Problems with Redemption Agreements 142
        10.35 Partnerships 142

11 Retirement Plans and Benefits 145

11.1 Background 146
11.2 Types of Retirement Plans 146
      11.21 Pension Plans 146
      11.22 Profit-Sharing Plans 147
      11.23 Money-Purchase Plans 148
      11.24 401(k) Plans 148
            11.241 Simple 401(k) Plan 149
      11.25 Self-Employed Persons 149
      11.26 SEP 150
      11.27 IRA 150
            11.271 Roth IRA 151
            11.272 SIMPLE IRA 151
11.3 Participation, Vesting, and Nondiscrimination 152
11.4 Top-Heavy Plans 153
11.5 Social Security Integration 153
11.6 Penalty Taxes 154
      11.61 Premature Distributions 154
      11.62 Minimum Distributions 154
11.7 Distributions 155
      11.71 Distributions during Lifetime 155
      11.72 Distributions at Death 156

12 Valuation of Assets 159

12.1 Background 159
12.2 Real Estate 160
      12.21 Cost Method 160
      12.22 Market Data Approach 160
      12.23 Income Approach 161
      12.24 Special-Use Valuation 161

12.3 Tangible Personal Property 163
12.4 Intangible Personal Property 163
    12.41 Valuation of Closely Held Stock 164
        12.411 Book-Value Approach 165
        12.412 Capitalization-of-Income Approach 166
        12.413 Discounts 167
        12.414 Buy-Sell Agreements 167

13 Postmortem Estate Planning 169

13.1 Background 169
13.2 Qualified Disclaimers 170
13.3 Will and Estate Litigation 171
13.4 Considerations Affecting the Estate Taxes 172
    13.41 Alternate Valuation Date 172
    13.42 Section 303 Stock Redemption 173
    13.43 Special-Use Valuation 174
    13.44 Deferred Payment of Estate Taxes 175
13.5 Considerations Affecting Income Taxes 177
    13.51 Medical Expenses 177
    13.52 Series E and EE U.S. Savings Bonds 177
    13.53 Selection of Estate's Tax Year 178
    13.54 Filing Joint Returns 178
    13.55 Administrative Expenses 179
    13.56 Termination of the Estate 179
    13.57 Waiver of Executor's Fee 180

14 Choosing Executors and Trustees 183

14.1 Choosing an Executor 183
14.2 Choosing a Trustee 187
14.3 Trustee Removal 188
14.4 Individual Trustees 190
    14.41 Powers over Principal 190
    14.42 Power to Discharge Trustee's Obligation of Support 191
    14.43 Power to Sprinkle Income 192
    14.44 Life Insurance on Trustee's Life 192

15 Sample Forms 195

- **15.1** Corporate Redemption Agreement 195
- **15.2** Stockholder Cross-Purchase Agreement 199
- **15.3** A-B Trust Planning Approach: Equalization of Estate between Husband and Wife 204
- **15.4** Marital Deduction Planning with Disclaimer Trust 224
- **15.5** Minor's or Educational Trust 228
- **15.6** Irrevocable Life Insurance Trust 233
- **15.7** Will, Trust, and Premarital Agreement 242
- **15.8** Special Needs Trust for Handicapped Child 254
- **15.9** Income-Only Trust 259
- **15.10** Charitable Remainder Trusts 264
- **15.11** Standby Trust 264
- **15.12** Living Trust 269

Index 273

Preface

This text is intended to provide a helpful introduction to the basics of estate planning. The text is written with an eye toward the needs of general practitioners and those who are seeking to develop a specialty in the estate-planning field. For this reason, the text is written in a user-friendly manner that provides basic text treatment of the subject along with cautions, examples, and planning pointers clearly denoted throughout the text. The cautions point out problem areas that must be considered to avoid an unwanted tax or other problem. The examples supplement the text and illustrate the point being discussed. The planning pointers show how to use the tax laws to benefit the tax and other planning needs of one's clients.

The text includes numerous will and trust forms, most of which are reproduced in the final chapter. Generally, the forms are written in the first person. These forms are annotated to make it clear why particular provisions are included in the will or trust. There are also cross-references between the text and the forms to aid readers. Readers are cautioned that these forms are based on the authors' experience with the state law in their home state of Kentucky. Even though much of estate planning deals with federal tax law, readers should be familiar with their own state laws before they make use of these forms. Kentucky is a common-law state; consequently, readers from community property states have to make appropriate modifications because of the uniqueness of will and trust law in those states. Also, the text makes reference to IRS forms. These forms are not reproduced; however, they are readily available and may be obtained at the IRS web site at www.irs.gov.

The intent of this book is to make the estate-planning area of law more accessible to nonspecialists. To that end, the authors would appreciate any comments by users of this text regarding areas that need better clarification and areas that should be added to the text. In this way, the quality of subsequent editions can be enhanced.

The fourth edition includes the estate and gift tax law changes made by the Tax Cuts and Jobs Act of 2017. The act simply doubles the estate and gift tax exempt amount; however, these provisions expire December 31, 2025. The law then reverts to the $5,000,000 ($10,000,000 with portability) inflation adjusted exempt amount. This complicates planning.

The authors' best hunch is that the law will be allowed to expire and planning will revert to the $5,000,000 ($10,000,000 with portability) inflation adjusted exempt amount. If so, wealthier clients should make larger gifts between now and 2025. We expect generation-skipping transfers and trusts for your wealthier clients will become an important planning tool. Otherwise, planning will largely be the same. Cautious practice will be to plan based on the $5,000,000 inflation adjusted exempt amount while ensuring flexibility in the estate plan to utilize the larger exempt amount permitted between 2018 and 2025.

About the Authors

L. Rush Hunt is currently engaged in the private practice of law in Madisonville, Kentucky, where he devotes much of his time to areas of estate and trust law. Mr. Hunt brings more than thirty years of experience in estate planning and related areas of the law to the writing of this text, including not only his legal experience but also his prior experience as a certified financial planner and as a vice-president of trust services for Citizens Bank of Kentucky, where he supervised trust administration and investments.

Mr. Hunt earned his B.S. in accounting from Murray State University, his J.D. from the University of Louisville School of Law, and his Ph.D. in public law at Southern Illinois University.

A frequent lecturer at continuing legal education seminars for both lawyers and accountants, Mr. Hunt is a member of the General Practice, Solo and Small Firm Division and Senior Lawyers Division of the American Bar Association and the Kentucky Bar Association.

Lara R. Hunt practices law with her father, L. Rush Hunt, in Madisonville, Kentucky, where she practices mainly in the areas of estate, trust, and tax law. Ms. Hunt earned her B.A. *cum laude* from Western Kentucky University and her J.D. *cum laude* from the University of Kentucky College of Law. Ms. Hunt is a former staff member of the *Kentucky Law Journal*. She is a member of the Kentucky and Indiana Bars and is active in several associations, including the American, Kentucky, and Indiana bar associations.

Acknowledgments

As was written in the first edition of this book, we deeply appreciate the confidence of the American Bar Association in publishing this book. Also, we appreciate the readers' interest in the prior editions being sufficient to merit an updated fourth edition. The encouragement and guidance of ABA Publishing is most gratifying, as is the skilled work of the editors. The professionalism and friendliness of ABA Publishing speaks well for both them individually and the ABA.

We also appreciate the willingness of the publisher of our first book to reprint in this book some of the same materials. In keeping with their request, we gratefully acknowledge that portions of this book are based on Baldwin's *Kentucky Wills and Trusts* and used with the permission of the publisher and copyright owner, previously Banks-Baldwin Law Publishing, Cleveland, Ohio, which is now currently owned by Thomson Reuters.

Obviously, the shortcomings of this book are our own fault. We welcome the criticism, inquiries, and suggestions of our colleagues, which can only serve to assure that the next edition goes even further in "demystifying" estate planning law and practice.

L. Rush Hunt
Lara Rae Hunt

 Chapter 1

Beginning the Process

1.1 Initial Client Contact
1.2 Initial Conference
    1.21 Client's Side of the Desk
    1.22 Lawyer's Side of the Desk
1.3 Formulating the Estate Plan
Appendix A   Family Questionnaire
                   Asset Questionnaire
Appendix B   Engagement Letter for Individual
                   Engagement Letter for Couple
                   Additional Terms and Conditions of Client Employment
                   Privacy Notice
Appendix C   Estate Tax Worksheet
Appendix D   Dispositive Checklist
Appendix E   Letter of Instructions

1.1 Initial Client Contact

The initial contact with the client usually begins with a telephone call. It may be received by the lawyer or the secretary. In either event, the client typically asks if anything should be brought to the first conference.

    Many lawyers prefer to keep the process as simple as possible for their clients and encourage the clients simply to come to the initial meeting and not be concerned with collecting any data in advance of the meeting. Indeed, many clients have procrastinated for years in even making the telephone call to set an appointment. Requiring them to collect a large amount of personal and financial data may delay them further. If the client has not known the lawyer previously and does not understand the confidential nature of the relationship, the client may be concerned about the lawyer's detailed interest in personal and financial affairs. Nonetheless, some initial data are essential.

Ideally, the lawyer should receive the initial telephone call from the client. The lawyer can then explain the estate-planning process in general terms, explain the need for thoroughness, and advise the client that a brief questionnaire will be mailed to the client, which the client needs to complete and bring to the first conference. If the secretary has made the appointment, the lawyer may want to forgo efficiency, telephone the client, and provide this explanation. Then a letter [email] should be mailed to the client, confirming the appointment and enclosing the questionnaire. The client should be asked to bring all deeds and other documents of title, life insurance policies, and retirement plan information, if possible.

Experience teaches that most clients really do not understand the differences in ownership of property. Even if they do, many times they will be incorrect in their recollection of how the title is held. Ideally, life insurance and retirement plan beneficiary designations will also be brought to the conference for review. It is the responsibility of the lawyer, not the client, to inquire as to title ownership and current status of beneficiary designations.

Lawyers seldom think in terms of marketing their services; however, they are in a customer service business. The service they provide will be as important to the client as the product. Certainly, the client rightly expects the documents to be properly drafted, but it is the manner in which the lawyer handles the entire estate-planning process that results in a satisfied client and future referrals of business. Therefore, the initial personal telephone call, followed by a personal letter confirming the appointment, enclosing the questionnaire, and explaining the estate-planning process is very important. To avoid overwhelming the client, the questionnaire should be brief. The details can be obtained later, during and following the first conference. A sample client questionnaire is included in Appendix A to this chapter.

1.2 Initial Conference

1.21 Client's Side of the Desk

The initial conference is another day at work for the lawyer, but it is a very important day for the client. Clients approach the estate-planning process quite differently. Some are very distrustful of the lawyer and do not want to divulge information. Clients simply want the lawyer to write the will as they instruct but using the basic legalese of the profession. Most clients are apprehensive about the costs of legal services yet are uncomfortable about bringing up the subject. This concern should be addressed by the lawyer early in the initial conference. The thought and discussion of one's own death seriously disturbs many clients, making the entire conference uncomfortable for them. Be sensitive.

There may be secrets that one spouse does not want divulged to the other spouse; thus, the lawyer's questions may be evaded. Also, there may be unexpressed concerns over the future stability of the couple's marriage. The lawyer who senses marital problems may wish to decline the representation or undertake to represent only one of the spouses. This fact should be made clear to the unrepresented spouse. If a lawyer is representing only one spouse, this fact should be noted in the lawyer's own file and be confirmed by a letter to the unrepresented spouse.

If the representation is a joint one of both spouses (which is the usual situation), then explain that this means anything disclosed by one spouse must be shared with the other spouse. No secrets! Letters of engagement are wise, as this will avoid a future ethics complaint if problems develop between the spouses that affect their estate plan. Sample engagement letters are shown in Appendix B.

Many clients have none of these concerns and are eager for the lawyer to lead them through the estate-planning process. Irrespective of how clients approach the first conference, they have a level of confidence in their choice of a lawyer. They have definite needs and are looking to the lawyer to guide them through the estate-planning process. It is the lawyer's function to accept clients' apprehensions as understandable and to proceed with both sensitivity and professionalism.

1.22 Lawyer's Side of the Desk

The lawyer should use the initial conference for several purposes. First, basic data gathering is needed to supplement the information brought by the client to the conference. Obviously, the dispositive intent of the client must be determined. This often involves a great deal more discussion than just asking, "Whom do you want to receive your estate?" How will the client's and the surviving spouse's financial needs be met in the event of disability? How is the client going to protect the estate for the children if the surviving spouse remarries? Are there special needs of the client's children to be considered? Does a child have a handicap? Are the children old enough to receive an inheritance outright? Will a child's spouse influence squandering of the inheritance? Should the children inherit in trust for life to protect their inheritance from a possible future creditor claim or a possible divorce? Can the child act as his or her own trustee? Although determining the dispositive intent of clients is not difficult, lawyers will find that when more time is devoted to this process, a more complete estate plan will result. On adopting a more thorough approach, the lawyer will begin to recognize the inadequacy of the quick-interview, simple-will approach.

The lawyer also needs to assess the client's general mental capacity to execute a will, as well as discerning any possible influence being placed on the client by others. If the will is challenged at a later date, the lawyer will be a prime witness. That can be an uncomfortable experience if you have not assessed these two concerns. Lawyers know from their law school days that the requirements for executing a valid will are minimal. About all that is required in most states is for the testators to have a general understanding of what they own, who their beneficiaries are, and to have formed a general plan for passing their estate on to those beneficiaries. When in doubt, cautious practice dictates having the client examined by a physician and retaining a written letter from the physician in your files. Some lawyers prefer to videotape or otherwise record the signing of a will in order to better document the testator signing the will; this approach provides the lawyer the opportunity to ask questions as well as to cover the formalities for execution of a valid will.

When these options are not available, the lawyer should consider asking a few pertinent questions to determine competency. A helpful resource is to utilize some or all of the questions found in the Mini-Mental State Examination (MMSE), which is a short test used by mental health professionals to assess cognitive impairment. That test is easy to use and can be found by searching online for "MMSE form."

Determining undue influence is more difficult. Obvious red flags include the prime beneficiary of the estate being the person who brought the client to your office, significant changes being made late in life that favor a person who has the closest daily contact with the client, or a significant change in the estate distribution from prior wills. When undue influence is suspected, but the client is insistent on making the change, the lawyer is faced with a difficult dilemma. Wise practice will be to obtain an ethics opinion from your state bar association before proceeding. Absent that option, many cautious lawyers would refuse the representation. A better option if the lawyer is not certain about undue influence is to question the client while having the interview videotaped or otherwise recorded as part of video recording of the execution of the will. In that way the lawyer creates a record that can be viewed by a court at the appropriate time.

The initial conference also offers an educational opportunity. In discussing the client's dispositive intent, the lawyer should explain the fundamentals of a will and contrast this with intestacy. Many clients are not sure they need a will. The explanation of this area of the law is helpful to the client. Explaining the fundamentals of wills is not only a mark of good professionalism but also provides a good marketing opportunity for the lawyer's services. Clients who are well satisfied with the service provided will be quick to refer other business to their own lawyer.

The lawyer should take time to discuss the probate process with the client. Clients need to understand how a will and trust fit in with the settlement of their estates. There is considerable misunderstanding over the probate process. Many people simply start with an impression in their minds that probate is "bad," terribly complicated, and expensive. The lawyer needs to demystify the probate process. The client should leave the office with a better understanding of the probate process and its costs. Clients should also be told that their executor will normally need to hire a lawyer to perform the legal work incident to the probate process. The lawyer's availability to perform that service is, perhaps, understood; however, the client should be assured of the lawyer's availability if the executor chooses to hire him or her.

1.3 Formulating the Estate Plan

Following the initial conference, collection of the necessary data, and any other required client conferences, the lawyer is ready to formulate the estate plan. Fortunately, creating an estate plan for most clients is no longer complicated by estate tax considerations. Yet, for larger estates, the lawyer must still take into account the amount of federal and state estate taxes that will be owed by the estate. The available tax savings options must be considered. The question of estate liquidity must be considered, as must the apportionment of the death tax liability among the estate beneficiaries. Consequently, the formulation of the estate plan requires the lawyer to be familiar with the various tax and nontax tools needed to implement an estate plan. These are discussed throughout this text. A worksheet for computing the federal estate tax liability appears in Appendix C. The state death tax should also be computed; no worksheet is provided, however, because state death tax structures vary from state to state.

After the lawyer has determined the death tax liability and formulated a general overall estate plan, another client conference is necessary to consider various dispositive provisions. The checklist that appears in Appendix D should be helpful. Following the client conference, the lawyer should be ready to draft the necessary wills and trusts. After the initial drafts of the documents are reviewed by the client and any revisions are made, the final drafts of the wills and trusts can be executed.

With the estate plan concluded and all documents executed, the lawyer will bill for any services that have not been prepaid. The lawyer should specify in the billing the amount of service that is for will and trust drafting and the amount that is for tax advice. Will and trust drafting is a nondeductible personal expense, but the portion of the billing that represents tax advice can be taken as an itemized deduction. For the client to be entitled to the income tax deduction, the lawyer's billing should separate the services.[1] A simpler approach is to submit two billings, one for the nontax services and the other for the tax services. No effort should be made to improperly apportion the billing between the tax and nontax services. After all, the client may assume that the lawyer who lacks integrity in apportioning the billing for tax purposes may also lack integrity in other areas of professional conduct. That is not the type of public relations a lawyer needs or wants. As a final consideration, the lawyer may wish to include with the billing a letter explaining various concluding matters, such as when the will should be reviewed. See Appendix E for an example of such a letter.

Note

1. Bagley v. Commissioner, 8 T.C. 130 (1947); Merians v. Commissioner, 60 T.C. 187 (1973); I.R.C. § 212.

Family Questionnaire

1. CLIENT FACTS

a. Full name

b. Name(s) commonly used

c. Social Security no.

d. Home address

e. Primary telephone

f. Secondary (cell) telephone

g. E-mail address

h. Occupation

i. Work address

j. Birthdate

k. Birthplace

l. Period of residence [state]

▶ **Additional Information (Client)**

a. Do you have any physical or mental health conditions? Yes / No
   If yes, please explain:

b. In what state do you vote, have your driver's license, have your car registered, own real estate, and file state income taxes? _____

c. Have you ever lived in a community property state (AZ, CA, ID, LA, NV, NM, TX, WA, WI)? Yes / No _____ If yes, please list: _____

d. Do you have a prenuptial or postnuptial agreement? Yes / No
   If so, please provide a copy of that agreement with this questionnaire.

e. Do you have a divorce decree affecting any of your property rights or imposing a current legal obligation to support a former spouse or child? Yes / No
   If so, please provide a copy of that divorce decree, property settlement agreement and any related court documents.

f. Are you a U.S. citizen? Yes / No
   If not, of what country are you a citizen? _____

2. SPOUSE/PARTNER FACTS

a. Full name	
b. Name(s) commonly used	
c. Social Security no.	
d. Home address	
e. Primary telephone	
f. Secondary (cell) telephone	
g. E-mail address	
h. Occupation	
i. Work address	
j. Birthdate	
k. Birthplace	
l. Period of residence [state]	

Additional Information (Spouse)
a. Do you have any physical or mental health conditions? Yes / No
   If yes, please explain:

b. In what state do you vote, have your driver's license, have your car registered, own real estate, and file state income taxes? _____
c. Have you ever lived in a community property state (AZ, CA, ID, LA, NV, NM, TX, WA, WI)?
   Yes / No _____ If yes, please list: _____
d. Do you have a prenuptial or postnuptial agreement? Yes / No
   If so, please provide a copy of that agreement with this questionnaire.
e. Do you have a divorce decree affecting any of your property rights or imposing a current legal obligation to support a former spouse or child? Yes / No
   If so, please provide a copy of that divorce decree, property settlement agreement and any related court documents.
f. Are you a U.S. citizen? Yes / No
   If not, of what country are you a citizen? _____

3. CHILDREN AND GRANDCHILDREN

Is there a physical possibility of your having more children? Yes / No
Please list all children, noting any who are illegitimate or non-U.S. citizens.
If a child is not of your present marriage, please note the name of the other parent (your prior spouse/partner).

▶ Child #1 Facts

Deceased? Yes / No		
Adopted? Yes / No		
Handicapped /Poor Health? Yes / No		
Full Name		
Date of Birth		
Address		
Spouse's Name		
Child's Children	Name: _____	Date of Birth: _____
	Name: _____	Date of Birth: _____
	Name: _____	Date of Birth: _____
	Physical possibility of further children? Yes / No	

▶ Child #2 Facts

Deceased? <u>Yes / No</u>	
Adopted? <u>Yes / No</u>	
Handicapped /Poor Health? <u>Yes / No</u>	
Full Name	
Date of Birth	
Address	
Spouse's Name	
Child's Children	Name: _____ Date of Birth: _____
	Name: _____ Date of Birth: _____
	Name: _____ Date of Birth: _____
	Physical possibility of further children? Yes / No

▶ Child #3 Facts

Deceased? Yes / No	
Adopted? Yes / No	
Handicapped /Poor Health? Yes / No	
Full Name	
Date of Birth	
Address	
Spouse's Name	
Child's Children	Name: _____ Date of Birth: _____
	Name: _____ Date of Birth: _____
	Name: _____ Date of Birth: _____
	Physical possibility of further children? Yes / No

▶ Child #4 Facts

Deceased? Yes / No	
Adopted? Yes / No	
Handicapped /Poor Health? Yes / No	
Full Name	
Date of Birth	
Address	
Spouse's Name	
Child's Children	Name: _____ Date of Birth: _____
	Name: _____ Date of Birth: _____
	Name: _____ Date of Birth: _____
	Physical possibility of further children? Yes / No

4. PARENTS

	FATHER	MOTHER
Client's Parents' Names		
Address		
Age		
State of health		
Financially dependent?		
Expected inheritance from parent?		
Spouse's/Partner's parents' name		
Address		
Age		
State of health		
Financially dependent?		
Expected inheritance from parent?		

5. ADVISORS

a. Accountant

b. Stockbroker

c. Financial Advisor

d. Insurance Underwriter

e. Banker

f. Other

g. Other

6. ADDITIONAL INFORMATION

a. Did you bring your existing estate planning documents? If not, please provide copies or originals for my review.

b. Have you or your spouse/partner made any gifts to any other person that require the filing of a federal gift tax return? If so, please provide a copy of all gift tax returns.

c. Are you or your spouse/partner beneficiaries under any trust agreements? If so, please provide a copy of those documents.

d. Are you or your spouse/partner the holders of a power of appointment under any legal document? If so, please provide a copy of that document.

e. Do you or your spouse/partner anticipate receiving an inheritance or a large gift in the future? If so, in what amount, and please explain the details. _____

f. Do you or your spouse/partner own any property in a foreign country? If so, please give full details. _____

g. Are you or your spouse/partner subject to any existing or anticipated litigation; or are you in any business arrangements or occupations in which such liabilities are a possibility? If so, please explain. _____

h. Do you or your spouse/partner have any relatives who are dependent on you for support? If so, please explain.
_____
_____

i. Are you going to be disinheriting any family members? If so, please explain who and the reason for the disinheritance. _____
_____

j. Do any of your children or grandchildren, or other family members who are inheriting from you, have special needs either due to being of young age, mental or physical health problems, substance abuse, marital problems, or other factors that should be taken into account in determining how such person should inherit? If so, please explain. _____
_____
_____
_____
_____

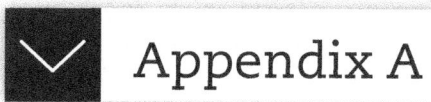

Appendix A

Asset Questionnaire

1. CASH EQUIVALENTS

Do you have any checking accounts and/or any other bank accounts or certificates of deposit?

	Name of Institution, Address, Account Number	Title in Whose Name	Approximate Balance
Checking Accounts	1.		
	2.		
	3.		
	4.		
Certificates of Deposit, Savings Accounts	1.		
	2.		
	3.		
	4.		
		TOTAL:	$

Safe deposit box no.

Location

2. STOCKS

Do you own any stocks?

Number of Shares	Company	Title in Whose Name	Current Market Value
		TOTAL:	$

3. BONDS

Do you own any bonds?

Maturity Value	Description	Title in Whose Name	Current Market Value
		TOTAL:	$

4. MUTUAL FUNDS

Do you own any mutual funds?

Number of Units	Company	Title in Whose Name	Current Market Value
		TOTAL:	$

5. REAL ESTATE (Please Bring Deeds)

Do you own a home or any other real estate? Indicate which is your residence.

Description and Location	Title in Whose Name	Current Market Value	Mortgage Amount
	TOTAL:	$	$

6. BUSINESS

Do you own an interest in any business?

Description of Business	Percentage of Ownership	Name of Co-owners	Market Value
		TOTAL:	$

Is there an existing buy-sell agreement? If so, please provide a copy of that agreement.

7. RETIREMENT BENEFITS

Do you have any IRAs, 401(K)s, or other retirement benefits?

Description	Beneficiary	Approximate Value
	TOTAL:	$

8. LIFE INSURANCE

Do you have any life insurance policies and/or annuities?

Insurance Company	Policy Owner	Insured	First Beneficiary	Second Beneficiary	Death Benefit

9. OTHER—TRUSTS, ANTICIPATED INHERITANCE, ETC.

10. PERSONAL PROPERTY

Do you own any other titled property such as a car, boat, etc?

Description	Title in Whose Name	Approximate Value	Amount of Lien
	TOTAL:	$	$

Do you own any other personal property that is not titled?

Description	Owner of Item	Approximate Value
Home Furnishings		
Jewelry		
Collections		
Other		
Other		
	TOTAL:	$

11. LIABILITIES

Description	Lender/Debtor	Approximate Value
Home mortgage		
Other mortgages		
Other debts		

12. CONTINUATION OF ASSETS FROM 1-11 ABOVE

Type of Asset	Description of Asset	Title in Whose Name	Current Market Value

Appendix B

Engagement Letter for Individual

Dear _____:

I am pleased that you have asked me and [name of firm] to assist you in developing your estate plan. This letter confirms my discussion with you regarding your employment of our firm and describes the basis upon which we will provide legal services to you. Accordingly, I submit for your approval the following provisions governing our employment. If you are in agreement, please sign a copy of this letter in the space provided below.

Scope of Representation. You have asked me to represent you with regard to the planning, preparation, and implementation of appropriate estate planning documents (such as wills, health care power of attorney, durable power of attorney, and revocable trust agreements). You may limit or expand the scope of my representation from time to time, provided that any substantial expansion must be agreed to by me. While our firm would be interested in assisting you in other matters, unless our firm is specifically engaged for some other future matter this letter shall confirm that our representation of you is limited to the foregoing matters and shall end when they are concluded.

Fees. Our fees are based primarily upon the time expended by our attorneys and paralegals on the engagement. Attorneys and paralegals have been assigned hourly rates based upon their experience and level of expertise. The present rates of those attorneys and paralegals likely to work on these matters range from $_____ in the case of the paralegal who will work on this matter, $_____ in the case of the associate who will work on this matter, and $_____ in my case. Our hourly rates are reviewed periodically and may be increased from time to time but will remain at these rates during this representation. We do not consider any billing for our services final until you are satisfied as to both the quality of our services and the amount charged. If you have any questions about a billing, please contact me directly.

Potential Conflicts. Our firm represents other businesses and individuals. This can create situations where work for one client on a matter may preclude us from assisting other clients on unrelated matters. It is at least possible that during the time that we are representing you some of our present or future clients may have disputes or transactions with you. In order to avoid the potential problems that this kind of restriction could have for our practice, we ask you to agree that we may continue to represent (or may undertake in the future to represent) existing or new clients in any matter that is not substantially related to matters in which we have represented you, even if the interests of such clients in those other matters might be adverse to yours. We do not intend, however, for you to waive your right to have our firm maintain confidences or secrets that you transmit to our firm, and we agree not to disclose them to any third party without your consent. We will, of course, take appropriate steps to ensure that such information is kept confidential.

Additional Standard Terms. Our engagement is subject to the policies included in the enclosed memorandum.

Privacy Policy. Enclosed is a copy of the Firm's privacy policy. Please let us know if you have any questions about it.

If these terms of our engagement are acceptable to you, please sign a copy of this letter for my records. You may keep the original letter for your records.

Sincerely,

_____

[name of firm]

_____

[name of attorney]

The foregoing is understood and accepted:

_____

Date: _____

Appendix B

Engagement Letter for Couple

Dear _____,

I am pleased that you have asked me and [name of firm] to assist you in developing your estate plan. This letter confirms my discussion with you regarding your employment of our firm and describes the basis upon which we will provide legal services to you. Accordingly, I submit for your approval the following provisions governing our employment. If you are in agreement, please sign a copy of this letter in the space provided below.

Scope of Representation. You have asked me to represent you with regard to the planning, preparation, execution, and implementation of appropriate estate planning documents (such as wills, health care power of attorney, power of attorney, and revocable trust agreements) for each of you concerning the management of your assets during your joint lives and the life of the survivor and the disposition of those assets to beneficiaries in connection with various contractual rights, such as life insurance policies and retirement plan accounts. You may limit or expand the scope of my representation from time to time, provided that any substantial expansion must be agreed to by me. While our firm would be interested in assisting you in other matters, unless we are specifically engaged for some other future matter this letter will confirm that our representation of you is limited to the foregoing matters and will end when they are concluded.

Joint Representation. Under the ethical rules that govern attorneys, I may represent both of you jointly so long as you are in agreement about your estate plan. It is normally quite beneficial for one attorney to represent both of you in the estate planning process, and my goal in doing so will be to help you implement a mutually agreeable plan for both the present and future. However, in the course of the estate planning process one or both of you sometimes develop differences in their choices of beneficiaries; appointments of trustees, executors, and representatives; and in their overall interests and desires. Occasionally, couples initially agree on a plan and then later change their minds and go in different directions. Consequently, please understand that if I undertake to represent both of you jointly, I cannot take sides or favor one of you over the other, either now or in the future.

During the planning process, I will obtain confidential information from each of you, whether in conference with both of you together or with one of you alone. If I undertake to represent you jointly, please understand that I cannot withhold any such information from either of you even if one of you asks me to do so. The alternative is for me to represent only one of you separately without open sharing of information. The other one of you would then have to either engage separate counsel or choose not to be represented at all. Such separate representation is usually not practical and having one party unrepresented is usually not desirable. If during the course of my joint representation of you a conflict should develop that in my opinion would keep me from adequately representing both of you, or if either of you asks me to take sides against the other, I will have no choice but to withdraw from further joint representation of the two of you and advise each of you to obtain separate counsel. By your signing this letter you are assuring me that you are comfortable with my representing both of you jointly.

Fees. Our fees are based primarily upon the time expended by our attorneys and paralegals on the engagement. Attorneys and paralegals have been assigned hourly rates based upon their experience and level of expertise. The present rates of those attorneys and paralegals likely to work on these matters range from $_____ in the case of the paralegal who will work on this matter, $_____ in the case of the associate who will work on this matter, and $_____ in my case. Our hourly rates are reviewed periodically and may be increased from time to time but will remain at these rates during this representation. We do not consider any billing for our services final until you are satisfied as to both the quality of our services and the amount charged. If you have any questions about a billing, please contact me directly.

Potential Conflicts. Our firm represents other businesses and individuals. This can create situations where work for one client on a matter may preclude us from assisting other clients on unrelated matters. It is at least possible that during the time that we are representing you some of our present or future clients may have disputes or transactions with you. In order to avoid the potential problems that this kind of restriction could have for our practice, we ask you to agree that we may continue to represent (or may undertake in the future to represent) existing or new clients in any matter that is not substantially related to matters in which we have represented you, even if the interests of such clients in those other matters might be adverse to yours. We do not intend, however, for you to waive your right to have our firm maintain confidences or secrets that you transmit to our firm, and we agree not to disclose them to any third party without your consent. We will, of course, take appropriate steps to ensure that such information is kept confidential.

Additional Standard Terms. Our engagement is also subject to the policies included in the enclosed memorandum.

Privacy Policy. Enclosed is a copy of the Firm's privacy policy. Please let us know if you have any questions about it.

If these terms of our engagement are acceptable to you, please sign a copy of this letter for my records. You may keep the original letter for your records.

If you have any questions regarding any of the matters discussed in this letter, please feel free to give me a call.

Sincerely,

_____

[name of firm]

_____

[name of attorney]

The foregoing is understood and accepted:

_____

_____

Date:_____

Appendix B

Additional Terms and Conditions of Client Employment

1. **Expenses.** Expenses we incur on the engagement are charged to the Client's account. Expenses include such items as court costs, charges for computerized research services and the use of our facsimile and photocopying machines, long-distance telephone calls, travel expenses, messenger service charges, overnight mail or delivery charges, extraordinary administrative support, filing fees, fees of court reporters and charges for depositions, fees for expert witnesses, and other expenses we incur on your behalf. Our charges for these services reflect our actual out-of-pocket costs based on usage and in some areas may also include our related administrative expenses.

2. **Monthly Statements.** Unless a different billing period is agreed upon with the Client, the firm will render monthly statements indicating the current status of the account as to both fees and expenses. In some situations we will need to bill at the conclusion of the legal work. The statements are payable upon receipt.

3. **Termination.** The Client has the right to terminate our representation at any time by notifying us of the Client's intention to do so. We will have the same right, subject to an obligation to give the Client reasonable notice to arrange alternative representation. If either party should elect to terminate our relationship, our fees and expenses incurred up to that point will still be due to us. Upon payment to us of any balance due for fees and expenses, we will return to the Client, or to whomever the Client directs, any property or papers of the Client in our possession. We will retain our files pertaining to any matters on which we have been engaged to represent the Client.

4. **Withdrawal.** Under the rules of professional conduct by which we are governed, we may withdraw from our representation of the Client in the event of (for example) nonpayment of our fees and expenses; misrepresentation or failure to disclose material facts concerning the engagement; action taken by the Client contrary to our advice; and in situations involving a conflict of interest with another client. If such a situation occurs, which we do not anticipate, we will promptly give the Client written notice of our intention to withdraw.

5. **Post-Engagement Services.** The Client is engaging our Firm to provide legal services in connection with a specific matter or matters. After completion of that matter or matters, changes may occur in the applicable laws or regulations that could have an impact on the Client's future rights and liabilities. Unless the Client engages us after completion of a matter to provide additional advice on issues arising from the matter, the Firm has no continuing obligation to advise the Client with respect to future legal developments.

6. **Authorization.** By the Client's agreement to these terms of our representation, the Client authorizes us to take all action we deem advisable on the Client's behalf on this matter. Whenever possible, we will discuss with the Client in advance any significant actions we intent to take.

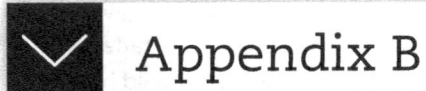

Appendix B

Privacy Notice

[Name of Firm] understands that your privacy is important. We are sure you are aware that your personal information will always be held in the strictest confidence within [Name of Firm]. You are receiving this notice in accordance with applicable federal law because you receive income, estate and gift tax advice, planning, or preparation services from [Name of Firm]. This privacy notice outlines what information we collect and how we use it. In serving you we are committed to maintaining your privacy.

We collect "nonpublic personal information" about you from multiple sources, including:

- Information we receive from you on questionnaires, forms, or other documents supplied by you to us;
- Information about your transactions with us or with others;
- Information we receive from others involved in your financial or tax planning activity, such as your accountant, banker, or stockbroker.

The rules governing lawyers' professional conduct prohibit a lawyer from disclosing information obtained in connection with representing a client, except in limited circumstances. These rules are very stringent. The lawyers and staff at [Name of Firm] take great care to adhere to these rules and have always protected your right to privacy. We do not disclose any nonpublic personal information about you or about former clients, except as agreed by you or as required by law or by the applicable rules governing lawyers' conduct.

We restrict access to nonpublic personal information about you to lawyers and employees at [Name of Firm]. Physical, electronic, and procedural safeguards that comply with rules governing lawyers' professional conduct are maintained to guard your nonpublic personal information.

Appendix C

Estate Tax Worksheet

▶ **Client Name**

	1st Death	2nd Death
Gross estate	$	$
Add: Gifts includable (within 3 years) plus gift tax (IRC Section 2035) (See Chapter 3)	$	$
Gross estate	$	$
Deduct: Expense of administration and probate	$	$
Deduct: Debts, funeral expenses	$	$
Deduct: Charities	$	$
Deduct: Marital deduction	$	$
Deduct: State death tax	$	$
Deduct: Taxable estate		
Add post-1976 taxable gift amounts (not IRC Section 2035)	$	$
Tentative Tax Base	$	$
Tentative Tax	$	$
Less: Gift tax payable on post-1976 gifts	$	$
Estate tax before credits	$	$
Less: Unified credit - current decedent		
Less: Unified credit - deceased spouse's unused exclusion	$	$
Less: Foreign death tax credit		
Less: Tax on prior transfer credit	$	$
Net Estate Tax Payable	$	$

Appendix D

Dispositive Checklist

A. Disposition of property other than residue
   1. Specific gifts
      a. Description
      b. Primary beneficiary
      c. Contingent beneficiary or gift lapses
      d. Survivorship period
   2. Tangible personal property
      a. Primary beneficiary
      b. Contingent beneficiary or gift lapses
      c. Survivorship period
   3. Residence
      a. Primary beneficiary
      b. Contingent beneficiary or gift lapses
      c. Survivorship period
      d. Subject to encumbrances?   Yes / No
      e. Tangible personal property included?   Yes / No
   4. Other real estate
      a. Primary beneficiary
      b. Contingent beneficiary or gift lapses
      c. Survivorship period
      d. Subject to encumbrances?   Yes / No
      e. Tangible personal property included?   Yes / No
   5. Does the client have power of appointment over any property?   Yes / No
   6. Are there any charitable gifts to be given?   Yes / No
B. Disposition of residue
   1. Outright to spouse
   2. Outright to children
   3. Outright to others
   4. Contingent gift
      a. Outright to children
      b. Trust for children
      c. Outright or otherwise to others
   5. Trust for spouse
   6. Trust for children
   7. Trust(s) for relatives or others

C. Tax clause
   1. Taxes only on probate assets paid from residue
   2. Taxes on probate and nonprobate assets paid from residue
   3. Other tax provision
D. Executor
   1. Name and address
      Alternate and alternate's address
   2. Surety waived?   Yes / No
   3. Special provisions
      a. Operate business
      b. Operate farm/ranch
      c. Other
E. Guardian
   1. Name   Address
      Alternate   Address
   2. Surety bond waived?   Yes / No
   3. Special provisions or bequests
F. Concluding provisions
   1. Disinheritance?   Yes / No
      Name(s)
   2. General survivorship: days
      Excludes spouse   Includes spouse
   3. Simultaneous death
   4. Other

II. Trust Provisions
   A. Spouse: A-B Trust
      1. Provisions of Trust A
         a. Marital deduction formula clause
         b. Income payable at least
            annually   more frequently
         c. Principal in trustee's discretion
         d. Principal at spouse's request
         e. Limited principal at spouse's request
         f. General inter vivos power to appoint
         g. Limited inter vivos power to appoint
         h. General testamentary power to appoint
            (Must use either f or h)
      2. QTIP trust in lieu of Trust A?   Yes / No
      3. Provisions of Trust B
         a. Income to spouse mandatory
            at least annually   more frequently
         b. Income to spouse discretionary
         c. Sprinkle income among spouse and children
         d. Principal in trustee's discretion

e. Trust A to be depleted before distribution of principal
   f. $5000 or 5% withdrawal power
   g. Limited inter vivos power to appoint
   h. Limited testamentary power to appoint
B. Children
   1. Division and allocation
      a. Family pot until youngest attains age
      b. Equal shares
         (If pot trust is used, consider potential generation-skipping tax, as explained in Chapter 4 at 4.31.)
   2. Dispositive provisions
      a. Income payable at least   annually   quarterly
      b. Income discretionary
      c. Other
      d. Principal in trustee's discretion
      e. Principal by ascertainable standard
      f. Principal/other
      g. Distribution at ages
      h. Provisions in the event of child's death before full distribution
         1. Child to have general testamentary power to appoint
         2. Child to have limited testamentary power to appoint
            Descendants
            Spouse
         3. To descendants of child
         4. To brothers and sisters
         5. Other
C. Grandchildren
   1. Use generation-skipping tax exclusion   Yes / No
   2. Outright distribution
   3. Separate trusts
D. Trust for relative or other person
   1. Beneficiary
   2. Terms
E. Other provisions
   1. Education to include
      a. Trade school
      b. College
      c. Postgraduate study
   2. Spendthrift clause
   3. Perpetuities savings clause
   4. Other
F. Trustee
   1. Name
   2. Cotrustee

3. Successor trustee
   4. Successor cotrustee
   5. Provisions for removal by spouse and/or current beneficiary
   6. Surety bond waived?   Yes / No
   7. Compensation
   8. Other special provisions regarding trustee
G. No-Contest/Arbitration Clauses   Yes / No

Appendix E

Letter of Instructions

Dear Mr. and Mrs. Doe:

It has been a pleasure working with you in establishing your estate plan. Enclosed is our firm's final billing. You will note that two billings have been included. The billing that specifies tax advice represents legal services that should be deductible as itemized deductions on your personal income tax return. The other billing, which is for the preparation of the wills and trusts, is a nondeductible personal expense.

It is important to review your estate plan periodically. It is surprising how quickly changes occur that may require some modification in your estate plan. This does not always require an amendment to the documents, but it is a wise practice to keep your estate plan current by a periodic review. I suggest we review your estate plan at least every other year.

In addition to periodic reviews there are some circumstances that should cause an immediate review of your estate plan. Examples of these circumstances are: (1) death of a beneficiary; (2) marriage, death, or remarriage; (3) birth or adoption of a child or grandchild; (4) death or change of circumstances of the executor; (5) death or change of circumstances of a child's guardian; (6) a significant change in your assets; (7) a change in your decision as to the distribution of your estate; (8) at your retirement; and (9) on the receipt of assets by gift or inheritance.

Any modifications to your estate plan can be done by an amendment to your trust or a codicil to your will. A codicil is simply an amendment to your will. Normally, any minor modifications will involve very little legal work, and thus the expenses should be modest.

Be sure your executor and successor executor know the location of your will. It is not necessary that they have a copy or know its contents, but they do need to know where the will can be found.

You will no doubt have questions in the future, and I encourage you to contact me to discuss those questions.

Very truly yours,

Chapter 2

Estate Tax Overview

2.1 Introduction
2.2 Gross Estate
   2.21 Gifts
   2.22 Transfers with Control Retained by Decedent
   2.23 Annuities and Retirement Benefits
   2.24 Joint Interests
   2.25 Powers of Appointment
   2.26 Life Insurance
2.3 Adjusted Gross Estate
2.4 Taxable Estate
2.5 Net Estate Tax
2.6 Filing and Payment
Appendix A   Unified Transfer Tax Rate Schedule

2.1 Introduction

[handwritten note: No state ~~death~~ inheritance tax in TN]

The federal estate tax is an excise tax levied on the estate owing to the transfer at death of an individual's property. It differs from an inheritance tax, which many states impose, in that an inheritance tax is levied on each beneficiary's inherited share rather than on the estate itself. The federal gift tax is also an excise tax and is levied on the transfer during an individual's lifetime of that individual's property. Before 1976, the estate tax and the gift tax were separate taxes, with the gift tax rate being 75% of the estate tax rate. The Tax Reform Act of 1976 merged these two taxes into one unified transfer tax. Now, owing to the unification of the two taxes, a transfer during lifetime or at death generally results in the same tax assessment. Yet the two taxes are not quite the same because the estate tax is tax-inclusive and the gift tax is tax-exclusive.

> **Example:** Assuming a taxpayer in the 40% bracket bequeaths $100,000 to a child, the bequest is taxed at $40,000, leaving the child $60,000

(tax-inclusive because the bequest includes the tax). The same lifetime gift also results in a $40,000 tax, but the tax is paid by the donor and not from the gift (tax-exclusive, as the gift excludes the tax). Stated differently, a lifetime gift of $100,000 costs a gift tax of $40,000 for a total cost to the donor of $140,000. To pass a net gift of $100,000 at death, the donor must bequeath $166,667 ($100,000 plus $66,667 estate tax). For an explanation of net gifts that shift the gift tax to the donor, see 3.61.

The federal estate tax can best be understood by considering four concepts: (1) gross estate, (2) adjusted gross estate, (3) taxable estate, and (4) net estate tax. These concepts are discussed in the following sections.

2.2 Gross Estate

The gross estate is the beginning point in determining what property is subject to the federal estate tax.[1] The gross estate includes both probate and nonprobate property and certain gifts made during one's lifetime. Probate property includes all property, real or personal, tangible or intangible, owned at death by the decedent, either in his or her sole name or in which the decedent owned an undivided interest that passes from the decedent to another by will, trust, or intestacy. Included are such properties as real estate, stocks, bonds, mutual funds, bank accounts, cash, vehicles, equipment, and household items. Nonprobate property includes various types of property in which the decedent had an interest at death but that do not pass from the decedent to another by will, trust, or intestacy. Instead, such property passes to another by beneficiary designation or the titling of the property, such as jointly with survivorship, payable-on-death, or transfer-on-death accounts. These types of properties, some gifted properties, and a few other property interests require further explanation.

2.21 Gifts

Before 1982, any gift made by a decedent to another within three years of death was subject to inclusion in the decedent's gross estate. The gift was presumed to have been made in contemplation of death and was taxed as part of the decedent's gross estate. The only exception was when the executor could establish sufficient lifetime motives for making the gift, in which event the presumption was overcome and the gift was not included in the gross estate. When included in the gross estate, the gift was valued at its value at the date of the decedent's death, rather than the earlier date-of-gift value. Thus, for assets that had appreciated in value, this treatment negated all tax advantages of the gift. The Economic Recovery Tax Act of 1981 significantly changed the tax treatment of gifts. Now, with only those few exceptions discussed in the "cautions" in this chapter, a gift is not included in the gross estate, even if made within three years of death.[2]

Although a gift made within three years of death is not included in the gross estate, it is considered in the estate tax computation. Such a gift, and any other lifetime gifts made after 1976, is considered in the estate tax computation owing to the unified nature of the present estate and gift tax law.[3] Regardless of when made, however, the gifts are valued in the estate tax computation at the earlier, date-of-gift value and not at the date-of-death value. Consequently, appreciation between the date of the gift and the date of death is not included in the estate tax computation.

Example: If a decedent made a $30,000 taxable gift in 2000 and died in 2018 when the gift property was valued at $50,000, the decedent's estate would consider the gift at its 2000 gift tax value in computing the current estate tax. Because the gift would have been reported, if any gift tax is paid on it, credit is given on the estate tax return for the previously paid gift tax. The effect of considering the gift in the estate tax computation is merely to push the estate higher up the progressive tax rate schedule owing to the earlier gift.

Planning Pointer 1

Property that is expected to increase in value is an excellent asset for gifting because the appreciation will escape taxation irrespective of when the gift is made. This can be seen in the prior example, in which $20,000 of appreciation escaped estate taxation.

Caution: There are several exceptions that must be recognized. Transfers within three years of death will be treated as part of the gross estate for the limited purpose of determining if the estate qualifies for the following special tax elections:[4]

1. The 35% of adjusted gross estate requirement for a Section 303 stock redemption to pay death taxes and administrative costs without the distribution being taxed to the estate as a capital transaction with the benefit of a stepped-up basis, rather than unfavorable dividend income tax treatment;

2. The 25% and 50% of the adjusted value of the gross estate requirement of the Section 2032A special use valuation for farms and closely held businesses;[5] and

3. The 35% of adjusted gross estate requirement of the Section 6166 extension of time to pay the estate tax for estates consisting of a large interest in a closely held business.[6]

Clarification: These three sections are intended to aid individuals whose estates consist of a large interest in a farm or closely held business. To qualify for each election, the farm or closely held business must represent a certain percentage of the gross estate or the adjusted gross estate. The exceptions are designed to prevent an individual whose estate does not meet these percentage requirements from qualifying by making gifts shortly before death.

Caution: There is another series of exceptions that also must be recognized:[7]

1. Any gift tax paid within three years of death is included in the gross estate.

2. Life insurance proceeds received from a policy owned by the decedent and given by the decedent to another within three years of the decedent's death are included in the gross estate.

3. Property that would be includable in the gross estate under the following sections of the Internal Revenue Code is included in the gross estate when the property rights are relinquished within three years of death: Section 2036—transfers with a retained life estate, Section 2037—transfers taking effect at death, Section 2038—revocable transfers, and Section 2041—powers of appointment.

2.22 Transfers with Control Retained by Decedent

Transfers made by the decedent during his or her lifetime may be included in the gross estate if the decedent retained control of the transferred property. Sections 2036, 2037, and 2038 of the Internal Revenue Code are the sections that cause such transfers to be included in the gross estate. A transfer included in the gross estate owing to the application of one of these sections is usually included at the full value of the property. Reductions in value due to intervening interests, however, may be appropriate, depending on the nature of the particular interest involved.[8] Also, the relinquishment of these retained controls by the decedent within three years of death will still result in the inclusion of the property in the gross estate at the full value of the property on the date of the decedent's death.

Section 2036 includes in the gross estate gratuitous transfers in which the decedent retains, by trust or otherwise, a life interest in the transferred property to:

- receive the income from the property;
- possess or enjoy the property; or
- designate, either alone or with another, who will receive the property.

Typical of these types of transfers are a life estate retained by the grantor in a conveyance of real estate to another or a transfer of property into a trust in which the settlor has retained the right to income for life or the right to designate who among a group of beneficiaries shall receive the income.

Caution: The retention by the decedent of the right to vote, directly or indirectly, shares of stock in a controlled corporation will result in the entire stock interest being included in the decedent's gross estate as a retention of possession or enjoyment of the property.[9] A corporation is considered controlled by the decedent if he or she owns 20% or more of the voting stock in the corporation. In computing this percentage, the attribution rules in Section 318 of the Internal Revenue Code apply.

These rules treat ownership by a spouse, parent, child, grandchild, and certain controlled entities, such as a partnership, estate, trust, or corporation, as if owned by the decedent.

Section 2037 includes in the gross estate gratuitous transfers in which the decedent retains a reversionary interest in the transferred property.[10] The section applies to transfers in which the transferee must survive the transferor-decedent to continue in possession of the property. It also includes any transfer that may revert to the decedent from the transferee during the decedent's lifetime or to his or her estate or that may be subject to a power of disposition by the decedent. For administrative convenience and to avoid overly harsh tax treatment of remote reversionary interests, this section applies only if the value of the reversionary interest immediately before the decedent's death exceeded 5% of the value of the transferred property.

Section 2038 includes in the decedent's gross estate any transfer of property in which the decedent retains, in trust or otherwise, the right to alter, amend, revoke, or terminate the transferee's possession and enjoyment of the property.[11] Thus, a transfer by the decedent into a trust for the benefit of another is included in the gross estate if the decedent retains the right to alter, amend, revoke, or terminate the trust. This is still the result, even though the trust could not revert to the decedent or to his or her estate.

Similarly, a transfer by the decedent into trust for the benefit of another is included in the gross estate if the decedent acted as trustee of the trust and had the right to withhold the distribution of income and principal. Section 2038 is broad in its application because it applies to any power reserved by the decedent that affects the time or manner of enjoyment of transferred property or its income.

> **Caution:** The nuances of these three statutes can be complicated. The point to remember is to avoid establishing deeds, trusts, or other instruments in which the donor retains "strings" over the donated property.

2.23 Annuities and Retirement Benefits

Annuities purchased by the decedent are included in the gross estate under Internal Revenue Code Section 2039. Inclusion occurs if (1) before death the annuity was payable to the decedent, or to the decedent and another, and (2) after death any payment is made to a beneficiary who has survived the decedent. Simply stated, if because of a contractual obligation to the decedent payment is made to a beneficiary who survived the decedent, the payment is included in the gross estate. This includes not only commercial annuities and private annuities but also the various types of qualified employee benefit plans, such as pension plans, profit-sharing plans, 401(k) and 403(b) plans, SEPs, and IRAs.

Frequently, the beneficiary of an annuity has the payment option of receiving a lump sum, in which event the lump-sum payment is included in the gross estate. If instead payment is receivable as a periodic payment, then the present value of the income right of the beneficiary is included in the gross estate of the decedent. This computation is made according to the regularly published Internal Revenue Service (IRS) valuation tables.[12] Interest factors are published monthly by the IRS.

> **Example:** The decedent was receiving a $30,000 per year payment from his retirement plan, which payment was to continue for the benefit of his daughter's lifetime following his death. The daughter is age 60 at the decedent's death; thus, the gross estate must include $479,190 for the value of the retirement annuity (15.9730 annuity factor x $30,000). This computation is based on a 2.4% interest factor. Current Treasury regulations and notices must be consulted in making calculations, because of monthly changes in the interest rate factor.[13]

In those rare situations in which someone other than the decedent and the decedent's employer contributed to the annuity, a proportionate reduction is allowed for those third-party contributions to the purchase of the annuity when valuing the annuity.

> **Example:** If in the preceding example the decedent and his daughter had purchased an annuity paying $30,000 per year for their joint lifetimes, with each paying one-half of the purchase price for the annuity, then the decedent's gross estate would include only $239,595, which represents his proportionate part of the annuity.

Planning Pointer 2

Purely voluntary employer payments to a beneficiary, such as a surviving spouse, that are not made pursuant to a contractual obligation are not subject to this rule. Therefore, such payments are not included in the gross estate and are not subject to the federal estate tax.

 Caution: Before 1983, death benefits under a qualified retirement plan were fully excluded from the estate tax. The exclusion was then reduced to $100,000. Since 1985, such benefits have been fully taxable, except for estates of decedents who were in pay status (retired) on December 31, 1984, and had irrevocably elected before July 19, 1984, the form for paying the remaining benefits. In this limited situation, the first $100,000 of plan proceeds is exempt from the federal estate tax. This exemption is of little benefit because the decedent's election must be irrevocable. Most elections are revocable; however, this fine point is in the law.

2.24 Joint Interests

Joint interests, as that term is defined in Section 2040 of the Internal Revenue Code, refers to property owned jointly with right of survivorship by the decedent and any other person or persons. It also refers to property held by husband and wife as tenants by the entirety in those states that permit such tenancies.

For all individuals other than spouses, the gross estate includes the entire value of all jointly owned property, not merely the decedent's proportionate interest. The full value of the property can be reduced, however, by the actual consideration furnished by the surviving tenant or tenants. If jointly owned property was received by the decedent and other tenants by gift or inheritance, the gross estate includes only the decedent's proportionate part of the gifted or inherited joint property. For example, if the decedent and his two brothers received property as joint tenants by will, inheritance, or gift, the decedent's gross estate includes only one-third of the value of the property.

 Caution: Actual consideration furnished by another joint tenant does not include consideration that was given to the joint tenant by the decedent.[14] For example, tenant A gives money to tenant B and then the two tenants purchase jointly owned property, they cannot then be allowed to treat the purchase as if both had furnished monetary consideration for the property.

Jointly owned property held by spouses as joint tenants with right of survivorship or as tenants by the entirety is treated more simply. Such property is treated as if one-half were owned by each spouse, irrespective of the actual consideration furnished. This simplification has some loss associated with it. Because only one-half of the property is included in the decedent's gross estate, only one-half of the income tax basis in the property receives a stepped-up basis to the date-of-death value of the property. This is particularly unfortunate because in most estates the unlimited marital deduction will preclude any estate tax being owed by the surviving spouse.

⌄ Planning Pointer 3

This planning concept is best understood by illustration. A couple jointly own a $1,000,000 rental property, which has an income tax basis of $100,000. Only $500,000 will be included in the husband's gross estate, even if he furnished the entire consideration for the purchase of the property. The income tax basis in the rental property to the wife following the husband's death will be $550,000 ($500,000 from the husband's estate and $50,000 for her half of the property). If she sells the property for $1,000,000, she must pay income tax on a taxable gain of $450,000, whereas if the entire property had been taxable in her husband's estate, her basis would be increased to $1,000,000 and she would owe no income tax on the subsequent sale of the property. Irrespective of whether the property is partly or fully taxable in the husband's estate, the wife will owe no estate tax on the jointly owned property, because of the unlimited marital deduction. Thus, the apparent advantage of reporting jointly owned property at one-half value is illusory. It is better for the husband to own the property in his sole name and pass it to his wife by will. She then receives a stepped-up basis (in this illustration) of $1,000,000, and income tax savings are possible when the property is later sold.

2.25 Powers of Appointment

The gross estate includes property over which a decedent holds a general power of appointment. Generally, a *power of appointment* is a device through which owners of properties reserve to themselves or to others the power to designate a transferee of a property or the shares or interests a transferee may receive. A *general power of appointment*, as the term is used in estate tax law, refers to a power that may be exercisable in favor of decedents, their estates, their creditors, or the creditors of their estates.[15] The value of the property over which a decedent possesses a general power of appointment is fully includable in the gross estate. This result applies even if the power is never exercised.

> **Caution:** The release of a general power of appointment within three years of the decedent's death will nonetheless result in the property subject to the power being included in the gross estate at the date-of-death value of the property.[16]

> **Example:** A wife's estate passes into a trust for the benefit of her husband and children with the husband named trustee and he being directed to pay income and principal as deemed appropriate in his sole discretion. The husband is also given the right to direct at his death without restriction who receives the trust property and in what percentages. Because each of these powers could be exercised in favor of the husband, his creditors, his estate, or the creditors of his estate, these powers are each general powers of appointment that will cause the property to be includable in the husband's gross estate.[17]

 Planning Pointer 4

A power of appointment that cannot be exercised in favor of the decedent, the decedent's estate, the decedent's creditors, or the creditors of the decedent's estate is not a general power of appointment and is not subject to inclusion in the decedent's gross estate. In the preceding example, if the wife had specified how income and principal were to be distributed and had given her husband only the power to appoint by his will who would receive the trust property at his death, the property would not be included in his gross estate, provided this power was expressly restricted to preclude exercise in favor of the husband, his estate, his creditors, or the creditors of his estate.[18]

Planning Pointer 5

A power of appointment limited to an ascertainable standard of relating to the "health, education, support, or maintenance" of the holder of the power is not a general power of appointment. Therefore, a husband could pass his estate into a trust for his wife's lifetime benefit and name her as trustee with the trust estate passing to their children at her death. If the wife's discretion as trustee in spending income and principal for her own benefit is limited by this standard, the power will not be a general power and will not cause the trust property to be included in her gross estate.

2.26 Life Insurance

The gross estate includes the full value of any life insurance on the decedent's life, the proceeds of which are payable to the decedent's estate or any other beneficiary, provided the decedent possessed at death any incidents of ownership in the life insurance policy.[19]

Incidents of ownership include:

- being the owner of the policy,
- having the right to change beneficiaries,
- having the right to cancel the policy,
- having the right to assign the policy, and
- having the right to borrow against the cash value of the policy or to pledge the policy as collateral.[20]

Caution: The entire proceeds of an insurance policy on the life of the decedent will be includable in the gross estate if the policy and the incidents of ownership were transferred by the decedent to another within three years of his or her death.[21]

 Planning Pointer 6

Insurance is a good asset to give because of its typically low cash value in relation to the proceeds payable at death. The three-year rule precludes so-called deathbed gifts of life insurance, but it is still a good asset to give if done early enough and before large cash values build up in the policy. Term life insurance is a particularly attractive gift because it has no cash value and thus its gift creates no gift tax. The gift tax consequences of giving life insurance with a cash value can be lessened if the decedent borrows the policy's cash value before making the gift. In this manner there is no value in the policy at the time of the gift and, consequently, no gift taxes to be paid.[22]

For example, if a father desires to give to his adult children a $500,000 life insurance policy he owns on his own life that has a $75,000 cash value, a gift of $75,000 has been made to the children. If the father borrows the $75,000 from the policy and then gives the policy, there is no gift. The obvious disadvantage of this approach is that the children will not have the cash value, which could be used in the years ahead to lessen the life insurance premium cost.

Insurance owned by the decedent on the life of another is included in the decedent's gross estate under the general taxing statute Internal Revenue Code Section 2033. The amount included in the decedent's gross estate is the replacement cost of the policy, which approximates the cash value of the policy.[23] Term life insurance provides death protection only and no cash value; therefore, term insurance owned by the decedent on the life of another will result in minimal, if any, value being included in the gross estate.

Caution: A policy owned on the life of another can cause unexpected gift tax consequences. If the owner of a policy on the life of another names a third party as the beneficiary of the policy, a gift tax problem exists because, on the death of the insured, the owner has inadvertently made a gift to the third party in the amount of the insurance proceeds.[24] To avoid this consequence, the owner and beneficiary of the policy should be the same.

2.3 Adjusted Gross Estate

The adjusted gross estate is determined by subtracting several types of estate-related expenses from the gross estate. The only importance of the adjusted gross estate is to calculate the percentage requirements to determine if the estate qualifies for a Section 303 redemption or a Section 6166 extension to pay the estate tax. The adjusted gross estate had greater significance in earlier years when the marital deduction was limited to 50% of the adjusted gross estate. Now that the marital deduction is an unlimited deduction, the adjusted gross estate has significance only for computing entitlement to these two elections.

The permissible deductions include the actual expenses incurred for funeral expenses, costs of administration, debts and unpaid mortgages of the decedent, and losses incurred during estate administration.[25] The deductible funeral expenses include not only the funeral home expenses but also other funeral-related expenses, such as grave markers, transportation, and lot maintenance.[26] *Administrative costs* is a broad category of estate settlement-related costs and includes such expenses as executor, legal, and accounting expenses; appraisal and brokerage fees; and court costs.[27] Since 2005, a tax deduction is permitted for the amount of state death taxes paid rather than for the tax credit, which had traditionally been allowed.

Any debts, including accrued but unpaid taxes, owed by the decedent at the time of death that are enforceable under state law are deductible.[28] Mortgages are likewise deductible, provided the decedent's interest in the underlying property is included in the estate.[29] Losses incurred during the administration of the estate are also deductible expenses to the extent that they are not reimbursed by insurance.[30]

2.4 Taxable Estate

In estates in which the election under Internal Revenue Code Sections 303 and 6166 is not used, the previously discussed deductions are allowed in determining the taxable estate. Two additional deductions also are allowed. The first deduction is allowed for the value of any property passing to public, charitable, and religious organizations.[31] The deduction is permitted for a bequest, devise, or transfer to (1) a federal, state, or local government for public purposes; (2) corporations or fraternal organizations whose exclusive purpose is religious, charitable, scientific, literary, educational, fostering national or international sports competition, or preventing cruelty to children or animals; or (3) qualified veterans organizations. The estate tax deduction is allowed for the fair market value of the property passing to the charity to the extent that such property is included in the gross estate.

A marital deduction is allowed for qualified property passing from the decedent to his or her surviving spouse.[32] The marital deduction, like the charitable deduction, is allowed for the full value of the property passing to the surviving spouse to the extent that such property is included in the gross estate. It is immaterial whether the property passes by the decedent's will, by intestacy, by beneficiary designation on a life insurance policy or retirement plan, by right of survivorship, or in some other manner. The basic requirements for entitlement to the deduction are that:

1. the property must pass from the decedent to the surviving spouse;
2. the survivor must be the decedent's spouse at the time of death; and
3. the property must pass outright to the surviving spouse, unless the qualified terminable interest property (QTIP) election discussed later applies.

Caution: Property passing from the decedent to the surviving spouse that is conditioned on the spouse's surviving for a limited period of time will not qualify for the deduction if the time period from the decedent's death exceeds six months.[33]

Caution: Property passing into trust or consisting of proceeds payable under a life insurance or annuity contract in which the surviving spouse receives only an interest for life will not qualify for the deduction unless the surviving spouse:

- receives all of the income from the property at least annually;
- receives a lifetime or testamentary general power of appointment over the property; and
- the power of appointment is exercisable (whether or not it is ever exercised) by the surviving spouse alone and in all events.[34]

The qualified terminable interest property (QTIP) election provides an important exception to requirement 3, discussed earlier in this section. Because of this election, property that does not pass outright to the surviving spouse may still qualify for the marital deduction if certain requirements are met. Examples of typical nonqualifying property are (1) a life estate to the surviving spouse with the remainder passing to the children or (2) a trust for the survivor's lifetime benefit in which he or she does not receive a general power of appointment. These types of properties will now qualify for the marital deduction under the so-called QTIP election if (1) the property qualifies for the marital deduction for reasons other than its being a terminable interest and (2) the executor elects on the decedent's federal estate tax return that the property qualifies for the marital deduction.[35]

The effect of this election is that the decedent's estate will receive a marital deduction, but to qualify for the election, the property will be taxable later in the surviving spouse's estate. Without the QTIP election, the property will not qualify for the marital deduction in the estate of the first spouse and will thus be taxable; however, the property will then not be taxable in the estate of the surviving spouse.

 Planning Point 7

The QTIP election provides planning flexibility when estate planning for couples who have children from prior marriages, or when one spouse is concerned that the survivor may remarry and the new spouse will receive part of the estate. Placing the estate in trust for the life of the survivor utilizing the QTIP election ensures the marital deduction while preserving that the ultimate estate distribution will be made as determined by the first spouse to die.

2.5 Net Estate Tax

The net estate is increased by gifts made by the decedent. Any gifts made by the decedent after 1976 that are not includable in the gross estate are added to the taxable estate.[36] The amount "added back" is the date-of-gift value of the gift, less any applicable gift tax exclusion, marital deduction, and charitable deduction. This is termed the "adjusted taxable gift."[37] The adding back is required because of the unification of the estate and gift taxes.

The federal estate tax is then computed.[38] The rate schedule is shown in Appendix A at the end of this chapter. The tax is then reduced by the gift tax previously paid on the "added-back" gifts.[39] Previously, the net effect of adding back the post-1976 gifts was to increase the estate tax owed on the estate because of the progressive nature of the estate tax rates. The corresponding deduction for the gift tax that was payable on the added-back gifts is allowed to give proper credit for the tax paid on the earlier gifts. Today's higher estate tax exemption precludes any estate tax at the lower rates. Thus, when an estate tax is owed, it is at a flat tax rate of 40%.

The resulting estate tax is then reduced by any of the three credits that are applicable to an estate. The application of these credits results in the net estate tax payable. The first is the *unified credit* (applicable credit amount), which in 2018 exempts from estate taxation an estate up to $11,200,000. This amount increases annually because it is indexed to future cost-of-living increases.

The amount of the exemption is further increased for the amount of the unused exclusion of a deceased spouse. For example, assume a husband died in 2014 when the exclusion amount was $5,430,000. He passed his entire estate to his wife and his estate utilized the marital deduction to eliminate the federal estate tax in his estate. Current law allows the $5,430,000 exclusion amount from the husband's estate to be added to the $11,200,000 exclusion amount for the wife's estate. Her estate now has a exclusion in 2018 of $16,630,000. This concept is termed *portability* in the estate tax laws; it was first added to the law in 2011 and made permanent in 2013.[40]

The second possible credit is a credit for the federal estate tax paid on a prior estate.[41] If property was subject to the federal estate tax in a prior decedent's estate, the property passes to the present decedent, and the property is included in the present decedent's estate, then the present estate is entitled to a credit. The credit is limited to the lower of the estate taxes paid on the transferred property in the first decedent's estate or the estate tax attributed to the transferred property in the second decedent's estate. Also, the credit is further reduced by 20% at two-year intervals beginning with the third year after the date of death of the first decedent. Therefore, after 10 years the credit ceases.

The third credit is for any foreign death tax that is paid.[42] This credit is available for estates of both U.S. citizens and resident aliens and is allowed for the amount of any foreign death taxes paid on property situated in a foreign country that is also included in the gross estate.

2.6 Filing and Payment

The federal estate tax return, which is filed on IRS Form 706, is due nine months after the date of death of the decedent, provided the gross estate exceeds the applicable exclusion amount ($11,200,000 in 2018).[43] No return is required for estates equal to or less than the applicable exclusion amount because no estate tax is owed on such estates. An extension of time to file the return may be obtained from the IRS district director's office for the decedent's service area for an additional six months upon filing an application and establishing reasonable cause for the extension.[44] An extension to file does not result in an extension of time to pay.

Normally, payment must be made within nine months of the death of the decedent. In situations in which there is a reasonable need or an undue hardship will result if the payment is made within nine months of death, the district director can permit extensions of time to pay, ranging from 12 months to a maximum of 10 years.[45] Typical situations meriting an extension include (1) an illiquid estate that would suffer a loss in value if a forced sale were required to pay the estate taxes; (2) an estate consisting largely of assets that will result in value being realized in the future, such as royalties or pending litigation claims; or (3) estate assets consisting largely of a farm or a closely held business that does not qualify for the Section 6166 extension.[46] Section 6166 provides for payment of estate taxes and a reduced interest rate over a period of 15 years for certain farms and closely held businesses when certain requirements are met.[47]

Notes

1. I.R.C. § 2031.
2. I.R.C. § 2035.
3. I.R.C. § 2001(b).
4. I.R.C. § 2035(c).
5. Section 2032A is discussed further in Chapter 12.
6. Section 6166 is discussed further in Chapter 13.
7. I.R.C. § 2035(a), (b).
8. Treas. Reg. §§ 20.2036-1(a), (b)(1)(ii); 20.2037-1(e)(3), (4); Notice 89-60, I.R.B. 1989-22 (May 1, 1989).
9. I.R.C. § 2036(b).
10. Treas. Reg. § 20.2037-1(c), (d), (e).
11. Treas. Reg. § 20.2038-1.
12. Valuation tables and interest factors are available in all major tax services.
13. This calculation is based on life expectancy and interest factors in effect at the time of writing. Current factors should be consulted when making calculations.
14. Treas. Reg. § 20.2040-1(c)(4).
15. I.R.C. § 2041(b)(1).
16. I.R.C. § 2041(a)(2).
17. For further planning considerations, see Chapters 6 and 7.
18. Treas. Reg. § 20.2041-1(c)(2).
19. I.R.C. § 2042.
20. Treas. Reg. § 20.2042-1(c)(2).
21. I.R.C. § 2035(d)(2).
22. For an explanation of valuing life insurance policies, see Treas. Reg. § 25.2512-6. (This information can also be obtained from the insurance company and is furnished by the company on IRS Form 712.)
23. Treas. Reg. § 25.2512-6.
24. Rev. Rul. 73-207, 1973-1 C.B. 409; Rev. Rul. 77-48, 1977-1 C.B. 292.

25. Treas. Reg. § 20.2053-1.
26. *Id.* § 20.2053-2.
27. *Id.* § 20.2053-3.
28. *Id.* § 20.2053-4.
29. *Id.* § 20.2053-7.
30. *Id.* § 20.2054-1.
31. I.R.C. § 2055.
32. *Id.* § 2056.
33. *Id.* § 2056(b)(3).
34. *Id.* § 2056(b)(5).
35. *Id.* § 2056(b)(7).
36. *Id.* § 2001(b).
37. *Id.* § 2001(b)(2).
38. *Id.* § 2001(c).
39. *Id.* § 2012.
40. I.R.C. § 2010(c).
41. *Id.* § 2013.
42. *Id.* § 2014.
43. *Id.* § 6075.
44. *Id.* § 6081.
45. *Id.* § 6161.
46. Treas. Reg. § 25.6161-1(b).
47. For a further discussion of I.R.C. § 6161, see Chapter 13.

Appendix A

Unified Transfer Tax Rate Schedule

Column A Taxable amount over	Column B Taxable amount not over	Column C Tax on amount in Column A	Column D Rate of tax on excess over amount in Column A Percent
0	$10,000	0	18
$10,000	20,000	$1,800	20
20,000	40,000	3,800	22
40,000	60,000	8,200	24
60,000	80,000	13,000	26
80,000	100,000	18,200	28
100,000	150,000	23,800	30
150,000	250,000	38,800	32
250,000	500,000	70,800	34
500,000	750,000	155,800	37
750,000	1,000,000	248,300	39
1,000,000	—	345,800	40

Chapter 3

Gift Tax Overview

- **3.1** Background
    - **3.11** Gift Tax Overview
    - **3.12** Advantages of Gift Giving
    - **3.13** General Requirements
    - **3.14** Special Considerations
        - **3.141** Gifts of Services
        - **3.142** Disclaimers
        - **3.143** Assignment of Income
        - **3.144** Delivery of the Gift
- **3.2** Annual Exclusion and Split Gifts
    - **3.21** Annual Exclusion
    - **3.22** Gift-Splitting
- **3.3** Income Tax Basis in Gift Property
- **3.4** Transfers not Subject to Gift Tax
    - **3.41** Marital Deduction
    - **3.42** Charitable Deduction
    - **3.43** Tuition and Medical Expenses
- **3.5** Gifts for the Benefit of Children
- **3.6** Special Situations
    - **3.61** Net Gifts
    - **3.62** Gift Subject to an Indebtedness
- **Appendix A** 2018 Individual Income Tax Rate Schedules
- **Appendix B** 2018 Income Tax Rate Schedules for Use by Estate and Nongrantor Trusts

3.1 Background

3.11 Gift Tax Overview

The gift tax is an excise tax imposed on the transfer of property by a donor during his or her lifetime to a recipient-donee. The donee of a gift may be an individual or other entity, such as a trust, partnership, corporation, or charity. However, recipients of gifts to a trust, partnership, or corporation are deemed to be the individual beneficiaries, partners, or stockholders, to the extent of their proportionate interest.[1] The gift tax is obviously a necessary complement to the estate tax. Otherwise, avoidance of the estate tax could be easily accomplished if individuals could give property away during their lifetime without any tax consequence.

Prior to 1977, the gift tax rate was 75% of the estate tax rate. Now, the tax rate is the same whether for gifts or estates. Prior to 2012, in the case of gifts during lifetime, any gifts in excess of the $1,000,000 amount were subject to gift tax even though the estate tax exclusion amount was higher.[2]

However, since 2013 the estate exclusion amount ($11,200,000 in 2018) may be used in whole or in part for lifetime gifts. Thus, in 2018 an individual could give $11,200,000 in lifetime gifts and owe no gift tax, or make no lifetime gifts and pass the same amount at death free of any estate tax. This change simplifies planning, as an individual may make large lifetime gifts or wait and pass the property at death. All that one must consider is that one has a total estate and gift tax exclusion that can be used as one chooses for lifetime or death giving.

Additionally, any present-interest gift in 2018 is entitled to an annual gift tax exclusion of $15,000 per donee. This annual gift tax exclusion is indexed for inflation and will increase in future years. Further, by both spouses joining in the gift, even if the source of the funds is only from one spouse, the annual gift tax exclusion in 2018 can be doubled to $30,000.

3.12 Advantages of Gift Giving

Although the advantages of gift giving are not as great as in prior years, there are still several significant tax advantages. There also are several nontax reasons for making gifts. The advantages of gift giving merit brief review.

1. Gift giving may accomplish the donor's purpose of assisting the donee with some special needs, such as educational, medical, or charitable needs.
2. Gift giving reduces the size of the donor's estate, which may, in turn, reduce the amount of probate expenses such as executor's and legal fees when these fees are calculated as a percentage of the estate.
3. An individual in 2018 may give $15,000 per year (indexed for inflation) to as many different donees as he or she chooses without any gift tax being owed on such gifts.[3] Over a number of years, this may enable a donor to reduce his or her estate significantly, thus reducing the estate tax owed at death.

4. The $15,000 annual gift tax exclusion in 2018 can be doubled to $30,000 per year per donee when the donor's spouse joins in the gift.[4] Again, these amounts are indexed for inflation. This technique, known as *gift-splitting*, is permitted even though the gift has been made from the assets of only one of the spouses. Obviously, gift-splitting permits more rapid gift giving.

5. When the donee is in a lower income tax bracket than the donor, there is an overall income tax savings when gifts are made. This advantage is not as great for lower-bracket taxpayers, but is an advantage for higher-bracket taxpayers.[5] This savings is not available when the donee is under 19 years of age, or a student under 24 years of age and has a certain level of investment income, owing to the so-called kiddie tax, which is discussed further in Section 3.5.[6]

6. When the donated property has increased in value from the time of the gift until the death of the donor, the appreciation is not taxed in the donor's estate when he or she dies. This is obviously a tax savings, compared with the tax that would be owed if the property had been held until death and was subject to the estate tax. However, the appreciation is subject to income tax if a subsequent sale of the property by the donee takes place.

7. In estates that consist largely of stock in a closely held business, farmland, or other business property, a stock redemption pursuant to Section 303 of the Internal Revenue Code to pay death taxes, funeral expenses, and administrative costs is a possible estate tax savings to the estate. The special-use valuation permitted under IRC Section 2032A and the installment payment election under IRC Section 6166 are other estate tax benefits. Each of these code sections requires certain percentage tests to be met to qualify for the tax benefit. A gift of property reduces the size of the estate, which may then enable these percentage limitations to be met, although any such transfer must not be made within three years before the decedent's death.

3.13 General Requirements

A gift tax is not owed until a complete gift has been made. A gift has three basic elements: (1) the intent of the donor to give the property, (2) delivery of the property to the donee, and (3) the acceptance of the property by the donee. Although these three elements must be satisfied for there to be a completed gift on which a gift tax is owed, the gift tax law tends to minimize these elements. For example, donative intent is determined based on the objective facts of the transfer, not the subjective motive of the donor.[7] In addition, the focus is not so much on delivery and acceptance as on the cessation of the donor's control.[8]

The gift tax is imposed based on the fair market value of the transferred property.[9] A present-interest transfer in 2018 subject to the gift tax is entitled to a $15,000 per donee annual gift tax exclusion,[10] which amount is indexed for inflation. Further, the donor's spouse may join in the gift, thus creating the possibility of so-called gift-splitting and increasing the annual gift tax exclusion to $30,000 per donee, or higher with future inflation adjustments.[11]

An unlimited marital deduction is allowed for transfers between spouses, thus eliminating any gift tax for most such transfers.[12] Additionally, transfers to charities receive a charitable deduction, thus eliminating gift tax for most of these transfers.[13] A final exclusion is allowed for certain tuition and medical expenses paid on behalf of another.[14]

Under prior law, gifts made within three years of the decedent's death were included in the donor's gross estate for estate tax purposes. This is no longer the law. The three-year rule has not been applicable since December 31, 1981; thus, any transfer subject to the gift tax will not be included in the gross estate.[15] (For an illustration of the interplay between the gift and estate taxes, see Appendix A in Chapter 2.)

Naturally, there are exceptions. A donor who within three years of death (1) relinquishes a life estate, (2) makes transfers taking effect at the donor's death, (3) makes revocable transfers, or (4) makes transfers in which the donor retains a general power of appointment will have such property included in his or her estate.[16] The transfer of a life insurance policy within three years of death still will result in the insurance proceeds being included in the estate, even if the policy value at the time of the gift was within the annual exclusion.[17] Also, the three-year rule still applies in determining qualification for the percentage requirements of a 303 redemption and a 6166 installment payment of the estate taxes.[18]

The donor is required to file a gift tax return and pay any resulting gift tax by April 15 following the calendar year in which the gift or gifts are made.[19] The return is not required for gifts with a value below the annual gift tax exclusion, gifts for certain educational or medical expenses, and gifts to a spouse that qualify for a marital deduction.[20] The tax rates are the same as those for the estate tax. (See Appendix A in Chapter 2.)

3.14 Special Considerations

3.141 Gifts of Services

Several types of gifts are not subject to the gift tax. For example, a donor who gratuitously renders services for the benefit of another has not made a taxable gift. This includes the gratuitous gift of a donor's time for the benefit of a donee, such as a donor's donating his or her services for the benefit of a charity, friend, or family member. Another example is an executor who chooses not to charge an executor's commission.[21]

3.142 Disclaimers

When a donee has been given property, but disclaims the property within nine months, as required for a qualified disclaimer under the Internal Revenue Code, the subsequent transfer of the property to the next donee is not subject to an additional gift tax.[22] In situations in which a disclaimer is properly used, a transfer can be made without the imposition of a second gift tax. Of course, a gift tax is still owed by the initial donor of the gift.

> **Example:** A widow makes a $60,000 gift to her son, to be used by him to pay for the college education of his children who are under 18 years of age. The gift is taxable to the widow because she is the donor of the gift. The income subsequently earned from the $60,000 gift will be taxed to the son, and gifts by him to each child in excess of the $15,000 annual exclusion will be subject to the gift tax, except to the extent the tuition exclusion applies.[23] If the son disclaims the gift, it will pass equally to his two children. There is no gift tax owed by the son because of the disclaimer, and the future income will be taxable to the children because they now own the gift property, unless the kiddie tax applies, in which case the income will be taxed at the trusts and estates tax rate. This example assumes that the estate and gift tax exclusion amount has already been used for prior gifts. In most situations it will not have been used. Thus, the $60,000 gift to the son will be reduced by the $15,000 annual gift tax exclusion and the balance of $45,000 will reduce the exclusion amount by $45,000. Thus, the 2018 exclusion amount of $11,200,000 will be reduced to $11,155,000.

3.143 Assignment of Income

The assignment-of-income doctrine should be considered.[24] This doctrine can create unintended income tax consequences when a donor gives income-producing property to a donee. In a typical situation, a parent gives his or her right to future income, such as future rentals from a building or future royalties from a mineral ownership, to the children. These transfers constitute completed gifts and are subject to the gift tax; however, for income tax purposes the assignment of the gift has no effect, and the income is still taxed to the parent. The only way the income tax can be shifted to the children is for the underlying asset to be given. In this example, the ownership of the building or minerals must be transferred to the children, not just the income from the asset.

3.144 Delivery of the Gift

The concept of delivery to the donee is simplistic, but several points must be recognized. For example, a gift of a check is not a gift until it has been either certified by the donor or cashed by the donee.[25] This is important because the annual gift tax exclusion is a calendar-year exclusion. Thus, a check given on December 31 must be cashed that day or posted by the bank that day; if this is not possible, the donor should certify the check.

A similar situation is involved when a donor executes a deed but does not have the deed recorded. This is not a completed gift until the deed is recorded, because the deed can always be destroyed during the donor's lifetime.[26] A possible alternative to recording the deed is to irrevocably transfer it to an escrow agent with directions to record the deed at some future date. The gift is then regarded as having been completed at the time the deed was delivered into the hands of the escrow agent.

A gift of stock is completed on the date it is delivered to the donee, to the corporation for transfer, or to the corporation's transfer agent.[27] A transfer of a U.S. government bond is a completed gift when the bond is presented for registration.[28]

A transfer into a joint bank account is not a completed gift. The transfer is completed when the donee withdraws the funds from the account.[29] Similarly, a transfer by the settlor into a revocable trust he or she created is not completed until such time as the settlor relinquishes control of the trust. This occurs when principal or income is transferred to a beneficiary or when the settlor amends the trust to make it irrevocable. At that point a gift occurs.[30]

These are only important points when the annual gift tax exclusion is needed for the year of the gift. If it is needed, don't delay gifting to the end of the year, or these rules may upset the donor's plan.

3.2 Annual Exclusion and Split Gifts

3.21 Annual Exclusion

As discussed previously, every donor is entitled to an annual exclusion in 2018 of $15,000 per year per gift for gifts to as many different donees as the donor chooses.[31] The exclusion is indexed for inflation and will increase in future years. The exclusion is allowed only for a present-interest gift, as opposed to a future-interest gift. A present-interest gift is one in which the immediate use of the property is available to the donee. A gift of a future interest, such as a reversionary or remainder interest, is not allowed an annual exclusion.[32] This requirement creates a problem when a gift is made to a trust for the benefit of the trust beneficiary.

> **Example:** A transfer of assets to a trust that pays income for the life of the life tenant and then distributes the remainder to the remaindermen on the life tenant's death is a gift of both a present interest and a future interest. The life tenant's interest is a present interest that can be valued and for which the annual exclusion is available; however, the

remaindermen do not come into possession of the property until the death of the life tenant. The remainder interest is a future interest, for which no annual exclusion is available.

 Caution: A trust that may withhold annual payments of income, such as the typical discretionary trust, will result in no annual exclusion being allowed for the gifts to both the life tenant and the remaindermen.[33]

> ### Planning Pointer 1

A limited exception to the denial of the annual exclusion for gifts of a future interest is allowed for a gift to an individual under age 21.[34] The use of this exception is illustrated in the example of a gift or series of gifts to an educational trust that is established when a child is age 5 and that terminates when the child attains age 21. To qualify for the annual exclusion, it must be possible for the trust principal and the income to be expended for the child before the child attains age 21. To the extent not expended, the trust principal must be paid to the child when he or she reaches age 21. If the child dies before age 21, the entire trust property must pass to the child's estate or to a donee pursuant to the child's exercise of a general power of appointment.

3.22 Gift-Splitting

Gift-splitting is an option in which a husband and wife join together in the making of a gift.[35] This election is made on IRS Form 709. The effect is that the entire gift is treated as though one-half were made by the husband and one-half by the wife. This option is available even though one of the spouses made no financial contribution to the gift. Gift-splitting permits the amount of the available annual exclusion in 2018 to be doubled from $15,000 to $30,000, or double the future inflation-adjusted exclusion amount. To qualify for gift-splitting, the spouse who does not actually contribute to the gift must consent to this tax treatment by signing the gift tax return.[36] This is necessary even if the combined annual exclusion results in no gift tax being owed and no unified credit being used, such as when making a $30,000 gift to a child. Of course, if each spouse makes a separate $15,000 gift, then gift-splitting is not involved because each spouse has made a gift from her or his own funds.

3.3 Income Tax Basis in Gift Property

When property is given to a donee, it is required that the donor's adjusted income tax basis be used by the donee as his or her own income tax basis in the property.[37] The adjusted basis can be increased for any federal gift tax that is attributable to the portion of the gift that represents appreciation in the value of the gift property.[38]

> **Example:** Property valued at $100,000 is given to a donee. The donor's adjusted income tax basis in the property is $10,000, and the gift tax paid on the gift is $40,000 (assuming a 40% rate and prior use of the entire exclusion amount). The donee will have an adjusted basis in the property of $46,000: the donor's adjusted basis of $10,000 plus the gift tax on the $90,000 appreciation, which is $36,000 ($40,000 x $90,000 / $100,000).

When the donor later sells the gift property at a gain, he or she then will pay income tax on the difference between the sales price and the adjusted basis of the property. In the event the property is sold at a loss, the donee's adjusted basis is modified somewhat, to the lesser of either the donor's adjusted basis or the fair market value of the property at the time of the gift.[39]

> **Example:** The donee in the preceding example later sells the property for $110,000. The taxable gain for income tax purposes is $64,000.

> **Example:** The donor gives property with a fair market value of $50,000, in which the donor has an adjusted basis of $100,000, to the donee. While the donee's basis for purposes of a gain is $100,000, for purposes of a loss the basis is $50,000. A subsequent sale of the property for $45,000 will result in a loss of only $5,000. A sale for between $50,000 and $100,000 will result in neither a gain nor a loss.

 Planning Pointer 2

One of the disadvantages of a gift is that the donee receives the donor's adjusted income tax basis. This basis is often much lower than the fair market value of the property given. Rather than giving highly appreciated property, it is better tax planning to give property with a higher adjusted basis and pass the highly appreciated but low-basis property to the donee at death. This action is preferable because property that is held until death will receive a basis stepped up to the value of the property on the date of death of the donor-decedent.[40] Obviously, if the property is held until death, it will be subject to the estate tax. The extent to which this is a true disadvantage can be determined by computing trial estate, gift, and income tax costs before making the decision either to give the property or to hold it until death.

Example: A parent owns property with a fair market value of $1,000,000 and with an adjusted income tax basis of only $100,000 that is going to be either given to the child in trust during the parent's life or bequeathed at the parent's death. Assuming that no gift tax is owed, due to use of both the annual gift tax exclusion and part of the estate and gift exclusion amount, the adjusted basis of the property in the hands of the donee-child is

$100,000 if the property is given to the child during the life of the parent. If held until death and bequeathed to the child, the child's income tax basis will be $1,000,000; and if the estate is valued at less than the remaining estate and gift tax exclusion amount, no estate tax is owed. If the property is later sold for $1,100,000, the gift approach will result in a gain of $1,000,000, whereas the bequest will result in a gain of only $100,000 (if the estate tax value of the property has remained $1,000,000). Assuming a 20% capital gain rate, the gift approach results in income taxes of $200,000, whereas the estate approach results in income taxes of $20,000. The gift approach costs $180,000 more in income taxes, thus indicating that a bequest is better if the property is likely to appreciate in value.

> ## Planning Pointer 3

A planning technique sometimes used to obtain the benefit of a stepped-up income tax basis is for the spouse with the larger estate to transfer low-basis property to the spouse with the smaller estate when that spouse is in poor health and facing death. The ill spouse then bequeaths the property back to the surviving spouse, who then receives the property with a stepped-up income tax basis. If the property is later sold, there will be little income tax to be paid.

Example: A husband and wife jointly own property with a fair market value of $1,500,000 that has a basis of only $300,000. The husband conveys his interest in the property to his wife, who is in poor health and is anticipated to predecease her husband. On her death she bequeaths the property to her husband. The property will receive a stepped-up basis to its value at the date of her death, which for this illustration is assumed to be $1,500,000. A subsequent sale of the property by the husband for $1,500,000 will result in no taxable gain for income tax purposes. If the husband had retained his one-half interest in the property, his basis following his wife's death would be $900,000 ($150,000 for his half interest and a stepped-up basis of $750,000 for her half). The sale would result in a $600,000 taxable gain, which at a 20% capital gain rate would result in income taxes of $120,000.

 Caution: This technique will not be successful if the donee-spouse dies within one year of the gift and the property returns to the original donor or the donor-spouse.[41] If more than one year elapses, then the technique will be successful. If the property passes to a beneficiary other than the original donor or the donor-spouse, however, the technique will be successful even though death occurs within one year.

3.4 Transfers Not Subject to Gift Tax

3.41 Marital Deduction

Under current law, a marital deduction is normally allowed for the full value of any property transferred from one spouse to another. The requirements for the gift tax marital deduction are generally the same as for the estate tax marital deduction. Basically, the property must be given outright to the donee-spouse, or if in trust, the donee-spouse must have the absolute right to income for life from the property coupled with a general power of appointment. Another option is that the gift meet the requirements to be treated as qualified terminable interest property. This option requires that the donee receive a lifetime income from the property without having to receive a general power of appointment. It also requires an irrevocable election on a timely filed gift tax return. If these requirements are met, the marital deduction is available for the entire interest given, and no gift tax is owed on the transfer.[42]

Caution: A transfer incident to a divorce generally is not subject to the gift tax.[43] There is also no gift tax for a transfer between spouses when the transfer is made before entry of the decree of divorce, owing to the unlimited gift tax marital deduction.[44] To avoid gift taxation for a transfer after entry of the divorce decree, however, (1) the transfer must be made pursuant to a written agreement relating to the property transferred and (2) the divorce must occur within a three-year period beginning one year before the date of the agreement. The transfer must be to one of the spouses in exchange for marital or property rights or to provide support for one or more of the children during their minority.[45]

3.42 Charitable Deduction

A deduction is allowed for the full value of any property passing to charitable, religious, governmental, and certain other nonprofit organizations.[46] This deduction is similar to the estate tax deduction, and, as with that deduction, it is not limited solely to tax-exempt organizations under the income tax law.

3.43 Tuition and Medical Expenses

Payments to an educational institution for an individual's tuition are excluded from the gift tax. The payments must be made directly to the institution and not to the donee. Also, the exclusion is available only for tuition and does not include other education-related expenses such as housing, meals, and books. A similar exclusion is available for medical expenses that are paid to the institution or the person providing medical care.[47]

3.5 Gifts for the Benefit of Children

The "kiddie tax" creates some difficulty in transferring assets to an individual's children to create an educational fund for their benefit. This was often done in the past because the children's income tax bracket was usually lower than the parent's, thus allowing a larger after-tax fund to build up over the years. This was particularly good planning for establishing educational funds for the donor's children. The current income tax rules are somewhat complicated and provide that most net unearned income (investment income) of a child who (1) has not attained the age of 19 before the end of the tax year, (2) is a full-time student under the age of 24 at the end of the tax year, and (3) has at least one parent alive at the close of the tax year will be taxed at the trusts and estates income tax rate.[48]

 Caution: This tax result applies to all net unearned income without regard to the source of the income, when it was transferred, or by whom. The tax payable by the child is essentially the amount of additional income tax the parent would have to pay if the net unearned income of the child were included in the parent's taxable income.

Planning Pointer 4

Because of the "kiddie tax" rules, the tax laws leave only a few choices for creating educational funds for children without incurring present income taxes. One option is to purchase Series EE U.S. savings bonds for the children. The income on these bonds is tax deferred until they are redeemed; therefore, the child could hold the bonds until reaching age 14 or later, then redeem the bonds and pay income tax at the child's personal income tax rate. The proceeds then could be invested in higher-return investments. A newer, limited alternative for middle-income families allows interest from Series EE savings bonds used for higher education to be excluded from income.[49]

Growth stocks or mutual funds are another option. Although any income is subject to the kiddie tax, growth investments typically have low dividends and should generate very little current income. Deep-discount income tax–free municipal bonds are another option. These bonds are sold for a large discount but at maturity pay the face amount. Because they are tax-free bonds, no income tax is owed when they mature. Unfortunately, the current low interest rates on bonds limits the use of this technique.

A minor's trust, as permitted under IRC Section 2503(c), is another possibility. This type of trust can accumulate income for beneficiaries who are under the kiddie-tax age limits and will avoid the kiddie tax; however, there will be little if any income tax advantage as the kiddie tax rates are now the trusts and estates income tax rates. An appropriate trust form is provided in Chapter 15 at 15.5.

Perhaps the best option is a qualified tuition program, commonly termed a 529 plan. Generally, the income is not taxable, nor are distributions as long as the distributions do not exceed qualified higher education expenses (which include tuition, fees, books, supplies, school-required equipment, and reasonable costs for room and board). The annual gift tax exclusion applies for contributions, though not the tuition expense deduction discussed earlier. These plans are offered by state agencies and by accredited colleges and universities.

3.6 Special Situations

3.61 Net Gifts

A *net gift* is a gift in which the donor requires the donee to pay the gift tax attributable to the gift. Such a gift often is made when the donor lacks liquidity with which to pay the tax or wants to shift the tax burden to the donee. The taxable amount is not the gross amount of the gift; it is the gross amount of the gift reduced by the amount of gift tax the donee must pay. The formula for determining the amount of the gift tax is "tentative" tax divided by (1.00 + donor's gift tax bracket).

> **Example:** A donor who has made sufficient lifetime gifts to use his entire unified credit desires to give a donee property that has a fair market value of $100,000 but wants the donee to pay the gift tax. The donor is in the 40% gift tax bracket. Therefore, the gift tax is determined as follows: tentative tax $40,000 / (1.0 + 0.40) = $28,571.[50]

 Caution: A net gift may have possible income tax consequences to the donor.[51] Such a gift is treated as a part-sale, part-gift transaction due to the donor's being relieved from paying the gift tax liability. The income to the donor is the amount of gift tax paid by the donee less the donor's basis in the property. Thus, the greater income tax problem is created when low-basis property is given. In the preceding example, if the property given had an income tax basis of $10,000, then the income to be reported by the donor is $18,571; however, no income is reported if the basis equals or exceeds the gift tax.

> ### ⌄ Planning Pointer 5

In 1968, the Ninth Circuit Court of Appeals decided the case of *Crummey v. Commissioner*.[52] This case offers the opportunity for the annual gift tax exclusion to be allowed for transfers into trust. Normally, a gift to a trust is a gift of a future interest for which no annual exclusion is permitted. In *Crummey*, however, the beneficiary of the trust was given the absolute right to withdraw the amount of the annual gift to the trust up to and through December 31 of each year. If the right was not exercised, it lapsed. The mere fact that the right of withdrawal existed created a present interest for the beneficiary in the property that was transferred into the trust; thus, the gift qualified for the annual exclusion.

Under the *Crummey* ruling, it is not necessary for the beneficiary to exercise the right. However, the beneficiary must receive notice from the trustee that the property has been placed in trust and that the beneficiary has the right to withdraw the gift. Further, the fact that the beneficiary is a minor and does not have a court-appointed guardian does not cause the loss of the annual exclusion.

Because of this case, it is possible to draft irrevocable trusts that still qualify for the annual gift tax exclusion for the amount transferred into the trust each year. This technique is useful when establishing life insurance trusts because the annual gift to the trust can be used to pay the life insurance premiums. It also can be useful when the donor wishes to make regular gifts to a trust over a number of years to build up a trust fund for the benefit of the donor's beneficiaries but does not want the beneficiaries to receive the property outright. See Chapter 15 at 15.6 for an appropriate trust form.

Planning Pointer 6

Life insurance offers several options for gift giving. An obvious option is for the insured donor to give an existing policy to a beneficiary. The beneficiary then can pay the premiums on the policy, and on the death of the insured the proceeds will not be included in the insured donor's estate. This technique also can be used by the beneficiary simply purchasing a new policy and being both the owner and the beneficiary of the policy.

If the life insurance policy is a term insurance policy, the only value of the gift is the unearned portion of the last policy premium determined as of the date of the gift. If a cash value policy is in a premium-paying stage at the time of transfer, its value is equal to the interpolated terminal reserve value (roughly equivalent to the cash value) plus any unearned premiums at the time of the gift.[53] If instead the policy is paid up at the time of the gift, the value is the amount the insurance company would charge for the same type of policy based on the insured's age at the date of the gift. This value can be obtained from the insurance company on IRS Form 712, which should be submitted with the gift tax return (Form 709) because a gift of life insurance with a cash value is a taxable gift.

Any premiums paid by the donor after the gift of the life insurance are subject to the gift tax, although the annual gift tax exclusion will usually exceed the amount of the premiums.[54] When the premiums on the policy are paid by an employer, the employee is treated as the donor of a gift to the donee in the amount of the premiums paid by the employer.[55]

Caution: A possible gift tax trap exists when the insured gives a life insurance policy to another. The donee of the policy then becomes the owner; if he or she names another party as beneficiary, a problem exists. At the death of the insured, the death proceeds are paid to a party other than the insured or the owner. This results in a taxable gift from the owner to the third-party beneficiary equal to the amount of the death proceeds.[56] Therefore, the owner and beneficiary should be the same when the insured is not also the owner of the policy.

3.62 Gift Subject to an Indebtedness

In making a gift, the donor must be aware of the adjusted income tax basis of the property and the effect of any indebtedness on the property. A gift of low-basis property that is subject to an indebtedness can create an unintended income tax result. Income tax is owed by the donor on the difference between the indebtedness assumed by the donee and the basis of the transferred property.[57]

Example: The donor gives rental property that is valued at $100,000 in which the donor's income tax basis is $10,000. The property is subject to a $70,000 mortgage. If the donee assumes the indebtedness, an unexpected income tax will result. The difference between the $10,000 basis and the $70,000 debt that has been assumed by the donee is treated as taxable income to the donor. Thus, the donor has made a $30,000 gift but also must recognize $60,000 in additional income. This could easily become an unexpectedly costly gift.

Notes

1. Treas. Reg. § 20.2511-1(h)(1).
2. I.R.C. § 2505.
3. *Id.* § 2503(b).
4. *Id.* § 2513.
5. I.R.C. § 1.
6. *Id.* § 1(i).
7. Treas. Reg. § 25.2511-1(g)(1).
8. *Id.* § 25.2511-2.
9. I.R.C. § 2512; Treas. Reg. § 25.2512-1.
10. I.R.C. § 2503(b). (See also 3.2 in this chapter.)
11. I.R.C. § 2513. (See also 3.22 in this chapter.)
12. I.R.C. § 2523. (See also 3.41 in this chapter.)
13. I.R.C. § 2522. (See also 3.42 in this chapter.)
14. I.R.C. § 2503(e). (See also 3.43 in this chapter.)
15. I.R.C. § 2035(d)(1).
16. *Id.* § 2035(a). (See also Chapter 2, at 2.21.)
17. I.R.C. § 2035(c), (d).
18. *Id.* § 2035(c). (See also Chapter 2, at 2.21, Planning Pointer.)
19. I.R.C. § 6075(b).
20. *Id.* § 6019. (See also 3.4 in this chapter.)
21. Rev. Rul. 56-472, 1956-2 C.B. 21; Rev. Rul. 66-167, 1966-1 C.B. 20.
22. I.R.C. § 2518; Treas. Reg. § 25.2518-1(b).
23. I.R.C. § 2503(e).
24. Lucas v. Earl, 281 U.S. 111, 50 S. Ct. 241, 74 L. Ed. 731 (1930).
25. Rev. Rul. 67-396, 1967-2 C.B. 351.
26. Whitt v. Commissioner, 751 F.2d 1548 (11th Cir. 1985).
27. Treas. Reg. § 25.2511-2 (h).
28. Rev. Rul. 68-269, 1968-1 C.B. 339.

29. Treas. Reg. § 25.2511-1(h)(4).
30. Commissioner v. Guggenheim, 288 U.S. 280, 53 S. Ct. 369, 77 L. Ed. 748 (1933).
31. I.R.C. § 2503(b).
32. Treas. Reg. § 25.2503-3.
33. *Id.* § 25.2503-3(c)(1).
34. I.R.C. § 2503(c). (See also Chapter 5, at 5.29.)
35. I.R.C. § 2513.
36. *Id.* § 2513(b).
37. *Id.* § 1015.
38. *Id.* § 1015(d).
39. *Id.* § 1015 (a).
40. *Id.* § 1014.
41. *Id.* § 1014(e).
42. *Id.* § 2523. (See also Chapter 2, at 2.4; and Chapter 7.)
43. I.R.C. § 2516.
44. *Id.* § 2323.
45. *Id.* § 2516.
46. *Id.* § 2522. (See also Chapter 2, at 2.4.)
47. I.R.C. § 2503(e); Treas. Reg. § 25.2503-6.
48. I.R.C. § 1(i).
49. *Id.* § 135.
50. Rev. Rul. 75-12, 1975-1 C.B. 310.
51. Diedrich v. Commissioner, 457 U.S. 191, 102 S. Ct. 2414, 72 L. Ed. 2d 777 (1982).
52. Crummey v. Commissioner, 397 F.2d 82 (9th Cir. 1968).
53. Treas. Reg. § 25.2512-6.
54. *Id.* § 25.2503-3(c), Ex. 6.
55. Rev. Rul. 76-490, 1976-2 C.B. 300.
56. Rev. Rul. 73-207, 1973-1 C.B. 409; Rev. Rul. 77-48, 1977-1 C.B. 292.
57. I.R.C. §§ 61(a)(12), 1015.

Appendix A

2018 Individual Income Tax Rate Schedules

SINGLE INDIVIDUAL

Over	but not over	Tax			of the amount over
$ 0	$9,525	$ 0		10%	$ 0
9,525	38,700	952.50	+	12%	9,525
38,700	82,500	4,453.50	+	22%	38,700
82,500	157,500	14,089.50	+	24%	82,500
1557,500	200,000	32,089.50	+	32%	157,500
200,000	500,000	45,689.50	+	35%	200,000
500,000	—	150,689.50	+	37%	500,000

MARRIED FILING JOINTLY OR QUALIFYING WIDOW(ER)

Over	but not over	Tax			of the amount over
$ 0	$19,050	$ 0	+	10%	$ 0
19,050	77,400	1,905.00	+	12%	19,050
77,400	165,000	8,907.00	+	22%	77,400
165,000	315,000	28,179.00	+	24%	165,000
315,000	400,000	64,179.00	+	32%	315,000
400,000	600,000	91,379.00	+	35%	400,000
600,000	—	161,379.00	+	37%	600,000

MARRIED FILING SEPARATELY

Over	but not over	Tax			of the amount over
$ 0	$9,525	$ 0	+	10%	$ 0
9,525	38,700	952.50	+	12%	9,525
38,700	82,500	4,453.50	+	22%	38,700
82,500	157,500	14,089.50	+	24%	82,500
157,500	200,000	32,089.50	+	32%	157,500
200,000	300,000	45,689.50	+	35%	200,000
300,000	—	80,689.50	+	37%	300,000

HEAD OF HOUSEHOLD

Over	but not over	Tax			of the amount over
$ 0	$13,600	$ 0	+	10%	$ 0
13,600	51,800	1,360.00	+	12%	13,600
51,800	82,500	5,944.00	+	22%	51,800
82,500	157,500	12,698.00	+	24%	82,500
157,500	200,000	30,698.00	+	32%	157,500
200,000	500,000	44,298.00	+	35%	200,000
500,000	—	149,298.00	+	37%	500,000

APPENDIX B

2018 Income Tax Rate Schedules for Use by Estate and Nongrantor Trusts

Over	but not over	Tax			of the amount over
$0	$2,550	$0	+	10%	$0
2,550	9,150	255.00	+	24%	2,550
9,150	12,500	1,839.00	+	35%	9,150
12,500	—	3,011.50	+	37%	12,500

Chapter 4

Generation-Skipping Transfer Tax

4.1 Background
4.2 Overview
    4.21 Skip Person
    4.22 Transferor
    4.23 Taxable Distribution
    4.24 Taxable Termination
    4.25 Direct Skip
4.3 Additional Cautions
    4.31 Pot Trusts
    4.32 Tax Apportionment Clauses
    4.33 Disclaimer
    4.34 Double Taxation
    4.35 Portability

4.1 Background

The generation-skipping transfer tax creates a minefield for the unwary. This tax was first enacted in 1976, was significantly revamped in 1986, and is now a permanent part of the Internal Revenue Code, in spite of earlier hopes that it might be repealed. Thus, it is necessary for lawyers to be familiar with the tax.

    The "evil" the tax seeks to end—if an "evil" at all—is illustrated in the situation of a father creating a trust for his daughter, which terminates on the daughter's death and is distributed to her children. The trust for the daughter could permit income and principal to be spent during her lifetime as needed for her health, education, and support or maintenance. She could withdraw annually the greater of 5% or $5,000 from the trust principal. She even could have a power to appoint the trust at her death to anyone she chooses other than her own estate and her creditors. Such a trust did not previously result in any estate tax to the daughter's estate, because she never owned a vested interest in the trust. The estate taxes on the assets in the trust were skipped. Now a tax is imposed.[1] Unfortunately, the tax laws that accomplish this result are technical.

4.2 Overview

A flat tax equal to the maximum federal estate tax rate, presently 40%, is imposed on all generation-skipping transfers.[2] Every individual is allowed a limited exemption for any generation-skipping transfers, whether made during lifetime or at death.[3] The exemption is in the same amount as the estate tax exclusion amount. For 2018 the exemption is $11,200,000, and it increases each year in the same amount as the estate tax exclusion. To determine when a generation-skipping transfer has occurred, consideration must be given to whether the transfer is considered to be (1) a taxable distribution, (2) a taxable termination, or (3) a direct skip. It is also helpful to define the technical terms skip person and transferor.

4.21 Skip Person

A *skip person* is a person assigned to a generation that is two or more generations beyond the generation of the transferor. A skip person may also be a trust, if all interests in the trust are held by skip persons.[4]

> **Example:** A father establishes a trust for his daughter that terminates at her death and is distributed to the daughter's children. The daughter's children (transferor's grandchildren) are skip persons.

In the normal case of lineal descendants, there is no difficulty in determining the generation to which each individual is to be assigned. Parent, child, grandchild, great-grandchild is a simple enough concept, even in the tax law. As would be expected, spouses are treated as being in the same generation.[5] Adopted individuals and relationships of half blood, such as stepchildren, are treated the same as full-blood relationships.[6]

In the case of nonlineal (unrelated) descendants, a fixed numerical rule is imposed. An individual who is within 12½ years of the age of the transferor is assigned to the transferor's generation. An individual more than 12½ years to 37½ years younger than the transferor is assigned to the next younger generation. Generation assignments continue thereafter at 25-year intervals.[7]

4.22 Transferor

The meaning of the term *transferor* is rather obvious. It is the decedent when a testamentary transfer is involved and the donor when the transfer is an inter vivos gift.[8] In the prior example, the father is the transferor.

As with the skip person, some of the finer points are more technical. The holder of a general power of appointment becomes a transferor upon the exercise or lapse of the power, including a lapse due to the holder's death. If a married couple utilizes the gift-splitting option so that a gift is treated as made one-half by each spouse, then each spouse is a transferor. That is, gift-splitting for gift tax purposes creates two transferors for generation-skipping transfer tax purposes.[9]

Also, when a qualified terminable interest property election[10] is made by the executor of the transferor's estate, the estate may also elect to be treated as a transferor for generation-skipping transfer tax purposes. If the election is not made, the surviving spouse will be treated as the transferor.[11]

4.23 Taxable Distribution

A taxable distribution is any distribution from a trust of income or principal to a skip person.[12] The tax is paid by the skip person[13] and must be paid by April 15 of the year following the taxable distribution.[14]

> **Example:** In a trust that permits the payment of income or principal among a group of beneficiaries including both the children and grandchildren of the transferor, the trustee distributes $10,000 of income to a grandchild. The grandchild is a skip person, and a generation-skipping tax of $4,000 is owed. The grandchild receives a net of only $6,000. This and the ensuing examples assume that the entire generation-skipping tax exemption has been used for prior transfers.[15]

> **Caution:** If the tax is paid by the trust, it is treated as an additional distribution in the amount of the tax. Thus, to net $10,000, a distribution of $22,725 is required.[16]

> **Caution:** It must be remembered that this tax is imposed on distributions of both income and principal. Before the Tax Reform Act of 1986, distributions of income were not taxed. Thus, a distribution of income now will be subject to both income tax and the generation-skipping transfer tax, although an itemized income tax deduction is allowed for the generation-skipping transfer tax.[17] This can be quite costly.

> **Example:** A $10,000 income distribution that is a taxable distribution results in a generation-skipping transfer tax of $4,000, plus an additional $1,500 in income taxes, assuming that a 25% income tax bracket applies and the $4,000 generation-skipping transfer tax is deducted as an itemized deduction for personal income tax purposes. This leaves a net distribution after both taxes of only $4,500.

4.24 Taxable Termination

A taxable termination is the termination—by death, lapse of time, release of a power, or otherwise—of an interest in property held in trust. For the termination to be taxable, there must be no nonskip persons having an interest in the trust.[18] The tax is paid by the trustee[19] and must be paid by April 15 of the year following the taxable termination.[20]

> **Example:** A father establishes a trust for his son, and following the son's death, the trust continues for the grandchildren until the youngest becomes 35 years old, at which time the trust terminates and is distributed to the grandchildren. A taxable termination occurs on the son's death. The generation-skipping transfer tax is paid by the trustee. Thus, if the trust held $1 million on the death of the son, the trustee would be required to pay $400,000 in generation-skipping transfer tax. The trust is reduced to $600,000.[21]

4.25 Direct Skip

A *direct skip* is a transfer subject to estate or gift taxes that is made to a skip person.[22] Direct skips were not taxable prior to the Tax Reform Act of 1986, but a tax is now imposed on the transferor.[23] The tax must be paid by the due date for the federal estate tax return if the transfer is testamentary or by April 15 of the year following an inter vivos gift.[24]

> **Example:** Grandfather dies and bequeaths $1,000,000 to his grandchildren because his son already has a large estate of his own and does not need the additional inheritance. This is a direct skip, for which a tax of $400,000 is owed.[25]

> **Caution:** Absent directions in the will to the contrary, the typical tax clause in a will that charges all taxes to the residue will cause the grandchildren in the preceding example to receive the entire $1,000,000 bequest, and the $400,000 generation-skipping transfer tax will be paid by the estate. Obviously, this could cause a significant problem in the distribution of the other estate assets. Additional consideration must be given to the fact that the bequest is subject to the estate tax. A will directing that all taxes be paid from the residuary estate could result in the $1,000,000 bequest passing to the grandchildren but the residuary estate being reduced by $800,000 for the generation-skipping transfer tax and the federal estate tax.

For example, an estate in the highest estate tax bracket of 40% would pay 80% in combined taxes because the generation-skipping transfer tax is also 40%. The obvious intent of the law is to discourage direct skips. Nonetheless, if it is desired to make a generation-skipping transfer in excess of the $1,000,000 exemption, some consideration must be given to the apportionment of the estate and generation-skipping transfer taxes. (Tax apportionment is discussed in Section 4.32.)

4.3 Additional Cautions

There are several areas where caution must be exercised. A failure to recognize these problem areas could be quite costly. These are examined throughout the remainder of this chapter.

4.31 Pot Trusts

Often a donor establishes one trust for the benefit of a number of beneficiaries. For example, in his will a father establishes a trust for his three children to pay income and principal as needed among them. The trust terminates on the youngest child attaining a specified age, such as age 30. A problem exists at termination of the trust if one of the children dies before termination and that child's share is payable to his or her issue. On distribution from the trust, those issue are subject to the tax because a taxable termination has occurred that affected their share. Because a taxable termination is a distribution to a skip person[26] and the issue of the deceased child are skip persons, the taxable termination has occurred.

Planning Pointer 1

The result just described can be avoided (1) if the decedent's executor makes the election to use the GST exemption for the assets in this trust[27] or (2) if the trust is divided into separate subaccounts or separate trusts for each beneficiary rather than having the so-called pot trust for all beneficiaries. This second approach will qualify the trust for the predeceased child exception.[28] Obviously, pot trusts should not be used if there is a possibility of a skip person becoming a trust beneficiary. The first approach must be taken by an election made by the executor at the time of filing the federal estate tax return, which is due within nine months of the decedent's death. The second approach obviously must be chosen when drafting the trust instrument. If the trust is for the lifetime benefit of the surviving spouse and the couple's children, the division of the trust into separate subaccounts or trusts for each beneficiary may be done at the death of the surviving spouse.

4.32 Tax Apportionment Clauses

The generation-skipping transfer tax specifies who is liable for the tax. The trustee is liable for the tax in a taxable termination or if there is a direct skip from the trust.[29] A direct skip, other than from a trust, must be paid by the transferor or estate. In the case of a taxable distribution, the tax must be paid by the skip person (transferee).[30] In the event of a taxable termination or distribution, the tax is paid from the transferred property. The tax on direct skips is paid by the transferor or estate, but is charged to the property transferred unless the will or trust specifies to the contrary.[31] (For a further discussion of the problems associated with direct skips, see Section 4.25).

Planning Pointer 2

A bequest that is a direct skip raises a problem. Does the testator intend that the generation-skipping transfer tax be paid from the residuary estate, or is it to be paid from the bequest? This is an important consideration and should be addressed in the will. If the tax is to be paid from the bequest, which usually is the desire when the bequest is of a portion of the residue, the tax payment clause in the will should specifically charge the payment of the generation-skipping transfer tax to the bequest.

Will Form to Charge Tax to Bequest

All inheritance, estate, or other death taxes assessed against my estate (except generation-skipping transfer taxes, which shall be paid from the bequest), including penalties and interest, shall be paid from my residuary estate.

In contrast, if the tax is to be paid from the residue, which may be the desire when a specific dollar amount is bequeathed, the tax payment clause should exonerate the bequest from payment of the generation-skipping transfer tax.

Will Form to Exonerate Bequest from Tax

All inheritance, estate, or other death taxes assessed against my estate, and any generation-skipping transfer taxes, including penalties and interest, shall be paid from my residuary estate.

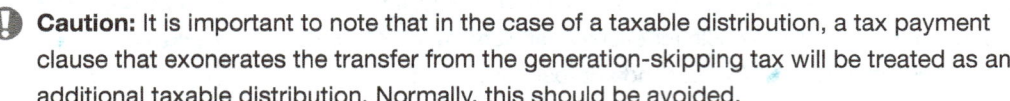 **Caution:** It is important to note that in the case of a taxable distribution, a tax payment clause that exonerates the transfer from the generation-skipping tax will be treated as an additional taxable distribution. Normally, this should be avoided.

Planning Pointer 3

Even though the tax on a taxable termination or distribution is required to be paid from the property, the beneficiary may be surprised at this result. Thus, to avoid both misunderstandings and interpretation problems with the estate-planning documents, a provision should be inserted in the trust instrument clarifying the tax burden.

Trust Form to Charge Tax to Property

In the event a taxable termination or taxable distribution occurs that is subject to the generation-skipping transfer tax as defined in Chapter 13 of the Internal Revenue Code, such tax shall be charged to and payable from the property transferred that gave rise to the generation-skipping transfer tax.

4.33 Disclaimer

A disclaimer can create an unintended result. If a child inherits property from a parent and then disclaims the property so that the property passes instead to the next generation, a direct skip has resulted. This causes both the estate tax and the generation-skipping transfer tax to be imposed on the transfer. In larger estates, this will result in both the 40% generation-skipping transfer tax and the 40% maximum estate tax being imposed on the same property. Thus, the total tax could be 80% of the value of the property. To further compound the problem, if the will provides that all taxes be paid from the residuary estate, the disclaimed property then passes without reduction for either tax, thus creating a potentially disastrous result.

 Planning Pointer 4

The use of a tax payment clause that specifically charges the generation-skipping transfer tax to the bequest in the event of a disclaimed bequest, as discussed in Section 4.32, could be used. More important, advance consideration must be given to the generation-skipping transfer tax before making a disclaimer.

4.34 Double Taxation

Another example of potential double taxation occurs with the interplay between the generation-skipping transfer tax and the gift tax. The following example shows the need to consider the generation-skipping transfer tax before making any transfer.

> **Example:** Assume grandmother makes a $1,000,000 gift to her grandson. A generation-skipping transfer tax must be paid by her of $400,000. However, a gift tax is also due, not only on the $1,000,000 gift, but also on the $400,000 generation-skipping transfer tax paid by the grandmother. If the grandmother is in the 40% gift tax bracket, $560,000 in gift taxes is owed. Thus, total taxes of $960,000 are owed on a $1,000,000 gift.

4.35 Portability

The current estate and gift tax law allows the unused estate and gift tax exclusion amount of the first spouse to die to be added to the exclusion amount for the estate of the surviving spouse. Thus, if the husband died in 2014 when the exclusion amount was $5,340,000 and he passed his entire estate to his wife, qualifying the wife's inheritance for the marital deduction and thereby eliminating all federal estate taxes, then his unused exclusion (which in this case is the entire amount) would then be added to the wife's estate and gift tax exclusion at her death. Assuming she dies in 2018, when the exclusion is $11,200,000, then her estate will be entitled to an estate tax exclusion of $16,540,000. This concept is termed *portability*. It is not available when one is making a generation-skipping transfer and using that exemption to offset any generation-skipping transfer taxes. Therefore, when making a generation-skipping transfer, trusts for the surviving spouse will typically be used in the estate of the first spouse in order to obtain the benefit of the generation-skipping transfer tax exemption. In most situations this will not be a significant disadvantage. It will simply complicate the drafting of the trust instrument in the estate plan.

Caution: Due to the complexity of the generation-skipping transfer tax, it is wise practice to delve more deeply into this complicated tax with a more specialized treatise, or to associate with an attorney experienced in drafting generation-skipping transfer trusts. Two excellent ABA publications are C. Cline, *Disclaimers in Estate Planning* (2d ed.; ABA, 2012) and J. Horn, *Flexible Trusts and Estates for Uncertain Times* (5th ed.; ABA, 2014).

Notes

1. I.R.C. §§ 2601, 2663.
2. *Id*. § 2641.
3. *Id*. § 2631.
4. *Id*. § 2613.
5. *Id*. § 2651(c).
6. *Id*. § 2651(b)(3).
7. *Id*. § 2651(d).
8. *Id*. § 2652(a).
9. *Id*. § 2652(a)(2).
10. See Chapter 7, at 7.24.
11. I.R.C. § 2652(a)(3).
12. *Id*. § 2612(b).
13. *Id*. § 2603(a)(1).
14. *Id*. § 2662(a)(2)(B).
15. This example assumes that the GST exemption has previously been used.
16. I.R.C. § 2621(b).
17. *Id*. § 164(a)(5).
18. *Id*. § 2612(a).
19. *Id*. § 2603(a)(2).
20. *Id*. § 2662(a)(2)(B).
21. This example assumes that the GST exemption has previously been used.
22. I.R.C. § 2612(c).
23. *Id*. § 2603(a)(3).
24. *Id*. § 2662(a)(2)(A).

25. This example assumes that the GST exemption has previously been used.
26. I.R.C. § 2612(a)(1).
27. *Id.* § 2631.
28. *Id.* § 2612(c)(2).
29. *Id.* § 2603(a).
30. *Id.* § 2603(b).
31. *Id.* § 2621(b).

Chapter 5

Trusts and Their Uses

5.1 Background
5.2 Types of Trusts
    5.21 A-B Trust
    5.22 QTIP Trust
    5.23 Premarital Trust
    5.24 Charitable Remainder Trusts
    5.25 Special Needs Trust
    5.26 Income-Only Trust
    5.27 Crummey Trust
    5.28 Disclaimer Trust
    5.29 Generation-Skipping Trust
    5.210 Living Trust
    5.211 Minor's or 2503(c) Trust
    5.212 Pot Trust
    5.213 Spendthrift Trust
    5.214 Standby Trust

5.1 Background

The primary tool in estate planning is the trust. There are many different types of trusts that can be used. Some trusts provide tax savings, whereas others are needed to fit the particular circumstances of the beneficiaries. Whether needed for tax reasons, nontax reasons, or both, the trust is the foundation of any estate plan.

    A trust may be inter vivos or testamentary. The *inter vivos trust* is a trust agreement executed by the settlor (often termed *grantor* or *trustor*) and the trustee during the settlor's lifetime. The trust can be funded during the settlor's lifetime, in which event assets are transferred to the trustee. The trust is then administered by the trustee for the beneficiaries during the settlor's lifetime and thereafter, if desired. If the trust is unfunded, no assets are transferred to the trust at the time of its creation. Assets are transferred to the trust at a later time, such as on the disability or death of the settlor. A *testamentary trust* is simply part of an individual's will and takes effect on the individual's death. The trust is funded following probate of the will and at some point during the settlement of the estate.

The inter vivos trust is merely a contract entered into between the settlor and the trustee. Thus, it is not a testamentary instrument that is subject to probate proceedings, filing in the public records, and court supervision. This added privacy is an advantage of an inter vivos trust. Because it is not subject to probate, there is the possibility of saving estate settlement costs. For example, if the trust is funded during the settlor's lifetime, those assets are not included in the probate estate. Any estate settlement costs charged as a percentage of the probate estate, such as executor or legal fees, are saved.

An inter vivos trust, even if not funded during the settlor's lifetime, ensures that the trustee will serve as fiduciary because the trustee has the opportunity to review and sign the trust before the settlor's death. A testamentary trust does not offer this opportunity. Thus, the named trustee could refuse to serve following probate of the will. This situation could occur, for example, if the will contained provisions that might create potential administrative difficulties or liabilities for the trustee. If a testamentary trust is desired, this disadvantage can be overcome by allowing the trustee to review the will in advance and sign a separate document in which he or she agrees to serve as trustee.

Because a testamentary trust lacks the advantage of privacy, the general nature of the estate is revealed in the probate court records. Further, the dispositive provisions of the trust are of public record, which may be undesirable when there is a need for unequal or unusual testamentary provisions. In some states, periodic reporting by the trustee to the local probate court also is required. This normally is considered a disadvantage, but it can be an advantage. For example, when the trustee is an individual rather than a corporate trustee, the supervision and bonding requirement of the probate court ensures disclosure and accountability. If the settlor desires to amend the trust during his or her lifetime, the testamentary trust can be easily amended by a codicil or new will, whereas an amendment to an inter vivos trust requires the trustee's consent.

5.2 Types of Trusts

5.21 A-B Trust

The A-B trust is a basic approach in estate planning used prior to the American Taxpayer Relief Act of 2012, which was designed to lessen the federal estate taxes owed by an estate. The A trust is sometimes referred to as the *marital trust*; and the B trust is often referred to as the *credit shelter, by-pass,* or *family trust*. Prior law required a married couple to use the marital deduction prior to using the exclusion amount ($11,200,000 in 2018).[1] Because the marital deduction eliminated the estate taxes on property passing to the surviving spouse, the exclusion amount was not used in the estate of the first spouse to die when the entire estate passed from the deceased spouse to the surviving spouse. The exclusion amount of the deceased spouse was, in effect, lost, resulting in the surviving spouse's estate being limited to his or her own exclusion amount. To obtain the use of both exclusion amounts, the "A-B Trust approach" was used.

In the A-B Trust approach, an estate is placed in trust and divided into two separate trusts termed Trust A and Trust B. Trust A must qualify for the federal estate tax marital deduction, whereas Trust B is designed intentionally not to qualify. If a Trust A is not desired, these assets can be given outright to the surviving spouse. Trust B is intended to equal the exclusion amount in the year of death, with the balance of the estate passing into Trust A.[2] The estate tax owed on Trust B is offset by the unified credit, thus resulting in no estate tax on Trust B. Because Trust A (or Share A if a trust is not desired) qualifies for the marital deduction, no estate tax is owed on it. A third option using a QTIP trust rather than a Trust A or Share A is discussed at 5.22.

If Trusts A and B are used, the surviving spouse can receive the entire income from both trusts if desired, but he or she must receive the income at least annually from Trust A. The principal from both trusts can be expended for the surviving spouse if necessary for his or her health care, maintenance, and support. Normally, the surviving spouse must be granted a general power of appointment over Trust A, but this is not essential if the QTIP trust discussed in 5.22 is elected. On the death of the surviving spouse, Trust A and that spouse's own property are subject to the estate tax on his or her own estate. The Trust B assets pass to the remaindermen of Trust B without any federal estate tax. Therein lie the estate tax savings. These savings will result even though the surviving spouse had the benefit of income and principal from Trust B. (There are a number of intricacies in an A-B trust estate plan. The discussions in Chapters 6 and 7 should be helpful, as should the annotated wills and trusts provided in Chapter 15 at 15.3 and 15.4.) Two additional resources providing drafting forms are R. Hunt, *Estate Planning Forms* (ABA, 2009) and J. Horn, *Flexible Trusts and Estates for Uncertain Times* (5th ed.; ABA, 2014).

Current law does not require this awkward approach to tax planning. The current law introduced a concept known as "portability," which simply means that the unused exclusion amount from the first spouse's estate can be transferred to the second spouse to be added to her or his exclusion amount.[3] This sensible and overdue legislative change enables a couple to have the benefit of both exclusion amounts without the complicated trust drafting that was required under the A-B trust planning approach. All that is required to ensure the portability option is the filing of a federal estate tax return making this election for the estate of the first spouse to die. Although the A-B Trust approach is not utilized as much today as it was under the prior law, there are still situations in which it will be the preferred planning approach. For example, if there is expected to be significant asset growth in the estate assets between the time of the death of the first spouse and the death of the surviving spouse, then this planning approach is still a wise one to use. In estates that are large enough to owe a federal estate tax, the tax rate is 40%. An estate today that is approximately $11,000,000 would not result in any federal estate tax at either death. However, if some of those estate assets grew significantly in value, it would have been a wise plan to place the growth assets in the B trust, as those assets would not be taxable at the death of the second spouse. If those assets grow in value in excess of the exclusion amount ($11,200,000 in 2018), then 40% of the growth will escape estate taxes. For example, if the assets placed in the B trust increased by $5,000,000 over the years between the death of the first spouse and the second spouse to die, then an estate tax savings of $2,000,000 would be possible. This savings is partially offset by a capital gains income tax on the gain above the income tax cost basis when the assets are sold. Further, if the assets did not grow in value, there is no advantage to the B trust. Indeed, there is a disadvantage because all of the assets owned by the second spouse to die will receive a step-up basis in the income tax costs basis, which will usually lessen income taxes.

Planning Pointer 1

Because it is difficult to know at the time of drafting the estate planning documents whether the estate tax or the income savings will be the bigger issue, a useful approach is to will all of the property outright to the surviving spouse or into an A trust or a QTIP trust, and then provide that any disclaimed assets will then pass into the B trust. In this way a decision can be made at the first death as to whether to pursue the income tax savings option or the estate tax savings option. An excellent ABA resource is C. Cline, *Disclaimers in Estate Planning* (2d ed.; ABA, 2012).

5.22 QTIP Trust

The qualified terminable interest property (QTIP) trust makes use of the marital deduction in much the same way as does the A-B Trust approach. The primary difference is that the QTIP trust does not grant the surviving spouse a general power of appointment over the A trust. The B trust remains the same.

A general power of appointment was traditionally granted to the surviving spouse so that the A trust could qualify for the marital deduction. Otherwise, the A trust was termed a terminable interest, for which no marital deduction was allowed. An amendment to the estate tax law effective in 1982 permits the marital deduction for most terminable interests if so elected by the executor.[4]

In a QTIP trust, the surviving spouse must be given income for lifetime from the A trust, but principal distributions can be restricted as desired by the settlor. The surviving spouse is not given a general power of appointment over the trust. The terms of the settlor's trust determine the manner in which the trust will be distributed following the death of the surviving spouse.

The QTIP trust is particularly important when planning estates for spouses who each have children from an earlier marriage. The settlor can determine the estate distribution and know that it will not be modified at a later date by the surviving spouse's exercise of a power of appointment in favor of his or her own children. The QTIP trust also prevents the surviving spouse from transferring the A trust to a new spouse should the surviving spouse remarry. See 15.3 regarding inclusion of QTIP trust provisions in the A-B trust.

5.23 Premarital Trust

A widow or widower often is concerned about the rights of inheritance of a new spouse should he or she remarry. A typical situation involves a widow who owns property that was inherited from her husband or that they owned jointly with right of survivorship, as well as life insurance proceeds and retirement benefits received by her owing to his death. The widow's desire is that this property pass to her and her deceased husband's children following her death. She may have no immediate plans to remarry, but she knows this is a possibility. A properly drafted premarital agreement executed by her and her prospective husband will waive his rights to the estate that she inherited from her previous husband; however, she may be uncertain of both her ability to discuss the subject and the willingness of her new husband to sign such an agreement.

The widow (or widower) in this example can establish an inter vivos trust and transfer into it all of the property that she does not want to be subject to the inheritance rights of a new spouse. The widow can act as trustee for herself and her children and name a corporate trustee to succeed her on her death, disability, or resignation. If she prefers, a corporate trustee can act as trustee, and she can reserve the right to change trustees. The trust can be revocable during her lifetime and become irrevocable only on her death. A renunciation of her will by her new husband should not reach the trust property because it is not probate property. Any claims by her new husband that the trust is a fraudulent device to circumvent his statutory rights of inheritance should not prevail if the trust is established and funded well before their marriage. The law of the practitioner's own state must be consulted, but this approach will prevail in some states. The wisest approach is a properly drafted premarital agreement coupled with the trust. (In Chapter 15, at 15.7, a will and trust to carry out this approach are provided. The will and trust offer no tax savings, but they provide an obvious, more important benefit for the children. A premarital agreement is also provided in 15.7.) A helpful ABA publication is L. Ravdin, *Premarital Agreements: Drafting and Negotiations* (2d ed.; ABA, 2017).

5.24 Charitable Remainder Trusts

There are two types of charitable remainder trusts: a charitable remainder annuity trust (CRAT) and a charitable remainder unitrust (CRUT). Generally, for either type of trust, the remainder interest must be at least 10% of the fair market value of the assets transferred to the trust. A CRAT is a trust in which a fixed percentage or dollar payment is paid to the annuitant at least annually.[5] The annual payment must be no less than 5% nor more than 50% of the initial fair market value of the trust property. The payment may be for either the lifetime of the beneficiary or a period not to exceed 20 years. The payment may not increase or decrease during the term of the trust, nor may additional gifts be made to the trust. Following the death of the annuitant, the remainder then is transferred to the charity or is held in trust and distributed for the charity. For example, a typical CRAT would be one paying a $5,000 annual payment, payable in monthly installments from an initial one-time gift to the CRAT of $100,000.

The CRUT has the same requirements as the annuity trust, except the annual payment is a fixed percentage that must be reset each year upon reevaluation of the trust property.[6] Thus, the annual payment will increase or decrease, depending on the value of the trust assets. A limited exception allows the unitrust to pay the lesser of 5% or trust income. The CRUT also permits additional gifts to the trust. A typical CRUT would pay out 5% of fair market value of the trust determined on December 31 of the prior year, payable in 12 monthly installments. Assuming a 5% payment and a $100,000 gift (as in the prior example), in the first year the donor receives the same amount as with a CRAT. If the value of the trust drops to $80,000, then the donor only receives $4,000 during the following year, but if instead the trust increases in value to $110,000, then the donor receives $5,500 in the following year.

Both types of trusts provide income and estate tax benefits for the charitably minded individual. The value of the charity's remainder interest is a deductible charitable contribution on the donor's individual income tax return for the year in which the asset is transferred to the trust. Any unused deduction can be carried forward for five years. Also, the value of the charitable gift is based on the fair market value of the remainder interest at the time of the gift. Thus, the appreciation on the gift is not subject to income tax, and the individual is allowed a deduction for the value of the remainder interest, including the untaxed appreciation. If a charitable remainder trust is established by the individual's will, it will generate an estate tax deduction for the remainder interest. In some situations the individual may find that the charitable remainder trust, when coupled with the purchase of life insurance, results in a larger estate passing to the estate beneficiaries than if the charitable gift had not been made. (A further discussion of charitable giving and the use of charitable remainder trusts appears in Chapter 9.) Prototype CRAT and CRUT forms have been preapproved by the IRS;[7] these simplify drafting. (See Chapter 15, at 15.10, for the references to these trust forms.)

5.25 Special Needs Trust

A *special needs trust* is a trust established for the benefit of a disabled beneficiary who is entitled to receive government assistance. The typical benefits are Supplemental Security Income (SSI) and Medicaid to pay for medical needs. The intent of the trust is to supplement government assistance. The correct drafting of this type of trust is very important; errors can result in the loss of government assistance, or the loss of trust income and principal.[8] The payment of income and principal should be entirely discretionary with the trustee. No cash payments should be made to the beneficiary; rather, the trust should pay for the items needed by the beneficiary.

Protective wording should be inserted in the trust to clarify that the trustee is to expend income and principal only after federal, state, and local public assistance is received and used for the benefit of the beneficiary. A spendthrift clause should be inserted in the trust to avoid the possibility of the government's attaching the trust property to be reimbursed for its public assistance payments. Although not essential, it is better practice to name a corporate trustee to administer this type of trust. A special needs trust form is provided in Chapter 15, at 15.8. This trust is a third-party special needs trust. Because the source of the funds is a third party, there are no limitations on this type of trust other than that the trust distributions may not be for basic support needs, as these payments will generally reduce SSI payments by a maximum of one-third.

A self-settled special needs trust is one in which the source of the funds is the disabled beneficiary.[9] Typically, the source of funds will be from a personal injury settlement or an inheritance. To remain eligible for SSI and Medicaid benefits, the trust must be established for a person disabled under Social Security definitions of *disability* who is under the age of 65 years at the time the trust is established. Further, the trust must provide that any funds remaining at the beneficiary's death must be repaid for the government benefits received. Again, the trust may not pay for basic necessities, which are defined as food or shelter. This drafting can become complicated. A helpful treatment of this "fine point" appears in C. Kruse, *Third Party and Self-Created Trust: Planning for the Elderly and Disabled Client* (3d ed.; ABA, 2002).

5.26 Income-Only Trust

An income-only trust is one in which property is placed in a trust with the beneficiary only being entitled to receive income from the trust.[10] This type of trust is sometimes used by persons concerned with preserving property from sale to pay long-term care expenses. Its use is limited, but in some situations it is very useful. Under no circumstances may principal be distributed to the beneficiary. The Medicaid 60-month look-back period applies to transfers into this type of trust. However, after the 60-month look-back period has elapsed, the property held in the income-only trust does not result in those assets being treated as a resource for determining Medicaid eligibility, nor are the assets subject to estate recovery after the beneficiary's death. A personal residence or income-producing property such as rental property or a farm are ideal properties to be placed in an income-only trust. Once the 60-month look-back period has elapsed, and assuming the beneficiary then has to go into long-term nursing home care, only the income from the trust will be paid to the nursing home, with the Medicaid program paying for any balance owed to the nursing home (assuming that there are no other resources then owned by the beneficiary outside of the trust). A sample trust form is shown in Chapter 15, at 15.9.

5.27 Crummey Trust

A Crummey trust[11] is not a poorly drafted trust, as its name might imply. Quite the contrary: it is a trust that, when properly drafted, entitles the settlor to use the annual gift tax exclusion for gifts to the trust.[12] Otherwise, the settlor is not entitled to the annual gift tax exclusion because that exclusion only applies to present-interest gifts. A gift to a trust is considered a future interest. The name of this type of trust stems from the court case of *Crummey v. Commissioner*.[13] The *Crummey* decision, which has been accepted by the Internal Revenue Service (IRS),[14] permits the annual gift tax exclusion, provided that the trust beneficiary has notice of the gift to the trust and has the right to withdraw the gift from the trust. This right can expire after a reasonable length of time (for example, 30 or 60 days).

A Crummey trust allows the buildup of a large trust fund over a number of years if the beneficiary does not withdraw the annual gifts to the trust. Obviously, if the beneficiary withdraws an annual gift, it is unlikely that the settlor will continue to make further gifts. Another good use of the Crummey trust arises when the trustee purchases life insurance on the life of the settlor and pays the premiums with the annual gift to the trust. This creates the potential that a large trust fund will be created when the insurance is paid to the trust on the settlor's death. Because a Crummey trust is irrevocable, the trust is not considered part of the settlor's estate and thus is not subject to the federal estate tax. (There is discussion of the use of a Crummey trust with life insurance in Chapter 8, at 8.4. A sample trust form appears in Chapter 15, at 15.6.)

5.28 Disclaimer Trust

A disclaimer trust[15] can be used in several different situations. It is designed to create flexibility. An example of where it might be used is when each spouse provides in his or her will that the estate will go outright to the survivor, but in the event the survivor disclaims some part or all of the estate, it will pass into a trust for the benefit of the children or grandchildren. A disclaimer does not result in the disclaimed property being subject to gift tax. Thus, with a larger estate the surviving spouse may choose to disclaim part of the estate to permit it to be transferred into a trust for the children, in anticipation that in the years ahead the property will grow significantly in value, resulting in a 40% estate tax at a later date. Obviously, use of a disclaimer trust is most likely with larger estates that exceed the exclusion amount for both spouses.

Another use of a disclaimer trust was referred to earlier in the discussion of the A-B trust planning option. For many couples, the portability of the exclusion amount to the surviving spouse will ensure there are no federal estate tax problems. In those estates where it is anticipated that there is a possibility of some part or all of the estate assets increasing in value significantly after the death of the first spouse, then the disclaimer trust is a viable option. For example, assume the wife dies first, with her will providing that the entire estate passes to her husband outright. In the event the husband disclaims any part or all of the property passing under the will, it will then go into a trust for the husband's lifetime benefit. The husband can be given rights to income for life and even distributions of principal if needed for his reasonable health care, maintenance, and support needs. The husband can even act as trustee of this trust. If the husband disclaimed assets in an amount equal to the exclusion amount (which is $11,200,000 in 2018) and those assets doubled during his lifetime, he will have saved $4,480,000 in federal estate taxes for his children when they receive the property at his subsequent death. The use of disclaimers is discussed in Chapter 13, at 13.2. A sample disclaimer trust is found in Chapter 15, at 15.4.

5.29 Generation-Skipping Trust

An estate-planning technique that often was used in the "golden days" of estate planning for larger estates was the generation-skipping trust. The planning technique simply required the testator to transfer his or her children's inheritance in trust for their lifetime rather than giving it to them outright. On the children's death, their trust terminated and was distributed to the grandchildren. The trust could continue for even more generations, provided the rule against perpetuities was not violated. Because the children did not own the trust property, none of the trust assets were included in the children's estate on their own death. Thus, no federal estate tax was owed by the children's estate on the trust assets. The children could receive the income and, if needed, the principal from the trust throughout their lifetime. They could even have the right (with only minor limitations) to direct the distribution of the trust at their own death.

A generation-skipping transfer tax is now imposed on such transfers at a flat rate equal to the highest current federal estate tax rate, which is 40%.[16] The generation-skipping tax permits one important exemption. Each individual is allowed an exemption from the tax equal to the estate and gift tax exclusion amount.[17] Thus, a husband and wife both dying in 2018 can use a generation-skipping trust for up to $22,400,000 of their estate. This is a $8,960,000 savings even if the assets never increase in value. A discussion of the generation-skipping tax appears in Chapter 4.

5.210 Living Trust

The *living trust* is a trust established by the settlor during lifetime. Typically, the settlor transfers some or all of his or her property to the trust during lifetime. The settlor may act as trustee of the trust or name an individual or corporate trustee. The trust pays income for life to the settlor and to the settlor's spouse and children, as the settlor directs. Principal can also be expended as directed by the settlor.

Following the death of the settlor, the trust can continue for the benefit of the surviving spouse and the children. The trust then terminates at some later date, such as on the death of the surviving spouse. Because the trust is funded during the settlor's lifetime, there is no delay in paying income to the trust beneficiaries when the settlor dies. (A delay would occur if the trust were not funded until during or after the settlement of the settlor's estate.) The living trust also saves estate settlement costs such as executor and legal fees because those costs are calculated as a percentage of the probate estate. Because the assets are already in the living trust, they do not make up a part of the probate estate on which those costs are calculated. An added benefit is that those trust assets do not have to be reported to the probate court, which ensures privacy. A sample living trust appears in Chapter 15, at 15.12.

5.211 Minor's or 2503(c) Trust

A minor's trust or, as it is sometimes termed, an educational trust, is designed to take advantage of the annual gift tax exclusion ($15,000 for the year 2018) in order to build up a fund for a child's benefit over a period of time.[18] Normally, a gift in trust is not entitled to the annual gift tax exclusion because it is a gift of a future interest, and the annual exclusion is available only for a present-interest gift. Section 2503(c) of the Internal Revenue Code provides an important exception.

The donor is entitled to the annual gift tax exclusion for any gift to a trust if the trustee (1) has the discretion to distribute income and principal to the donee before age 21, irrespective of whether any income or principal is in fact distributed; (2) must distribute the entire trust principal and any accumulated income to the donee when the donee reaches age 21; and (3) must distribute the trust to the donee's estate should the donee die before reaching age 21, or pursuant to the terms of a general power of appointment granted to the donee in the trust. The trust can continue beyond age 21 if the donee is granted the right to withdraw the entire trust at age 21 but elects not to do so.[19]

This type of trust permits regular gifts to a trust, for example, to establish an educational fund for a child. The income earned from the investments is taxed to the trust and not to the settlor. This is the tax result irrespective of the so-called kiddie tax.[20] For a discussion of the minor's trust and the kiddie tax, see Chapter 3, at 3.5. A minor's or 2503(c) trust sample form is provided in Chapter 15, at 15.5. Two helpful ABA publications are N. Shurtz, *Education Planning: Taxes, Trusts, and Techniques* (ABA, 2007); and C. D'Aversa, *Tax, Estate, and Lifetime Planning for Minors* (ABA, 2006).

5.212 Pot Trust

A *pot trust* is a type of trust typically used for the children of the settlor when the trust estate is not large. For example, the settlor may establish a trust for the lifetime benefit of his or her spouse and children. On the surviving spouse's death, the trust continues for the benefit of the children if the youngest is under a particular age, such as age 25 or 30. The trust grants the trustee broad discretion to make unequal distributions of income and principal among the children. Further, any distributions of income and principal are not required to be equalized among the children on termination and final distribution of the trust.

This type of trust grants the trustee the same discretion to provide for the children's needs that the settlor and his or her spouse exercised during their lifetime. Because the children's financial needs will vary over the years, there will be times when some children receive large trust distributions whereas others receive very small distributions. For example, children during their college years normally will receive large distributions, whereas those who have graduated from college will receive much smaller distributions, or possibly no distributions. The pot trust is best suited for situations in which the trust fund is small and may not be large enough to provide for the educational and living expenses of the younger children if equal distributions are required for the older children. For much larger estates in which the federal estate tax is a factor, the generation-skipping transfer tax may also create some potential and unintended tax problems that may weigh in favor of the use of separate share trusts for the children. These problems are discussed in Chapter 4, at 4.31.

5.213 Spendthrift Trust

A spendthrift trust is one of the more common types of trusts. Such a trust simply extends for the lifetime of the beneficiary and is distributed at his or her death to the next generation or to some other distributee. The trust can provide for the entire income to be paid to, or on behalf of, the beneficiary. If preferred, the trustee can be given discretion in deciding what amount of income to pay to the beneficiary. The trust can prevent the principal from being invaded under any circumstances, or the trustee can be permitted to invade principal for extraordinary needs, such as health care.

Although there are some classic spendthrifts who do need the protection of such a trust, there are several other reasons for establishing a spendthrift trust. A child may have a drug or alcohol dependency and need this protection. Similarly, a spendthrift trust can protect a child from loss of the trust property to business and personal creditors, because they cannot levy on the trust to collect debts owed them by the child. The possible commingling of trust and marital assets and the problem this may create in the event of divorce is another reason the settlor-parent (and the child) may prefer the protection of a spendthrift trust. A sample spendthrift trust is not provided in the text; however, spendthrift clauses are contained in the trusts in Chapter 15, at 15.3 and 15.6. All that is required to create a spendthrift trust is to extend the term of the trust for the lifetime of the child, preclude the right of creditors to levy on the trust, and provide for the distribution of the trust on the death of the child.

5.214 Standby Trust

A standby trust is established in anticipation of a period of disability or poor health. The settlor establishes a revocable living trust. The trust normally contains most of the same provisions as a living trust. The trust provides for the income and principal to be expended for the support, maintenance, and health care of the settlor and his or her spouse. On the death of the settlor, the trust continues for the benefit of the surviving spouse and terminates on the survivor's death.

The primary difference between a standby trust and a living trust is that the standby trust is not funded until disability occurs. For example, the settlor establishes a standby trust naming a corporate or individual trustee but does not transfer any property into the trust. A relative, friend, or the trustee is given a power of attorney that will enable the attorney-in-fact to transfer the settlor's property to the trustee should the settlor become disabled. The determination of disability is normally made by the settlor's treating physician. If the settlor never becomes disabled, the trust will not be funded and will remain inactive. The trust simply "stands by" until needed. Often the trust is funded following the settlor's death for the benefit of the surviving spouse, but this is not essential. A sample standby trust is provided in Chapter 15, at 15.11.

Notes

1. I.R.C. § 2056.
2. *Id.* § 2010.
3. *Id.* § 2010(c)(4).
4. *Id.* § 2056(b)(7).
5. *Id.* § 664(d)(1).
6. *Id.* § 664(d)(2).
7. Rev. Procs. 2003-53 through -60; Rev. Procs. 2005-52 through -59.
8. A helpful resource is CLIFTON B. KRUSE JR., THIRD PARTY AND SELF-CREATED TRUSTS (ABA, 2002).
9. *Id.*
10. *Id.*
11. A helpful resource is LAWRENCE BRODY ET AL., THE IRREVOCABLE LIFE INSURANCE TRUST (ABA, 2011).
12. I.R.C. § 2503(b).
13. Crummey v. Commissioner, 397 F.2d 82 (9th Cir. 1968).
14. Rev. Rul. 73-405, 1973-2 C.B. 321.
15. A helpful resource is C. CLINE, DISCLAIMERS IN ESTATE PLANNING (ABA, 2012).
16. *Id.* § 2641.
17. *Id.* § 2631.
18. *Id.* § 2503(b).
19. Rev. Rul. 74-43, 1974-1 C.B. 285.
20. I.R.C. § 1(i).

Chapter 6

Powers of Appointment

6.1 Background

6.2 Estate and Gift Tax Provisions

6.3 Effective Uses of Powers

    6.31 Limited Power of Appointment

    6.32 Power Limited to Ascertainable Standard

    6.33 5 or 5 Power

6.4 Interpretation and Drafting Considerations

    6.41 Miscellaneous Forms

6.1 Background

Powers of appointment can be useful in estate planning, from both a tax and a nontax standpoint. A *power of appointment* is a device through which the owner of property (the donor) reserves to himself or herself or transfers to another (the donee) the power to designate, within the limits set by the donor of the power, the person or entity (the appointee) who will receive the property and the interest that will be received.[1] Although a definition is a helpful beginning point, it must be recognized that powers of appointment may take numerous different forms and that no particular wording is necessary to create a power of appointment.

    The utility of a power of appointment comes from the flexibility it adds to an estate plan. Although not limited in usage to trust instruments, powers of appointment are most frequently used in trusts. Because changes in circumstances may occur after the creation of a trust, the power of appointment provides a convenient and effective way to respond to those changed circumstances.

    Several typical uses of powers of appointment can be seen in the examples that follow.

    Example 1: John, a widower, has two daughters, one of whom has two children; the other has no children. John wants to provide for his two daughters and any grandchildren through a trust. He passes his estate into two trusts—one for each daughter. Each trust pays income and principal to the daughter as life beneficiary of the trust, and on each daughter's death her trust terminates and is distributed to her children. Because one of John's daughters does not presently have any children, and it is uncertain whether she will have children at the time of her death, John needs greater flexibility in providing for the distribution of this daughter's trust upon termination. In this daughter's trust, John could grant her a power to direct the disposition of her trust fund at death, should she die without children. A sample form follows.

Trust Form Granting Power of Appointment

In the event the Settlor's daughter, _____, dies without issue, the Settlor's daughter may appoint outright or in trust in her last will and testament, by making specific reference to this power, the person or persons, or entities, including charitable entities, who shall receive the trust principal and any accumulated income at her death; provided, however, the Settlor's daughter may not exercise this power of appointment in favor of herself, her estate, her creditors, or the creditors of her estate.

Example 2: Jane, a widow, is the life income beneficiary of a trust established for her by her husband on his death. The trust provides that on Jane's death the trust terminates and is to be distributed equally among the couple's children. To provide greater flexibility to respond to future changes in the children's needs, Jane is granted both an inter vivos and a testamentary power to appoint the trust in such amounts and in such manner as she directs among a limited group of beneficiaries, including the children and their spouses; more remote descendants and their spouses; and any charities exempt from estate taxation under IRC Section 2055. In this manner Jane can meet any number of changes in circumstances that may occur between the time of her husband's death and her own death. If she does not exercise this power of appointment, then the trust is simply distributed equally among the children at her death. A form granting this type of power of appointment follows; however, the inter vivos exercise of this power may be subject to a gift tax. Thus, the discussion at 6.31 must also be considered.

Trust Form Granting Inter Vivos and Testamentary Power of Appointment

The Settlor's wife, _____, may appoint this trust fund, in such amounts and in such manner, whether in trust, outright, or otherwise, as she may elect among that limited class consisting of the Settlor's children and their spouses, more remote descendants and their spouses, and charities exempt from taxation under IRC Section 2055. The exercise of this power of appointment must make specific reference to this power, and if exercised during lifetime the exercise must be by a written instrument filed with the Trustee and if at death by the last will and testament of the Settlor's wife. In the event the Settlor's wife does not exercise this power of appointment, at her death the Trustee shall distribute this trust following her death to the Settlor's children in equal shares.

Example 3: Sue is the beneficiary for her lifetime of a trust established for her by her parents. She receives income for life, and the principal, if needed, can be spent for her health, maintenance, and support. On her death the trust terminates and the trust passes to her children. Sue's parents know she wants to provide for her husband should she predecease him, and they are in agreement with this desire. Nonetheless, they are concerned about the possibility of divorce; thus, they do not want to name him in their trust as a life beneficiary or remainderman. They grant Sue a testamentary power of appointment to direct the trust property at her death among a limited group consisting of her children, grandchildren, and her husband. If the power is not exercised, the trust will pass equally to Sue's children on her death. Sue can now make the decision of whether to pass any of the trust property to her husband, and if so, in what amount. The power of appointment can even permit Sue to exercise it in such a way as to create a life estate, or a trust for life, or a trust until the remarriage of her husband. A sample form follows.

Trust Form Granting Testamentary Power of Appointment

The beneficiary, _____, on her death, may direct the distribution of this trust in such amounts or proportions and in such manner, whether outright, in trust, or with any other restrictions, to or for the benefit of that limited class consisting of her husband, children, or more remote descendants, as she may choose to direct by her last will and testament; and should she fail to exercise this power by specific reference to it in her last will and testament, the trust shall pass equally among her children, in fee simple and per stirpes.

These examples reflect only a few of the uses of powers of appointment. The possible uses of powers of appointment are limitless. Before using powers of appointment, the estate and gift tax consequences must be considered.

6.2 Estate and Gift Tax Provisions

The pertinent provisions of the tax laws classify powers as (1) general powers and (2) nongeneral or limited powers. A *general power of appointment* is defined as a power exercisable in favor of:

(1) the decedent,

(2) his estate,

(3) his creditors, or

(4) the creditors of his estate; except that the following shall not be deemed a general power:

   (A) a power to consume, invade, or appropriate property for the benefit of the decedent which is limited by an ascertainable standard relating to the health, education, support, or maintenance of the decedent;

   (B) a power created on or before October 21, 1942, which is exercisable only by the decedent jointly with another;

   (C) a power created after October 21, 1942, which is exercisable only by the decedent jointly with another, provided that:

      (i) such other person is the creator of the power;

      (ii) such other person has a substantial adverse interest against the exercise of the power, including a joint holder who has a power to appoint to himself after the death of the decedent;

      (iii) if the joint holder does not have a substantial adverse interest against the exercise of the power, the power will be deemed a general power only in respect of a fractional part of the property subject to the power, determined by dividing the value of the property by the number of persons, including the decedent, in favor of whom the power is exercisable.[2]

A nongeneral or limited power of appointment is simply a power that does not meet the definition of a general power of appointment. From the preceding definition, several useful concepts can be derived. Basically, a general power of appointment is one in which there is no restriction on who may receive the property subject to the power. The power holder can exercise the power to benefit whomever he or she chooses, thus causing the property subject to the power to be includable in the holder's estate on death because the holder of the power could exercise it in favor of himself or herself. If a general power of appointment lapses or is released during the holder's lifetime, a gift tax will be imposed.[3]

6.3 Effective Uses of Powers

6.31 Limited Power of Appointment

For federal estate tax purposes, a general power of appointment is a power that can be exercised in favor of the holder, his or her estate, his or her creditors, or the creditors of his or her estate. A power will not result in an estate tax, no matter how broad the group for whom it can be exercised, if it cannot be exercised in favor of the holder, his or her estate, his or her creditors, or the creditors of his or her estate.[4] A power so limited is termed a *nongeneral* or *limited power of appointment*, which is not taxable to the holder. This presents a good planning opportunity.

Property can be transferred by the settlor into a trust for the lifetime benefit of the beneficiary. The beneficiary can be given a limited power of appointment exercisable during lifetime or at death, and this power will not result in an estate or gift tax to the beneficiary, whether or not the power is exercised. Typically, this power will be limited to being exercised in favor of the power holder's spouse, children and children's spouses, more remote descendants and their spouses, and tax-exempt charities.

> **Caution:** While the holding of a limited power of appointment does not result in the property subject to the power being included in the gross estate for federal estate tax purposes, it may make the holder subject to the gift tax.[5] If the holder of the power also has an interest in the property, a taxable gift will result from the inter vivos exercise of the limited power. For example, a widow who receives income for life from a trust makes a taxable gift when she exercises a limited power of appointment during her lifetime in favor of her children. She has passed part of the principal of the trust to them, which has the effect of the widow giving away part of her income right to her children. The value of the gift is not the principal that passes to the children due to the exercise of the power but, rather, the present value of the life interest forfeited by the widow due to the exercise of the power of appointment.

Trust Form Granting Limited Power of Appointment

The Trustee shall distribute this trust in such amounts or proportions and in such manner, outright or in trust, to or for the benefit of the Settlor's children and their spouses, more remote descendants and their spouses, and charities exempt from taxation under IRC Section 2055, as directed by the Settlor's wife during her lifetime by a written instrument filed with the Trustee, or upon her death by her last will and testament; provided, any exercise of this power of appointment must make specific reference to it. In the event the Settlor's wife has not exercised this power during her lifetime and does not exercise it at her death in her last will and testament, the Trustee shall distribute this trust following her death as follows: _____.

Note: If desired, references to the lifetime exercise of the power may be deleted.

6.32 Power Limited to Ascertainable Standard

A power of appointment is not a taxable power if its exercise is limited to an ascertainable standard relating to the "health, education, support, or maintenance" of the power holder.[6] A power limited to an indefinite standard such as the holder's "comfort, welfare, or happiness" does not qualify. Thus, great care must be taken in choosing the correct wording. The Treasury Regulations provide excellent guidance for properly limiting a power of appointment to an appropriate ascertainable standard.[7]

> **Example:** A husband creates a trust for his wife following his death and names her as trustee. The trust requires that the wife receive the entire income from the trust quarterly. Additionally, she, as trustee, may distribute the principal to herself as trust beneficiary if the principal is needed for her "health, education, support, or maintenance." This power is not taxable to the wife. That is, at her death the existence of the power will not cause the trust property to be includable in her gross estate, because the power is limited to an ascertainable standard. However, if the standard for invasion of principal were "comfort, welfare, and happiness," the standard would not be considered ascertainable. This results in the inclusion of the trust assets in the wife's estate. In this instance creativity is not wise; rather, the practitioner should use the following sample form or vary from it only after reading the Treasury Regulations previously cited.

Trust Form Creating a Power Limited to Ascertainable Standard

During the lifetime of the Settlor's wife, _____, the Trustee shall have the right at any time and from time to time to distribute from the principal of the trust estate such amounts as may be reasonably necessary to provide for the health, education, support, or maintenance of the Settlor's wife.

6.33 5 or 5 Power

A power is not taxable if the holder of the power (whether or not exercised) can demand and receive property in a calendar year of no more than the greater of $5,000 or 5% of the assets subject to the power.[8]

> **Example:** In the preceding example, the wife could have been given the unrestricted right to withdraw annually from the principal of the trust the greater of $5,000 or 5% of the trust principal, in either of which events there would be no estate or gift tax consequences to her, due to the creation or exercise of the power. At her death this power will not cause the trust property to be includable in her gross estate.

Trust Form Granting 5 or 5 Power

During her lifetime, the Settlor's wife, _____, shall have the right during the last month of any calendar year to withdraw from the principal of the trust an amount not to exceed the greater of $5,000 or 5% of the market value of the principal of the trust valued on the day the Trustee receives written request for withdrawal. This right of withdrawal shall be noncumulative.

6.4 Interpretation and Drafting Considerations

The exercise of a power of appointment can create questions of interpretation that must be considered. For example, does a typical residuary clause in a will exercise a power of appointment? The answer to this question will vary, depending on state law.

If under state law the residuary clause in the will does exercise the power of appointment, an inadvertent result may occur. A will that bequeaths the residue of the estate to someone other than those beneficiaries who receive the trust estate when the power of appointment is not exercised (the takers in default) will cause the trust estate to pass under the terms of the will. Thus, the intended beneficiaries—the takers in default—will not receive the trust estate.

> **Example:** Mary dies and passes her estate into trust for the lifetime benefit of her husband, John, and grants him a limited testamentary power of appointment to direct the trust to anyone other than his estate or creditors. If the power of appointment is not exercised, the trust estate passes to the takers in default (their two children). John later remarries, and on his death he makes no reference to the power in his will, but his will passes his residuary estate to his second wife. John has inadvertently exercised his power of appointment, and both his probate estate and the trust estate pass to his second wife if under state law a residuary clause in a will exercises a power of appointment. Thus, the practitioner should be familiar with the law of his or her state.

 Planning Pointer 1

To solve the problem of an inadvertent exercise of a power of appointment, the creator of the power should add protective language to the grant of the power, such as that contained in the sentence preceding Comment One in the following form. The form that follows is a general power of appointment.

Trust Form Granting Power of Appointment

Upon the death of the Settlor's husband, the trust property then remaining, including any accrued and undistributed income, shall be distributed by the trustee, to or for the benefit of such appointee or appointees, in such manner and in such proportions, as the Settlor's husband may appoint by specific reference in his last will and testament, including the right of the Settlor's husband to appoint said property to his own estate.

> **Comment One:** This wording creates a general power of appointment that causes the trust property to be included in the husband's gross estate for federal estate tax purposes. If this result is not desired, the wording should be modified to create a limited power of appointment. The discussion on limited powers of appointment and the form in 6.31 should be consulted.

The trustee may rely upon an instrument admitted to probate in any jurisdiction as the last will and testament of the Settlor's husband, or may assume he died intestate if it has received no written notice of the existence of a will of the Settlor's husband within six months after his death.

> **Comment Two:** This sentence is needed to clarify what action the trustee must take following the death of the holder of the power of appointment and when it must take that action. It also protects the trustee from liabilities when making distribution.

If the Settlor's husband fails to exercise the power of appointment herein conferred upon him, then upon his death that portion of the trust property not appointed shall be distributed as follows: _____.

> **Comment Three:** This sentence is essential, because it specifies who receives the trust property if the power is not exercised. In most situations, the power of appointment is not exercised; thus, care must be taken to clearly designate who receives the trust property.

6.41 Miscellaneous Forms

Several other provisions may be helpful in adding clarity to the exercise or non-exercise of a power of appointment. The appropriate form should be inserted in the will of the donee of the power of appointment.

Will Form: Donee Exercising Power of Appointment

I am the donee of a power of appointment under [the Last Will of _____, executed on the _____ day of _____, 20____] / [a trust agreement, dated the _____ day of _____, 20____, wherein_____ is the Settlor and _____ is the Trustee]. I hereby expressly exercise such power by appointing the appointive property thereunder as follows: _____.

Will Form: Donee Not Exercising Power

I am the donee of a power of appointment under [the Last Will of _____, executed on the _____ day of _____, 20___] / [a trust agreement, dated the _____ day of _____, 20___, wherein _____ is the Settlor and _____ is the Trustee]. I hereby expressly do not exercise such power of appointment and direct that none of the provisions of this will shall be deemed or construed to be an exercise of such power.

Notes

1. RESTATEMENT OF PROPERTY § 318 (AM. LAW INST. ____).
2. I.R.C. §§ 2041(b), 2514(c).
3. *Id.* § 2514(e).
4. I.R.C. § 2041(b), Treas. Reg. § 20.2041-1(c); I.R.C. § 2514(c), Treas. Reg. § 25.2514-1(c).
5. *In re* Estate of Regester, 83 T.C. 1 (1973).
6. I.R.C. §§ 2041(b)(1)(A), 2514(c)(1).
7. Treas. Reg. §§ 20.2041-1(c)(2), 25.2514-1.
8. I.R.C. §§ 2041(b)(2), 2514(e).

Chapter 7

Marital Deduction Planning

7.1 Background
7.2 Basic Requirements
    7.21 Survived by a Spouse
    7.22 Property Must Pass to Survivor
    7.23 Includable in Gross Estate
    7.24 Terminable Interest Rule
        7.241 General Requirements
        7.242 Exceptions
7.3 Marital Deduction and Portability

7.1 Background

The federal estate tax marital deduction is a cornerstone of estate tax planning. It is a deduction from the gross estate of a decedent who is a citizen or resident of the United States at the time of death that is equal to the value of the property passing from the decedent to the surviving spouse. Use of the marital deduction is somewhat more complicated than it appears from this definition. A review of the development of the marital deduction will be helpful in fully understanding this important deduction.[1]

The marital deduction was enacted in 1948 to correct an estate tax advantage that community property states held over common-law states. Generally, community property states treat property of a marriage as owned one-half by each spouse. Common-law states treat the property as owned by the spouse in whose name it is titled, subject to common-law dower or curtesy or statutory interests in lieu thereof.

For example, in the case of a husband who owns all of a couple's property valued at $500,000, differing results occur in community property and common-law states. In a community property state, the wife is treated as owning $250,000 and the husband as owning the remaining $250,000. Contrast this with a common-law state, which treats the husband as owning the entire $500,000. On the husband's death in a community property state, only $250,000 is subject to the federal estate tax, whereas the entire $500,000 is subject to the federal estate tax if he resides in a common-law state. To end this inequity, a marital deduction equal to one-half of the value of the property passing from the decedent to the surviving spouse was allowed in the estate of decedents residing in common-law states.

Then, in 1977, the marital deduction was modified to permit a deduction for the greater of $250,000 or one-half of the value of the property passing to the surviving spouse. The final modification came in 1982, when Congress decided there should be no estate tax on property passing from one spouse to another. To carry out this purpose, the estate marital deduction was modified to permit a deduction for the entire value of any property passing from the decedent to the surviving spouse.

7.2 Basic Requirements

The estate tax marital deduction is allowed for the full value of the property passing to the surviving spouse to the extent that such property is included in the gross estate. It is immaterial whether the property passes by the decedent's will, by intestacy, by beneficiary designation on a life insurance policy or retirement plan, by right of survivorship, or in some other manner.

For the estate of a decedent to qualify for a marital deduction, the following basic requirements must be met:[2]

1. The decedent must be survived by a spouse;
2. The property must pass from the decedent to the surviving spouse;
3. The property must be included in the decedent's gross estate; and
4. The property must not be transferred as a life estate or other terminable interest unless specific requirements are met.

Caution: Property passing from the decedent to the surviving spouse that is conditioned on the spouse surviving for a limited period of time will not qualify for the deduction if the time period exceeds six months from the date of the decedent's death.[3]

Caution: Property passing into a trust or consisting of proceeds payable under a life insurance or annuity contract in which the surviving spouse receives only an interest for life will not qualify for the deduction unless (1) the surviving spouse receives all of the income from the property at least annually, (2) the surviving spouse receives a lifetime or testamentary general power of appointment over the property, and (3) the power of appointment is exercisable (whether or not it is ever exercised) by the surviving spouse alone and in all events.[4]

The qualified terminable interest property (QTIP) election provides an important exception to the preceding caution and to the fourth requirement listed earlier. Because of this election, property that does not pass outright to the surviving spouse may still qualify for the marital deduction if certain requirements are met. Examples of typical nonqualifying property are (1) a life estate to the surviving spouse with the remainder passing to the children, or (2) a trust for the surviving spouse's lifetime benefit in which he or she does not receive a general power of appointment. These types of interests will qualify for the marital deduction under the so-called QTIP election if (1) the property qualifies for the marital deduction for reasons other than its being a terminable interest and (2) the executor elects on the decedent's federal estate tax return for the property to qualify for the marital deduction.[5]

The effect of this election is that the decedent's estate receives a marital deduction; however, to qualify for the election the property will be taxable in the surviving spouse's estate. Without the QTIP election, the property will not qualify for the marital deduction in the estate of the first spouse and thus will be taxable there, although it then will not be taxable later in the estate of the surviving spouse.

7.21 Survived by a Spouse

The requirement to be survived by a spouse obviously requires that the parties be married. This determination is made as of the date of death of the decedent. Thus, the marital deduction is still available even if the parties are separated at the time of the decedent's death. As long as the parties are married at the date of death, this requirement for the marital deduction is met. Also, any interpretation of the meaning of marital status is determined by reference to the state law of the state in which the decedent is domiciled at the time of death.

Normally, the requirement that the decedent be survived by his or her spouse creates no problems of interpretation. In the unusual situation in which the deaths of the parties occur simultaneously, a problem arises. How is the will to be interpreted, especially in regard to the marital deduction, which requires that the decedent be survived by his or her spouse?

If the decedent's will establishes a presumption as to which spouse survived, the presumption will be followed for purposes of this requirement of the marital deduction.[6] Thus, when death is simultaneous, the marital deduction will be allowed for the decedent's estate if the will contains a presumption that the decedent's spouse was the survivor.

Will Form: Simultaneous Death Clause

If my wife and I die under circumstances creating any doubt as to which of us survived the other, then my wife shall be presumed to have survived me.

When no presumption of survivorship is established in the decedent's will, the Uniform Simultaneous Death Act will be followed in those states in which it has been enacted. This act provides that in the event of a simultaneous death, it is presumed that each spouse survived the other. Therefore, no marital deduction is available for either estate. In states that have not enacted this Uniform Act, the property law of that particular state must be consulted to determine the entitlement to the marital deduction.

When the estates of the spouses are similar in size, the result under the Uniform Act should create the better estate tax result. However, a presumption of survivorship is important when the estates are unequal in size.

Example: The husband's estate totals $15,000,000 and his wife's estate totals $3,000,000. Assume that both die simultaneously in 2018 and his will contains no presumption of survivorship. Both estates pass to the children. His estate will owe $1,520,000 in estate taxes, and his wife's estate will not owe any estate tax. If his will presumed that his wife survived him and his estate made proper use of marital deduction and portability planning, his and his wife's estate would owe no estate tax, a total estate tax savings of $1,520,000.

Planning Pointer 1

Normally the spouse with the smaller estate should be presumed to have survived. When the estates are equal in size, no presumption is usually needed.

 Caution: In no event should the same presumption of survivorship be used in the wills and trusts of both spouses. A common mistake is a survivorship clause in the husband's will and trust that presumes the wife is the survivor; and the wife's will and trust presumes the husband survives. This creates an inconsistent result and an interpretational quagmire. A clause should be inserted in the will of the spouse who is to be presumed to survive that creates consistency with the other spouse's will, such as the following clause.

Will Form: Simultaneous Death Clause

If my husband and I die under circumstances creating any doubt as to which of us survived the other, then my husband shall be presumed to have predeceased me.

As seen in these examples, the determination of the use of a survivorship clause is best made after making trial tax computations to determine the effect on each estate, both with and without the presumption of survivorship. Once these computations are made, a proper decision can be made as to whether a presumption of survivorship is needed or if the result of the Uniform Simultaneous Death Act is preferable.

7.22 Property Must Pass to Survivor

An interest is treated as passing from the decedent to the surviving spouse and meets the second requirement if any one of the following conditions is met:[7]

1. The interest is bequeathed or devised to the survivor.
2. The interest is inherited by the survivor.
3. The interest received by the survivor is dower or curtesy, or a statutory interest in lieu thereof.
4. The interest is transferred to the survivor during lifetime by the decedent.
5. The interest is held by the decedent and the survivor jointly with the right of survivorship.
6. The decedent transfers property to the survivor pursuant to a power of appointment or the surviving spouse receives the property owing to the decedent's release of or failure to exercise a power of appointment.
7. The interest represents the proceeds of life insurance on the decedent's life that are payable to the surviving spouse.

Therefore, property that passes to the surviving spouse, whether testate or intestate, whether passing through probate or outside probate, will qualify for the marital deduction as long as the property does pass to the surviving spouse. The property can pass directly to the surviving spouse or in some other fashion, as long as the surviving spouse has the sole beneficial ownership of the property transferred. Also, property that passes to a surviving spouse following a will contest or owing to an election to receive a statutory interest in the estate will qualify for the marital deduction, provided the transfer is bona fide and enforceable under state law.[8]

7.23 Includable in Gross Estate

The third requirement of the marital deduction is that the property qualifying for the deduction must be includable in the decedent's gross estate. Thus, any property that generates deductions such as funeral expenses and administrative costs or claims against the estate, as well as casualty loss deductions, is not deductible, to the extent of such deductions. Only the net value of such property qualifies for the marital deduction.[9]

7.24 Terminable Interest Rule

7.241 General Requirements

The fourth requirement involves the terminable interest rule and creates the greatest difficulty and complexity in understanding the marital deduction. The terminable interest rule exists because of an advantage common-law states otherwise would have over community property states. In a community property state, each spouse owns an undivided one-half interest in the whole of the community property. As was explained earlier, in 7.1, this is not so in common-law states.

If a decedent in a common-law state transfers property to the surviving spouse in a manner that does not vest in the survivor, such as a life estate, there would be an easy method of tax avoidance were it not for the terminable interest rule. This method would exist because the decedent's estate would receive a marital deduction for the value of the property passing to the surviving spouse. Then, on the death of the surviving spouse, the property would not be included in his or her estate because at the first spouse's death the property vested in the remaindermen, subject to the surviving spouse's life interest. Thus, no estate tax would be owed on the property in either estate.

To eliminate this result, the terminable interest rule was enacted. Basically, any interest in property passing to a surviving spouse that is deemed a terminable interest (i.e., not vested in the surviving spouse at the decedent's death) is not deductible for purposes of the estate tax marital deduction.

A *terminable interest* is defined as an interest that will terminate or fail, after the lapse of time, on the occurrence of an event or contingency or on the failure of an event or a contingency to occur. This includes such property as life estates, term of years, annuities, patents, copyrights, and interests passing into trust for the lifetime benefit of the surviving spouse.[10]

Although a terminable interest does not qualify for the marital deduction, the determination of whether or not an interest is considered terminable is made according to state law. For example, a bequest to a surviving spouse that is to be distributed if the survivor is living at the time of distribution of the decedent's estate is terminable because the survivor has no vested right to the bequest at the time of the decedent's death.[11] However, if state law interprets such an interest to be vested at the time of death, as opposed to being vested at the time of distribution, state law controls and the interest is not terminable. Thus, a property interest that under a state law interpretation is not a terminable interest will qualify for a marital deduction.[12]

> **Exception:** An interest passing to a surviving spouse that is conditioned on survival of that spouse for a period of time constitutes a terminable interest. If the condition is limited in time to no more than six months after the decedent's death, then the terminable interest rule is not violated, provided such an event does not in fact occur.[13] This is a limited exception, but it can have great benefit when the decedent desires to insert a time clause in the will to delay the passing of the first estate in an effort to reduce the additional costs of administering two estates. Owing to this exception, such clauses can be used and the marital deduction will not be lost when the survivor lives beyond the time set in the time clause.

Will Form: Time Clause

If my wife does not survive me by six months, then this will shall be interpreted as if she predeceased me.

7.242 Exceptions

A key exception to the terminable interest rule exists when a life estate for the surviving spouse is coupled with a general power of appointment. This exception is most often utilized for property passing into trust for the benefit of the surviving spouse. If the surviving spouse receives the property in trust and is given sufficient authority over the property, it will still qualify for the marital deduction. Such property then will be subject to inclusion in the surviving spouse's estate on that spouse's subsequent death.

The five requirements for this exception to apply are:

1. the surviving spouse must be entitled to all of the income from the property for life;
2. the income must be payable to the surviving spouse in annual or more frequent installments;
3. the surviving spouse must have a power of appointment to appoint the property to the survivor's own self or estate;
4. the power of appointment must be exercisable solely by the surviving spouse without limitation, although the power can be limited to being exercised either during lifetime or at death; and
5. the property qualifying for the deduction must not be subject to the power of any other person to appoint the property to anyone other than the surviving spouse.[14]

In the case of periodic payments from the proceeds of life insurance, endowment, or annuity contracts, a similar exception is provided for such payments to qualify for the marital deduction.[15] Proceeds payable from an installment sale also can qualify for the marital deduction.[16] Basically, the same five requirements just discussed apply, and if met, a marital deduction is allowable.

The other key exception to the terminable interest rule was created by the 1981 amendments to the federal estate tax law, and it applies to estates of decedents dying after 1981. One of the amendments permits a qualified terminable interest property election. Because of this amendment, an executor can now elect on the federal estate return to treat terminable interest property as qualifying for the marital deduction.[17] Once the executor makes this election, the marital deduction is allowed for this property, but the property will subsequently be includable in the surviving spouse's gross estate. Other requirements for the terminable interest to qualify for the marital deduction are (1) the surviving spouse is entitled to all income from the property, which must be payable at least annually, and (2) there can be no power in any other person to appoint any part of the property to any person other than the surviving spouse during the survivor's lifetime.[18] Once these requirements are met, the marital deduction is available, even though the property will pass to the ultimate beneficiaries as directed by the decedent rather than by the surviving spouse, as when the general power of appointment exception is used.

> **Planning Pointer 2**
>
> This exception simplifies planning for those couples who have children from a prior marriage and fear that the survivor might exercise the power of appointment only for the survivor's children. By using this election, assets can be placed in a trust that qualifies for the marital deduction even though the survivor only has rights to trust income and cannot direct the disposition of the assets at death. Typically, the trust terminates at the survivor's death and is distributed to the remaindermen selected by the spouse who created the trust.

7.3 Marital Deduction and Portability

Prior to the introduction of "portability" into the federal estate tax law, it was essential that trusts be utilized to take advantage of the marital deduction and use of the full exclusion amount of both spouses. Trusts were the preferred vehicle for this type of planning, as discussed in Chapter 5, at 5.21, under the A-B trust planning approach. There is no longer a basis for this concern. Utilization of the full marital deduction no longer results in the loss of the exclusion amount from the estate of the first spouse to die. This portability, or carrying over, of the exclusion amount from the first spouse to die to the estate of the second spouse to die ensures the maximum use of the exclusion amounts without the awkwardness of what was rather technical trust drafting.

Tax planning today involves a consideration of both income tax consequences and potential estate tax consequences. With the larger exclusion amount ($11,200,000 in 2018), most estates will not face an estate tax. Thus, will and trust drafting is largely based on nontax considerations. These are still significant as large wealth is passing from one generation to the next. Due to high divorce rates and potential lawsuits, it is always wise for a child to inherit in trust for her or his lifetime. In some situations, they can serve as their own trustees. For most estates, upon the death of the first spouse those assets owned by the first spouse to die will receive a step-up basis for income tax purposes. The step-up in income tax cost basis means that the date-of-death value of the assets now become the cost basis. This is a real benefit, as a subsequent sale of property that had appreciated significantly during the decedent's lifetime will escape most, or perhaps all, of the capital gains tax. For example, a $1,000,000 asset that is now worth $2,000,000, if sold by the decedent, would have resulted in $1,000,000 of capital gains with a capital gains tax of $200,000 in most situations. The step-up in cost basis increases the income tax cost basis to $2,000,000. Thus, a subsequent sale for $2,000,000 by the surviving spouse results in no income taxes.

In those larger estates that will still owe a federal estate tax, portability may not be the best result. For example, if property appreciated $500,000 in value between the death of the first spouse and the death of the second spouse, there is a maximum $100,000 federal income tax savings to the children by inheriting the property at the second death and later selling it. However, if the surviving spouse's estate is large enough to owe a federal estate tax, that $500,000 increase in value will cause there to be an estate tax of $200,000. Thus, portability cost an additional $100,000 in taxes that could have been saved. The savings would occur by the first spouse's estate going into a trust for the surviving spouse, similar to the B trust discussed at 5.21. In this manner the survivor has use of the property, but it is not taxable in the survivor's estate. By forgoing portability, the assets pass into the B trust and are used for the surviving spouse throughout her lifetime. At the survivor's death, when the assets have increased in value, there is no estate tax owed on the assets because the assets remain in the B trust and are not part of the survivor's estate. Of course, when the assets are sold, a higher capital gains income tax is owed; but, as shown in this illustration, the estate tax rate is twice that of the income tax rate. Thus, there is an overall tax savings.

Planning Pointer 3

Several approaches should be considered. The simplest is an outright gift to the surviving spouse coupled with a disclaimer. The surviving spouse can then exercise the disclaimer to pass property into a trust (such as the B trust discussed at 5.21 and the trust form at 15.4); the survivor gets the use of the disclaimed property throughout lifetime but then the property passes on to the children without the estate tax. If at the settlement of the first estate the survivor believes the income tax savings are more important, as there will not be an estate tax, then there will be no need to disclaim.

In a second marriage, when the parties do not have common heirs, the matter is more complicated. Don't let the "taxtail" wag the dog. The A-B trust planning approach may be the best alternative coupled with the QTIP election for the A trust.

Notes

1. The discussion in this chapter centers on the estate tax marital deduction; however, the principles stated apply equally to the gift tax marital deduction in I.R.C. § 2523.
2. I.R.C. § 2056.
3. *Id.* § 2056(b)(3).
4. *Id.* § 2056(b)(5).
5. *Id.* § 2056(b)(7).
6. Treas. Reg. § 20.2056(e)B2(e).
7. I.R.C. § 2056(c)(1)(B)(7).
8. Treas. Reg. § 20.2056(d)(2).
9. *Id.* § 20.2056(a)B2(b).
10. I.R.C. § 2056(b)(1).
11. Fried v. Commissioner, 445 F.2d 979 (2d Cir. 1971), *cert. denied*, 404 U.S. 1016, 92 S. Ct. 676, 30 L. Ed. 2d 663.
12. Tilyou v. Commissioner, 470 F.2d 693 (7th Cir. 1972).

13. I.R.C. § 2056(b)(3), Treas. Reg. § 20.2056(b)B3.
14. I.R.C. § 2056(b)(5).
15. *Id*. § 2056(b)(6).
16. Rev. Rul. 79-224, 1979-2 C.B. 334.
17. Treas. Reg. § 22.2056-1.
18. I.R.C. § 2056(b)(7)(B).

Chapter 8

Life Insurance Planning

8.1 Basic Types of Life Insurance
    8.11 Term Life Insurance
    8.12 Whole Life Insurance
    8.13 Universal Life Insurance
    8.14 Variable Life Insurance

8.2 Taxation of Life Insurance Benefits
    8.21 Benefits Received during Lifetime
    8.22 Benefits Received following Death

8.3 Special Types of Life Insurance
    8.31 Split-Dollar Insurance
    8.32 Key-Man Insurance
    8.33 Group Life Insurance

8.4 Life Insurance Trusts
    8.41 Revocable Life Insurance Trusts
    8.42 Irrevocable Life Insurance Trusts

Appendix A   Uniform Premiums for $1,000 of Group Term Life Insurance Protection

8.1 Basic Types of Life Insurance

There are numerous life insurance products in today's marketplace. The types of life insurance fall within several broad categories, although this is somewhat misleading because there are many variations in products within each category. Only the general characteristics of the basic types of life insurance are considered here. Two excellent ABA resources are H. Skipper et al., *The Advisor's Guide to Life Insurance* (ABA, 2011); and L. Brody et al., *Federal Gift, Estate and Generation Skipping Transfer Taxation of Life Insurance* (3d ed.; ABA, 2012).

8.11 Term Life Insurance

Term life insurance, as its name implies, is life insurance written for a specific term. Examples are term policies written for a 10-year term to cover life insurance needs for a limited period of time or decreasing-term policies intended to pay for a home mortgage or other debt if the insured dies before the debt has been paid.

Term insurance provides only death benefits and no buildup of cash value. Therefore, the premiums are lower in earlier years when the probability of death is less, but the premiums increase with the insured's age. Because of this feature, term life insurance often becomes too expensive to continue as the insured becomes older. Often the need for life insurance has not decreased in the later years of life, as is often expected when initial low-cost term insurance is first purchased. Thus, term life insurance, though initially inexpensive, is not always the best option.

8.12 Whole Life Insurance

Whole life insurance is sometimes referred to as permanent life insurance. Unlike term insurance, whole life is purchased with the intent of keeping the insurance protection throughout life or until retirement. The disadvantage is that the premiums in the early years of the policy are higher than term life insurance premiums. This cost difference occurs because whole life premiums remain level throughout the life of the policy. In the early years, the premiums are greater than the cost of death protection; thus, the excess premiums build up with compound interest in reserve to supplement the premiums in later years when the death protection costs are more than the annual premiums.

Whole life products vary but generally consist of single premium payment, limited premium payment, and continuous premium payment plans. Each type of whole life insurance offers an income tax–free buildup of cash value, the certainty that the policy cannot be terminated owing to future contingencies such as future uninsurability, and a buildup of cash value that can be borrowed or withdrawn later in life, such as at retirement.

8.13 Universal Life Insurance

Universal life insurance was first introduced into the life insurance market by Hutton Life in 1978. This product was introduced largely in response to the economic situation that had developed during the 1970s. Because of the high level of inflation that existed during this period, there was a demand for life insurance that provided higher interest rates than traditional whole life insurance.

The universal life insurance product was offered to meet this demand. Basically, universal life combines term life insurance protection with a cash value fund that accumulates interest income tax free. The earnings of the cash value fund are based on short-term interest rates; thus, the risk of interest rate performance is shifted to the policy owner. In times of high interest rates, the return on the policy is good, making this an attractive alternative to traditional whole life insurance. The universal life insurance product is not nearly as attractive when interest rates fall.

A universal life insurance policy offers added flexibility because the policy owner can determine how much of the premium is to be applied to death protection and how much to the cash value fund. Thus, the policy owner can actually vary life insurance coverage based on current needs. Further, the amount of premium payments can be varied from year to year. The ability to vary the premium payments, cash value, and death benefits is an attractive feature of universal life insurance.

There is also an important income tax consideration. The universal life insurance policy must meet the requirements of the Internal Revenue Code if it is to be treated as life insurance and not as an investment for income tax purposes.[1] This is critical for the policy owner because the cash value accumulates income tax free in a life insurance policy, but it will be taxed annually if it is treated as an investment. Also, if the policy is not treated as life insurance under the Internal Revenue Code, the exclusion of life insurance proceeds from income tax on the death of the insured is lost.[2]

8.14 Variable Life Insurance

In a typical variable life insurance policy the policy premium is fixed, and it offers a guaranteed minimum death benefit. The cash value of the policy is not guaranteed; it varies with the investment performance of the investment fund into which the premiums have been invested. This also results in a varying death benefit; however, the death benefit will not fall below the guaranteed minimum.

The variable life insurance product thus allows greater investment opportunity than universal and whole life insurance because the cash value fund can be invested in common stocks and bonds. Typically, the owner can direct the investment among various investment funds, such as money market funds, growth stock funds, balanced stock and bond funds, and bond funds. The variable life insurance product is desirable if the insured wants more aggressive investments for the policy's cash value fund in hopes of increasing the death benefits.

Because of the risk inherent in investments, the variable life insurance product results in a death benefit and a cash value that vary—as its name implies. Again, just as with universal life insurance, the risk of performance of the policy is on the owner. This concept of varying death benefits is at odds with the normal reason for purchasing life insurance, which is to be assured of a definite death benefit to provide for family members' other needs.

8.2 Taxation of Life Insurance Benefits

8.21 Benefits Received during Lifetime

If the owner of a life insurance policy elects to receive the cash benefits that have built up in the policy during lifetime, income tax will be owed. The difference between the cost of the policy to the owner and the amount received is taxed as ordinary income.[3] The owner's cost is simply the total gross premiums paid.[4] Any premiums paid for accidental death benefits or for the option of waiver of premiums in the event of disability must be excluded from the cost of the policy because this portion of the premiums does not contribute to the cash value of the policy. Any policy dividends that were received in cash or used to reduce premium payments must also be excluded from the gross premiums.[5]

If the owner of the policy elects to receive policy benefits other than as a lump sum, the benefits are taxed under the annuity rules of Section 72 of the Internal Revenue Code. These rules simply tax the portion of each payment that represents gain in excess of the cost paid by the owner for the annuity. To determine the amount of the payment that represents the owner's cost and is excluded from ordinary income, the following formula can be used:

Amount Excluded = Annual Annuity Payment × [Owner's Total Cost / Annual Annuity Payment × Owner's Life Expectancy per IRS Tables][6]

8.22 Benefits Received following Death

The life insurance proceeds received by a beneficiary of a decedent's life insurance policy are not subject to income tax.[7] In the event the beneficiary elects a settlement option other than a lump-sum payment, the interest portion of each payment is subject to income tax, but the principal continues to be income tax free.[8]

Caution: The "transfer for value" rule creates a potentially troublesome problem. Basically, in those rare situations in which, before death, the insured transfers for value (i.e., sells) a life insurance policy on his life, an income tax will be owed by the purchaser on the subsequent receipt of the insurance proceeds at the insured's death. The taxable amount is the difference between the life insurance proceeds received and the amount paid for the policy plus the premiums paid by the purchaser.[9]

 Planning Pointer 1

A transfer of a policy between family members should be handled strictly as a gift to avoid the "transfer for value" problem. No consideration should be involved.

A transfer of the insured's own life insurance policy to the insured, his or her partner, a partnership in which the insured is a partner, or a corporation in which the insured is a stockholder or officer is excepted from the "transfer for value" rule.[10] The exception involving partners, partnerships, and corporations is essential owing to transfers of insurance that may be necessary for valid business purposes, particularly those involving buy-sell agreements. A discussion of insurance when used in a buy-sell agreement appears in Chapter 10, at 10.31.

Caution: A transfer of an existing policy between corporate stockholders to fund a corporate cross-purchase agreement creates a "transfer for value" problem. The transfer does not fall within the exceptions just discussed. No exception exists for transfers between corporate stockholders as it does for partners. Therefore, a cross-purchase agreement between stockholders should not be funded with existing life insurance policies. If this is nonetheless done, the death benefits payable at the death of a stockholder will be subject to income tax to the transferee (surviving stockholder). Only the amount the transferee paid for the policy plus the premiums paid since the transfer will offset the gross income.

Caution: A similar problem exists when a corporation transfers a policy to its stockholders. This could easily occur when a corporation replaces a corporate redemption agreement with a stockholder's cross-purchase agreement. There is no exception for this transfer. Such a transfer should be avoided because it also will be subject to the "transfer for value" rule.

The proceeds of life insurance are normally subject to the federal estate tax.[11] The basic rule is that life insurance proceeds are includable in the gross estate for federal estate tax purposes if (1) the proceeds are payable to the insured's estate; (2) the insured was the owner of the policy; (3) the owner was not the owner but retained incidents of ownership in the policy, such as the right to change beneficiaries; or (4) the insured transferred the policy and died within three years of the transfer.[12]

Planning Pointer 2

A gift of a life insurance policy by the insured to another family member will often be a good planning idea, as long as the insured survives the three-year time limit. The proceeds then will pass at the insured's death to the family member without any federal estate tax being owed. The value of the policy is subject to gift tax at the time of the gift, but often this value is rather low, particularly in the early years of owning a policy.[13] Another idea is for the family member to purchase a new policy on the insured's life. This will avoid the three-year rule. In either situation, the insured can make gifts of the premiums to the owner of the policy. Such gifts are subject to a gift tax, but normally the per-donee annual exclusion (currently $15,000) is sufficient to shield the gift from taxation. It should be recognized that there is no need for spouses to give life insurance policies to each other. Owing to the unlimited marital deduction, there is no estate tax to a surviving spouse on receipt of the insurance proceeds at the death of the insured spouse; thus, there is no tax advantage in giving a policy to the surviving spouse.

Caution: An unintended gift tax results when the insured, policy owner, and beneficiaries are each different.[14] For example, assume the wife owns a life insurance policy on her husband's life and she names the children as beneficiaries. On the husband's death, the proceeds are paid directly to the children. Although the proceeds are not includable in the husband's estate for estate tax purposes, the wife is deemed to have made a gift to the children of the life insurance proceeds. The wife not only has a gift tax to pay, but she also has no money with which to pay the tax, because the children have the life insurance proceeds. A transfer from the children to her to pay the gift tax results in another taxable gift.

8.3 Special Types of Life Insurance

8.31 Split-Dollar Insurance

Split-dollar insurance is one of the few employee benefits that can be offered to particular key employees without running afoul of too many tax law restrictions.[15] There are variations with split-dollar plans, but basically, life insurance is provided to a particular employee with the employer paying the part of the insurance premium representing the increase in the current year's cash value and the employee paying the balance. The amount paid by the employer is typically a significant part of the premium. The employer then receives the cash value of the policy at the employee's death, and the employee's beneficiary receives the balance of the death benefit. Obviously, while the plan remains in effect, the death benefit received by the employer increases and that received by the employee's beneficiary decreases.[16]

Caution: The taxation of these plans is complicated. You should check with a certified public accountant (CPA) or financial planning professional when dealing with split-dollar insurance.

8.32 Key-Man Insurance

Key-man insurance is simply insurance purchased by a business on the lives of certain key employees, including the principal owners. The insurance is purchased in recognition of the economic loss to the business on the death of a key employee. Not only will a new, qualified employee be needed, but the business may also falter during the time needed for the new employee to learn the business and develop rapport with its customers. In many businesses, particularly small businesses, the loss of a key employee is difficult to overcome.

Because the life insurance is for the protection of the business, the business is the owner of life insurance, pays the premiums, and is the beneficiary of the insurance. The insurance premiums are not a deductible business expense, but the life insurance proceeds received should the insured die are not treated as taxable income.[17] Although the receipt of the life insurance proceeds by the business will not directly result in an estate tax, it will indirectly result in an estate tax because it increases the value of the business.[18] Thus, if the key employee is also a stockholder, his or her estate will be assessed an estate tax on the value of the key employee's stock ownership in the business, and this value will increase due to the receipt of the insurance proceeds.

> **Caution:** If the key employee is a sole or controlling stockholder (owns 50% or more of the voting stock) and rather than naming the corporation as beneficiary names a third party, the corporation's incidents of ownership in the insurance will be attributed to the key employee. This will result in the entire death proceeds being included in the key employee's estate.[19]

8.33 Group Life Insurance

Group life insurance is a term life insurance benefit provided by an employer for all of its employees. The payment of premiums by the employer is a deductible business expense and is not taxable income to the employees to the extent that the death benefit does not exceed $50,000.[20] To the extent that greater benefits are provided, the employee must treat the life insurance benefits in excess of $50,000 as giving rise to taxable income. The amount taxable is determined from the IRS tables.[21] (See Appendix A at the end of this chapter.)

8.4 Life Insurance Trusts

8.41 Revocable Life Insurance Trusts

A revocable life insurance trust is a useful estate planning tool when estate tax savings are not a consideration. In a typical situation, the insured has purchased life insurance to provide for the financial needs of the surviving spouse and/or minor children. In either situation, the insured is the owner of the insurance, and the proceeds will be taxable in the insured's estate for federal estate tax purposes.[22]

The insured may choose not to have the life insurance proceeds payable directly to the beneficiary for various reasons. For example, if the insurance is intended to provide for the support and education of minor children, the insured may be unwilling for the insurance to be payable to the children's guardian. The guardian may not be well versed in financial matters, or in many cases the guardian may be an ex-spouse with whose judgment the insured is uncomfortable. Even if the guardian is otherwise competent to handle financial and investment matters on behalf of the children, a guardianship must terminate on the age of majority, which is age 18.

Few parents want their children to receive a large inheritance at 18 years of age. They are more comfortable with a trustee's investing the insurance proceeds for the benefit of the children and paying income or principal as needed for the children's support and education. When the children reach a specified age, such as 25 or 30 years, the trust can terminate and be paid outright to the children.

If the life insurance proceeds are intended to provide for the financial needs of a surviving spouse, a trust may still be a good choice. The financial expertise of a trustee may be invaluable. Even if the insured feels comfortable with the surviving spouse's handling of financial matters, a trust arrangement may be useful to care for the survivor's financial needs later in life, particularly during periods of disability. Additionally, a trust often lessens the probate costs that the survivor's estate otherwise will incur. Finally, a trust prevents the insurance proceeds from being subject to the inheritance rights of a future spouse, should the survivor remarry.

Planning Pointer 3

An inter vivos revocable trust is the preferable type of trust to use; however, a testamentary trust may also be used. An inter vivos trust is executed by both the settlor and the trustee; thus, the insured knows in advance that the trustee will serve as trustee. A testamentary trustee often does not know it is named as trustee and may refuse to serve when notified of the trusteeship after the decedent's death, for example, if the trust contains provisions with which it is uncomfortable. The inter vivos trust avoids this dilemma because the trustee can review the trust document and sign it during the settlor's lifetime. Any problem with the trust then can be resolved. The trust document in Chapter 15, at 15.3, is a revocable life insurance trust drafted to save estate tax through the proper use of the marital deduction.

 Caution: A revocable trust becomes irrevocable at the death of the settlor. Although the terms of the trust may vary widely, special care should be taken if the trust is to continue for the lifetime of the beneficiary. In that situation the trust instrument must consider the ultimate beneficiaries and specify when and how they are to receive their shares. Normally, if the life beneficiary is someone other than the surviving spouse, he or she should not be granted a general power of appointment—that is, a power that can be exercised in favor of the holder (donee) of the power, his or her estate, or the creditors of either. This will result in the trust's being taxed in the life beneficiary's estate. A limited power of appointment without adverse estate tax consequences can be granted to give the life beneficiary the opportunity to direct who are the ultimate beneficiaries. Of course, if flexibility is not needed, no power need be granted. If the life beneficiary is the surviving spouse, consideration must be given to the marital deduction and the overall planning of the estate between the two spouses; thus, a general power of appointment or QTIP provisions may be necessary for at least part of the estate.[23]

Caution: Care must be taken to ensure that properly executed beneficiary designations have been executed for all life insurance that is to be payable to the trust on the death of the insured. Beneficiary designation forms should be obtained from each of the insured's life insurance companies and be filled out, together with the trust document. A failure to designate the trust as beneficiary will cause the insurance to be payable outside the trust. This makes it essential that the practitioner stress to the client that all life insurance beneficiary forms must designate the trust as beneficiary. The suggested language for designating the trust as beneficiary follows.

Beneficiary Designation

The life insurance proceeds shall be payable to the insured's trustee, XYZ Bank and Trust Company, _____[city], _____[state], pursuant to the insured's trust executed on _____, 20____, including any amendments thereto.

8.42 Irrevocable Life Insurance Trusts

In some situations, the planning need is for the life insurance to be excluded from estate taxation in the insured's estate, yet the insured does not want to give the life insurance policy outright to the beneficiary. Some of those reasons are the same as discussed in the preceding section on revocable life insurance trusts. An additional factor calling for an irrevocable trust is the need for the insured to reduce the federal estate tax on his or her estate.

This estate tax savings can be accomplished either by the insured's establishing an irrevocable life insurance trust and giving existing life insurance policies to the trust or by the trust itself purchasing a new policy on the insured's life. The insurance will be excluded from the insured's estate because the insured will not own the insurance at the time of death; rather, the trust will own the insurance. Obviously, the same general rules for excluding life insurance from the estate must be met.[24] Thus, (1) the insured must not own or retain any incidents of ownership in the insurance;[25] (2) the proceeds must be payable to the trust rather than the estate;[26] and (3) if policies are given by the insured to the trust, the insured must survive the gift by three years.[27]

With most irrevocable life insurance trusts, no income-producing property is transferred to the trust. This creates an obvious problem in paying the premiums on the life insurance. An additional problem is that a gift to the trust (from which the premiums can be paid) is a gift of a future interest and does not qualify for the $15,000-per-donee annual gift tax exclusion.[28] Thus, any gift will result in the use of part of the insured's unified credit.

Under a court decision in *Crummey v. Commissioner*[29] and subsequent IRS rulings,[30] the insured now can make annual gifts to a trust from which the insurance premiums can be paid and still qualify for the annual gift tax exclusion. The basic requirement is that the trust grant the trust beneficiary the noncumulative right to withdraw the gift from the trust. Thus, the beneficiary must have the right to withdraw the amount given to the trust at the time it is given and for a reasonable time thereafter (such as 30 or 60 days), but this right then can lapse.[31] Of course, each time a new gift is made, the right of withdrawal applies to the new gift.

Caution: Because of the "incidents of ownership" requirement, the insured should not act as the trustee of an irrevocable life insurance trust. Even though the incidents of ownership are held in a fiduciary capacity, this may result in inclusion of the insurance in the insured's estate.[32]

Planning Pointer 4

Any trust must have, as a minimum, the right for the beneficiary to withdraw the annual gift. Further, it should be recognized that the right of withdrawal and the availability of the annual exclusion exist for each trust beneficiary. Thus, a trust could pay premiums in excess of the current $15,000 annual gift tax exclusion if there were multiple beneficiaries.[33] Also, the benefits of gift-splitting are available if the donor is married.

Caution: Each beneficiary must be given notice of his or her right of withdrawal. Failure to inform the beneficiary could result in the loss of the annual exclusion.[34] Notices should be given by the trustee on receipt of each gift for premium payments.

Caution: The *Crummey* right of withdrawal is a general power of appointment. If the power exceeds in value the greater of $5,000 or 5% of the trust principal, the "5 or 5" exception for powers of limited value does not apply.[35] This results in a gift tax due to the lapse of the power. The power holder is deemed to have made a gift to the trust to the extent that the gift exceeds $5,000 (the 5% exception seldom applies because these trusts usually hold no assets). Further, the gift will not qualify for the power holder's annual exclusion, because the gift is a future interest. To avoid this problem, a right of withdrawal can be limited to withdrawals of no more than $5,000 or 5% of the trust principal. The limit applies separately to each beneficiary who holds a demand power. This restriction is not troublesome unless the annual insurance premiums exceed $5,000 multiplied by the number of beneficiaries.

Planning Pointer 5

When the power of withdrawal exceeds $5,000 or 5%, the gift tax problem can be avoided if the beneficiary who fails to exercise the demand power will receive the trust principal in any event. In this situation the trust has to vest in the beneficiary at a certain age. If the beneficiary dies before that age, the trust must be payable to the beneficiary's estate or pursuant to a testamentary limited or general power of appointment held by the beneficiary.[36] This solution will work in most situations other than when the insurance trust is being structured as a generation-skipping trust.

Planning Pointer 6

Another option is to create a "hanging power" of withdrawal. This technique utilizes the 5% part of the "5 or 5" power. The concept is to allow demand rights to lapse annually in the amount of $5,000 per beneficiary ($10,000 if gift-splitting is elected), with the excess continuing to be subject to withdrawal. When the trust principal grows in size sufficiently for 5% of principal to be greater than $5,000, then those previously unexercised demand rights (which have been "hanging around") begin to lapse. For example, a trust that has grown to $300,000 will result in $15,000, rather than $5,000, annually being subject to lapse.

Planning Pointer 7

Owing to the flexibility lost in any irrevocable trust, the settlor may wish to add some flexibility by granting the trustee the power to sprinkle income among the trust beneficiaries. This may be particularly important when the beneficiaries include the surviving spouse and the children. Flexibility also is added by granting the surviving spouse a limited power of appointment over the trust principal, exercisable at the death of the surviving spouse. This will not result in inclusion of the trust in the surviving spouse's estate, but it will enable the survivor to modify the disposition of the trust if circumstances change in the future.[37]

Caution: If the noninsured spouse is a beneficiary of the trust, he or she could be deemed a grantor of part or all of the trust, resulting in inclusion in his or her estate because of allowing the withdrawal power to lapse. Eliminate a *Crummey* withdrawal power for this beneficiary if it is not necessary, or limit it to $5,000 to comply with the "5 or 5" exception.

Caution: Because divorce is a possibility and the trust is irrevocable, consideration must be given to this possibility. A possible solution is to refer to the insured's spouse in the trust instrument not by name, but rather as "my spouse at the time of my death."

Caution: If it is desired that the insurance proceeds be available to pay the insured's debts, taxes, and other estate obligations, the trust should be given the right to purchase assets from the estate or to make loans to the estate. The trust cannot be given the right to make such payments directly without the life insurance proceeds being included in the insured's estate for estate tax purposes.

Notes

1. I.R.C. § 7702.
2. *Id.* § 101.

3. *Id.* § 72(e)(2).
4. *Id.* § 72(e)(6).
5. *Id.* § 72(e)(4)(B).
6. *Id.* § 72(a), (b), (c); Treas. Reg. §§ 1.72-5, 1.72-9.
7. I.R.C. § 101(a)(1).
8. *Id.* § 101(c).
9. *Id.* § 101(a)(2); Treas. Reg. 1.101-1(b)(5).
10. I.R.C. § 101(a)(2)(B).
11. *Id.* § 2042; Treas. Reg. § 20.2042-1.
12. I.R.C. § 2035(b)(2).
13. Treas. Reg. § 20.2512-6.
14. Rev. Rul. 73-207, 1973-1 C.B. 409; Rev. Rul. 77-48, 1977-1 C.B. 292.
15. Rev. Rul. 64-328, 1964-2 C.B. 11.
16. Notice 2001-10.
17. I.R.C. § 101.
18. Treas. Reg. § 20.2031-2(f).
19. *Id.* § 20.2042-1(c)(6); Dimen v. Commissioner, 72 T.C. 198 (1979), *aff'd*, 633 F.2d 203 (2d Cir. 1980).
20. I.R.C. § 79(a).
21. Temp. Reg. § 1.79-3T.
22. I.R.C. § 2042.
23. See Chapter 6 on powers of appointment and Chapter 7 on marital deduction planning.
24. See the discussion of gift tax in Chapter 3.
25. Treas. Reg. § 20.2042-1(c).
26. I.R.C. § 2042(1).
27. *Id.* § 2035(d)(2).
28. *Id.* § 2503(b). See also Chapter 3, at 3.2 and 3.61, Planning Pointer 5.
29. 397 F.2d 82 (9th Cir. 1968).
30. Rev. Rul. 73-405, 1973-2 C.B. 321.
31. Rev. Rul. 81-7, 1981-1 C.B. 474.
32. Rose v. United States, 511 F.2d 259 (5th Cir. 1975); Terriberry v. United States, 517 F.2d 286 (5th Cir. 1975); *contra*, Estate of Fruehauf v. Commissioner, 427 F.2d 80 (6th Cir. 1970).
33. Rev. Rul. 80-261, 1980-2 C.B. 279.
34. Rev. Rul. 81-7, 1981-1 C.B. 474.
35. I.R.C. § 2514(e).
36. Ltr. Rul. 8229097.
37. See Chapter 6 at 6.31 for a limited power of appointment.

Appendix A

Uniform Premiums for $1,000 of Group Term Life Insurance Protection

Five-year age bracket	Cost per $1,000 of protection for one-month period
Under 25	$0.05
25 to 29	$0.06
30 to 34	$0.08
35 to 39	$0.09
40 to 44	$0.10
45 to 49	$0.15
50 to 54	$0.23
55 to 59	$0.43
60 to 64	$0.66
65 to 69	$1.27
70 and above	$2.06

Chapter 9

Charitable Giving

9.1 Background

9.2 Estate and Gift Tax Requirements

9.3 Income Tax Requirements

  9.31 Cash and Ordinary Income Property

  9.32 Long-Term Capital Gain Property

  9.33 Tangible Personal Property

  9.34 Future-Interest Property

  9.35 Tax-Exempt Organizations

9.4 Special Types of Charitable Gifts

  9.41 Remainder Interest in Farm or Personal Residence

  9.42 Qualified Conservation Contributions

  9.43 Gift Annuities

  9.44 Gift of Undivided Interest

  9.45 Pooled Income Fund

9.5 Charitable Remainder Trusts

9.6 Charitable Lead Trust

9.7 IRA Distribution

9.1 Background

Most of the practitioner's clients are unlikely to be charitably minded when they begin considering the distribution of their estates. Thus, the practitioner seldomly tends to mention charitable giving to a client, and when it is discussed it is usually to consider only a specific modest bequest to a charity. However, the area of charitable giving is one in which the practitioner can provide a significant service to his or her client as well as a benefit to the charity. To make the best use of the tax benefits of charitable giving, a review of the income, estate, and gift tax requirements for gifts to charities is needed. This chapter offers the reader an overview of charitable giving. The nuances are many. The reader who is interested in a more detailed treatment of charitable planning may want to read Thomas J. Ray Jr., *Charitable Gift Planning: A Practical Guide for the Estate Planner* (ABA, 2009).

9.2 Estate and Gift Tax Requirements

If a gift is made to a qualified charity during the donor's lifetime, it is deductible for gift tax purposes;[1] if made at the donor's death, it is deductible for estate tax purposes.[2] The charity must be a qualifying organization. Qualifying charities include organizations operated exclusively for religious, scientific, literary, or educational purposes, including the encouragement of the arts or national or international amateur sports. Also qualifying are groups that aid or prevent cruelty to children or animals; fraternal societies; veterans' organizations; and national, state, or local government units.[3]

9.3 Income Tax Requirements

The requirements for deductibility of gifts to public charities for income tax purposes is more detailed. The requirements are most easily understood by looking at the type of property given: (1) cash, (2) ordinary income property, (3) long-term capital gain property, (4) tangible personal property, and (5) future-interest property.

9.31 Cash and Ordinary Income Property

Prior to the Tax Cuts and Jobs Act of 2017, gifts of cash to a public charity were a deductible itemized deduction up to a maximum of 50% of the taxpayer's adjusted gross income. This cap has been increased to 60% of adjusted gross income. The text in this chapter is based on the 2017 law. Thus, the reader should note this change throughout this chapter. This act is not popular with most charities; thus, the reader is cautioned to expect additional changes in the tax laws affecting charities in the next several years. Any excess of the cash gift can be carried forward and deducted in future years for a maximum of five years.[4] *Ordinary income property* is property that, if sold, will give rise to ordinary income and not a capital gain. Thus, it includes such items as inventories, short-term capital gains (capital assets sold within one year of acquisition), and works of art or copyrighted materials given by the individuals who created them. Ordinary income property that is given to a public charity is subject to the same 50% of adjusted gross income and five-year carry-forward rule.[5] The appreciation on gifts of ordinary income property, however, is not deductible because the gift is limited to the donor's basis in the property.

9.32 Long-Term Capital Gain Property

Long-term capital gain property, which includes such items as stocks, real estate, and other investment properties that have been held by the donor in excess of one year, is deductible at the fair market value of such property. Thus, the appreciation in addition to the donor's basis is included in the value of the gift for purposes of the income tax deduction. The maximum deduction, however, is limited to 30% of the donor's adjusted gross income, with the same five-year carry-forward.[6]

> **Example:** A donor wishes to make a $10,000 gift to a favorite charity. The donor owns stock currently valued at $10,000 with a basis of $1,000. If the donor sells the stock and gives $10,000 to the charity, he or she will have a tax benefit from the itemized deduction of $2,800 offset by an income tax cost of the sale of $1,350, resulting in a net tax benefit of $1,450, assuming a 28% ordinary income tax rate and a 15% capital gains rate. If the donor gives the stock to the charity, he or she can deduct $10,000 as a charitable contribution without recognizing any income due to the appreciation of the stock, resulting in a tax benefit of $2,800. The charity can sell the stock and then have the $10,000 for its needs.

 Planning Pointer 1

Whenever possible, the donor should make gifts of appreciated long-term capital gain property. Being able to avoid any income tax on the appreciation in value of the capital asset is an important benefit.

9.33 Tangible Personal Property

A gift of tangible personal property is deductible at the fair market value of the property only if the use of the personal property is related to the tax-exempt purpose of the charity.[7] The maximum itemized income tax deduction is 30% of the donor's adjusted gross income, just as with long-term capital gain property. When the use of the tangible personal property is unrelated to the purpose of the charity, the deduction is further limited to the lesser of the donor's basis or the fair market value of the property.[8]

> **Example:** A gift of a painting for which the donor paid $10,000 and that is presently valued at $50,000 will result in a $50,000 charitable deduction if made to a museum (use-related), but only $10,000 if made to a YMCA (nonuse-related).

9.34 Future-Interest Property

A gift of a future interest to a charity does not normally result in a charitable deduction.[9] Thus, a gift by a donor of a painting to a museum to be received following the death of the donor does not qualify as a charitable gift for purposes of entitlement to an income tax deduction. An income tax deduction for a gift of a future interest is permissible if the gift is structured as required by the Internal Revenue Code for gifts of a remainder interest, such as charitable remainder annuities and unitrusts, as discussed later (see 9.5).

9.35 Tax-Exempt Organizations

The tax-exempt organizations for which these income tax rules apply can be grouped into 10 basic types of organizations, as follows:

1. Churches or conventions or associations of churches;
2. Educational institutions;
3. Hospital or medical research organizations (not including a home health care organization, convalescent home, homes for children or aged, or vocational institutions that train handicapped individuals);
4. Endowment foundations in connection with a state college or university;
5. A government unit, state, federal, or local, if the contribution is made exclusively for public purposes;
6. An organization normally receiving a substantial part of its support from the public or government unit;
7. A private operating foundation;
8. A private nonoperating foundation that distributes all contributions it receives to public charities and private operating foundations (or makes certain other qualifying distributions) within 2-1/2 months after the end of its tax year;
9. Organizations normally receiving (a) more than one-third of their support in each tax year from the public and other organizations previously listed in (1)-(7) in the form of grants, gifts, contributions, or membership fees, and gross receipts from an activity that is not an unrelated trade or business and (b) not more than one-third of their support from gross investment income and unrelated business taxable income; and
10. Private foundations that pool all contributions into a common fund and allow a substantial contributor to designate a recipient charity, income from the pool being distributed within 2-1/2 months after the tax year in which it was realized and principal attributable to any donor's contribution being distributed to a charity not later than one year after the death of the donor.[10]

⚠ **Caution:** To be entitled to the 50% and 30% limitations, the gift must be made to the group of charities just described. Contributions to other nonprofit organizations, such as grant-making organizations, veterans' organizations, fraternal organizations, or other nonprofit organizations, are deductible, but the limitations are different. These organizations are sometimes referred to as *private foundations*. The distinction between public charities and private foundations is largely drawn on the size of the donor base, not the purpose of the charity. The contribution limit for these charities for capital gain property is 20% of the donor's adjusted gross income, although this is further limited to the donor's basis in the capital gain property.[11] Generally, the contribution limit for cash and ordinary income property is 30% of the donor's adjusted gross income.[12]

9.4 Special Types of Charitable Gifts

9.41 Remainder Interest in Farm or Personal Residence

Whereas charitable gifts of a future interest are not normally deductible for income tax purposes, an exception exists for a gift to a charity of a remainder interest in a farm or personal residence.[13] The donor computes the actuarial value of the charity's remainder interest based on IRS tables and then deducts that amount as an itemized charitable deduction on his or her personal income tax return.[14] If the intervening life interest is to someone other than the donor or his or her spouse, a gift tax will be owed on the interest of the life tenant.

> **Example:** A husband gives a life estate to his wife in a personal residence with the remainder to a charity. There is no gift tax on the gift to the wife, because of the gift tax marital deduction. The value of the remainder interest is deductible by the husband on his personal income tax return. If the gift were granted instead to the husband's son, a gift tax would be owed on the value of the son's life interest.

9.42 Qualified Conservation Contributions

Facade Easement. A donor can deduct the value of a conservation restriction or easement granted to a charity for certain property.[15] This deduction is permitted even if the donor contributes the property itself to a family member. To qualify, the conservation restriction must include one or more of the following purposes:

1. Education or recreational purposes,
2. Protection of environmental systems,
3. Open space for scenic enjoyment, or
4. Historically important land areas.[16]

Example: A woman gives a building in the downtown business district to her son. The value of the building is $100,000; however, the mother gives to the city a perpetual easement for the exterior of the building to ensure that its original architecture will never be disturbed. The easement lessens the value of the building by $20,000. She receives a charitable deduction for income tax purposes of $20,000 and also lessens the value of the gift of the building to her son to $80,000. If the mother is in a 24% income tax bracket, she has saved $4,800 in income taxes.

Other Conservation Contributions. Donors who make partial contributions of real estate by placing conservation easements on the partial land may reap substantial tax benefits. At its simplest, a donor gives an easement to a public agency or qualified charity permanently limiting the use of the land to protect its conservation value. The donor can retain income from the real property and can even pass the property at death to his or her heirs. An appraisal of the gift will be needed, as the gift is less than the fair market value of the real estate because some rights are retained by the donor.

If qualified, the value of the gift is subject to a 50% adjusted gross income limitation and not the 30% limitation. Further, the five-year carryover rule is extended to 15 years. If the gift is made by qualifying farmers and ranchers, the 50% limitation is increased to 100% of adjusted gross income. A further excellent resource is C. Dietrich, *Conservation Easement for Tax and Real Estate Planning for Landowners and Advisors* (ABA, 2011). IRS Publication 526 is also helpful.

Example: A landowner earning $50,000 a year, who donates a $1,000,000 conservation easement, could normally only take a $15,000 deduction with a 5-year carry-forward for a total deduction of $90,000. This tax incentive allows a $25,000 deduction with a 15-year carry-forward for a total deduction of $400,000. If the donor is a farmer or rancher, the deduction increases to $50,000 with a 15-year carry-forward for a total deduction of $800,000.

9.43 Gift Annuities

A *gift annuity* is an arrangement with a charity by which the donor transfers property to a charity in exchange for an annuity payment from the charity. The donor's charitable deduction is based on the fair market value of the property transferred in excess of the annuity payment based on the payout rate and the donor's life expectancy.[17] If cash is transferred, the 50% rule applies, but the 30% rule applies if appreciated long-term capital gain property is transferred. As with any annuity, the payout will be subject to income tax under the annuity rules, which prorate the payment between a nontaxable return of capital and taxable interest.[18]

9.44 Gift of Undivided Interest

Although a future interest qualifies for an income tax deduction only in those few situations discussed at 9.41 and 9.42, a gift of an undivided interest in the donor's property is not a future interest, so an itemized deduction is allowed.[19] For example, the donor can give an undivided interest in a farm or other real estate, such as a one-half interest in a farm to the YMCA, and the other one-half interest to his children. The income, gift, and estate tax results are the same as with an outright gift of a 100% interest to a charity. Thus, the donor's gift is equal to one-half of the value of the farm or real estate.

A slight variation on this approach with the same tax result is available with a gift of a winter residence or a work of art. For example, the donor can give a museum the right to a work of art for the first six months of the year, and the donor can have the work of art for the last six months of the year. Similarly, the donor can give a charity the use of a winter residence for part of the year, and the donor can retain it for the other part of the year. Obviously, some valuation adjustment may be necessary if the location of the residence is such that the months the donor retains are the prime months and the charity has the residence for only the less desirable months.

9.45 Pooled Income Fund

A *pooled income fund* is a common trust fund established and administered by a charity.[20] A donor simply transfers property to the charity's pooled income fund, where the transferred property is commingled with that of the other donors to the fund. Typically, the transferred property will be sold and the proceeds invested by the charity in additional investments in the common trust fund. The donor receives an annual annuity payment from the fund, based on the investment return of the pooled income fund. At the donor's death, the remainder interest in the property vests in the charity.

The donor is entitled to an income tax deduction for the present value of the remainder interest to the charity. Appreciated property can also be transferred to the charity without an income tax being imposed on the appreciation.

9.5 Charitable Remainder Trusts

One of the better estate-planning techniques for an individual who is at least somewhat charitably minded is the use of a charitable remainder trust.[21] This type of trust permits an interest in the transferred property to be split. Thus, it is possible to provide income to a noncharity beneficiary (the donor or another), and at the end of a specified period of time have the property be distributed to the charity. Even though the charity does not receive the property until a future date, the donor is allowed a current income tax deduction for the actuarial value of the future interest. The only gift tax imposed is on the value of the intervening interest of the noncharitable beneficiary. There are a number of specific requirements that must be met to be entitled to the income tax deduction. For one who meets these requirements, some rather impressive income tax results are available.

There are two types of charitable remainder trusts: a charitable remainder annuity trust (CRAT) and a charitable remainder unitrust (CRUT). Both types of charitable remainder trusts must (1) be created under a written instrument; (2) pay at least annually a fixed sum or a sum certain to the noncharitable beneficiary for lifetime, or a period not to exceed 20 years; and (3) on expiration of the term, the principal must be held or distributed for the use or benefit of the charitable organization.[22] In addition, each type of trust has specific requirements it must meet. (IRS sample charitable annuity trust forms are found in Revenue Procedures 2003-53, 2003-54, 2003-55, 2003-56, 2003-57, 2003-58, 2003-59, and 2003-60; IRS sample charitable unitrust forms are found in Revenue Procedures 2005-52, 2005-53, 2005-54, 2005-55, 2005-56, 2005-57, 2005-58, and 2005-59.[23])

A CRAT pays the noncharitable beneficiary a fixed annual annuity calculated as a fixed percentage of the property transferred or as a fixed dollar amount. Either type of annual annuity payment must be at least 5% of the initial value of the trust. If the income is insufficient to pay the annuity, then principal must be spent. No additional property may be transferred to the CRAT after it is established.[24]

A CRUT pays the noncharitable beneficiary a payment that varies because it is computed annually as a percentage of the current value of the trust. As with the CRAT, the CRUT percentage payment must be at least 5% of the value of the trust.[25] It is permissible to set the payment at the lesser of the annual income from the trust or 5% of the value of the trust. If current income is less than the percentage payout, it can be made up in later years when the income exceeds the percentage limitation.[26] Because of its fluctuating formula, the CRUT must be valued annually to redetermine the current year's payment. Also, the CRUT permits additional property to be transferred to it, unlike the CRAT, which does not allow property to be transferred to the trust following the initial gift.[27]

Caution: The charitable remainder trust must not pay an amount in any year greater than 50% of (1) the initial fair market value of the trust's assets in the case of a CRAT, or (2) the net fair market value of the trust's assets, valued annually, in the case of a CRAT.[28]

Caution: The value of the charity's remainder interest in the gift to the trust must be at least 10% of the net fair market value of the property transferred to the trust.[29]

Planning Pointer 2

Owing to the fundamental difference in the two trusts, there are several planning considerations. Does the donor want to be allowed to make future transfers to the trust? Does the donor want a fixed or a fluctuating payment? Will revaluations of the trust create a great difficulty or an added expense? The effect of future appreciation on each type of trust and the resulting payout should also be considered, as reflected in the following examples.

Example: Charitable Remainder Annuity Trust. Assume that a $500,000 CRAT pays 5% ($25,000) per year to the beneficiary, beginning when he is age 50 and terminating when he dies, at age 75. The dividends from the trust investments average 5% annually, and the investments have an average rate of growth of 8% annually. At the life beneficiary's death the charitable trust is valued at approximately $3,425,000, and the beneficiary has received an annual payment for 25 years of $25,000.

Example: Charitable Remainder Unitrust. A $500,000 CRUT pays 5% per year to the beneficiary, but because it is a unitrust, the annual annuity payment is reset each year. Assuming the same ages and investment return as in the preceding example, the unitrust is valued at approximately $2,436,500 at the beneficiary's death, and the annual payment has increased by the age of 75 to $154,550 per year.

Planning Pointer 3

Another consideration in establishing a charitable remainder trust is that the trust is exempt from income tax. Therefore, appreciated property can be transferred to the trust and sold without any income tax. This prevents the charitable remainder trust from being reduced by an income tax on the appreciation of the property given, as would be required if the donor sold the property, paid income tax on the appreciation, and transferred the after-tax proceeds to a charitable remainder trust.

Example: Gifts of Appreciated Property. A donor, aged 65, transfers a $100,000 real estate investment with an income tax basis of $10,000 to a charitable remainder unitrust for a 5%-per-year annuity. The trust sells the real estate, invests the proceeds, and pays the donor the annuity. If the donor had sold the real estate, a federal income tax of $18,000 would have been owed (assuming a 20% capital gain rate), thus leaving only $82,000 to invest. If the investment returns 5%, the donor's annual income will be only $4,100. In addition to increasing annual income with the charitable remainder gift, the donor will have an itemized charitable deduction of $44,454 with which to further reduce personal income taxes. This deduction is based on a 2.6% IRS interest factor being in effect for the month of the gift.

Planning Pointer 4

Although the trust does not pay an income tax on the sale of any property held in the trust, the beneficiary will pay an income tax on the payments from the trust. Payments from the charitable remainder trust to the beneficiary are taxed in a specified manner. First, they are taxed to the beneficiary as ordinary income to the extent of current or accumulated income; then they are taxed as a capital gain to the extent of current or accumulated capital gains. Next, the payment is taxed as tax-exempt income to the extent of current or accumulated tax-exempt income. Finally, it is taxed as a tax-free payment of principal.[30]

This method of taxing the beneficiary creates a very good tax planning option. If the trust purchases all tax-exempt investments, the payments to the beneficiary will be tax-exempt. There is an important exception: When the donor transfers appreciated property to the trust, the payments from the trust will be taxed to the beneficiary as capital gain under the rule discussed earlier until all of the capital gain has been taxed. Thereafter, the remaining payments will be tax-exempt.[31]

Planning Pointer 5

One spouse can establish a charitable remainder trust for the couple's joint benefit. It is not necessary for the trust to benefit only the donor. The trust can pay an annuity for the couple's joint lifetime with the remainder passing to the charity following the death of the surviving spouse. The husband and wife will receive a current income tax deduction for the gift to the charity. There will be no gift or estate taxes because of both the charitable deduction and the marital deduction.[32]

Planning Pointer 6

The use of life insurance with a charitable remainder trust creates a tremendously effective estate-planning strategy. A couple with highly appreciated property faces a large personal income tax when they sell the property and invest the sales proceeds for their own benefit. Additionally, the after-tax proceeds that remain after the sale are subject at their death to estate tax. This will further reduce the amount of the estate passing to their ultimate beneficiaries. In most situations the couple can transfer the appreciated property to a charitable remainder trust, and they can then receive an annuity payment for their joint lives that will exceed the return they would have earned on the after-tax investment of the sales proceeds. The couple can purchase a joint and survivor's life insurance policy on their lives and use this extra income to pay the premiums on the policy. The policy can be payable to the couple's ultimate beneficiaries and thus replace the asset transferred to charity. If the policy is also owned by the ultimate beneficiaries, the proceeds are not subject to estate tax on the death of the surviving spouse. As seen from the following example, when the right situation exists, a gift to a charitable remainder trust that is replaced with life insurance can benefit the charity with no cost to the family. This approach is not inequitable to the government because the charity's use of the funds will be in furtherance of the public welfare and will often avoid additional, more costly government programs.

Example: A husband and wife, both age 65, own a parcel of real estate valued at $200,000 with an income tax basis of $10,000. The couple plan to sell the real estate and invest the proceeds at 5% interest. If their combined state and federal income tax rate is 26%, they will net only $150,600, which will yield them $7,530 per year. Further, if their estate tax rate is 40%, the sales proceeds will be reduced to $90,360 when passing to their children on the death of the survivor. Instead, if a gift of real estate is made to a charitable remainder trust in exchange for a 5% unitrust payment, the couple will receive $10,000 income per year, adjusted annually. The couple's children can then purchase a $200,000 joint and survivor's life insurance policy on the couple's joint lives. The premiums will be approximately $2,400 annually. The premiums can be paid by annual gifts from the parents to the children. The annual gifts will reduce the couple's income to $7,600, which slightly exceeds the annual income that would be earned if the remainder trust were not used. On the death of the surviving spouse, the $200,000 life insurance proceeds will be paid to the children without any estate tax, resulting in their receiving $119,640 more, owing to the charitable remainder trust coupled with the life insurance. In addition, the couple will have a charitable income tax deduction in the year of the gift to the charitable unitrust trust for the value of the remainder interest of $$66,570. Because the income tax calculation for this deduction is somewhat complicated, it is recommended that the client's regular income tax return preparer be involved in the planning of such a gift.

9.6 Charitable Lead Trust

A charitable lead trust (CLT) is the opposite of the charitable remainder trust. In a lead trust, the charity receives an annual payment for a term of years, at the conclusion of which time the remainder passes to a family member or other beneficiary of the donor. Aside from philanthropic motives, the trust can be used to lessen the gift or estate tax costs of transferring property to a beneficiary.[33] Of course, the lesser gift or estate tax cost occurs because the charity has an intervening right to the income from the transferred property.

A charitable lead trust is subject to most of the same requirements as the charitable remainder trust; however, there are several differences. There is no 5% minimum payment requirement. Any income not paid to the charity is taxed to the trust. Also, any capital gains are taxed to the trust. Furthermore, the donor does not receive an income tax deduction.[34] The prime use of the charitable lead trust is for those situations in which a gift or estate tax deduction is needed.

> **Example:** Lead Trust to Reduce Gift Tax. A father, aged 65, gives property worth $300,000 to a CLT for his lifetime, paying 5% annually to the charity, and at his death the property passes to his daughter. Assuming a 2.4% Section 7520 rate, the father will receive a charitable

gift tax deduction of $166,638, resulting in a taxable gift to his daughter of only $133,362. Although the daughter does not have the use of the property during her father's lifetime, the father has transferred the property to his daughter for a significantly lower gift tax cost. If the investments earn in excess of 9%, the daughter will inherit well over $300,000 at termination of the trust.

Example: Lead Trust to Reduce Estate Tax. A mother establishes a charitable lead trust in her will, passing property worth $300,000 to a CLT paying 5% annually to a charity for a term of 15 years and then terminating and passing to her children. Assuming a 2.4% IRS Section 7520 rate, the estate will receive an estate tax charitable deduction of $161,013, resulting in only $138,987 being subject to estate tax. Assuming the estate is in a 40% estate tax bracket, the estate tax is only $55,595, rather than $120,000—a savings of $64,405.

A charitable lead trust has the disadvantage that the ultimate beneficiary does not have the present use of the property and also that the purchasing power of the transferred property may not increase in value sufficiently to offset future inflation. One solution is the use of a payment rate to the charity that is less than the earnings from the investment of the transferred property. The excess after-tax earnings can then accumulate in the trust until termination of the trust, or in the case of an inter vivos lead trust can be used to purchase life insurance on the donor's life.

9.7 IRA Distribution

An individual age 70-1/2 or older may distribute up to $100,000 tax free from his or her individual retirement accounts (IRAs) to 50% charitable organizations, except supporting organizations and donor advised funds.[35] The gift is not subject to being reported for income tax purposes. The percentage limitations do not apply.

Notes

1. I.R.C. § 2522.
2. *Id.* § 2055.
3. Treas. Reg. §§ 20.2055-1, 25.2522(a)-1.
4. I.R.C. §§ 170(b)(1)(A), 170(d).
5. *Id.* § 170(e).
6. *Id.* § 170(b)(1)(C).
7. *Id.* § 170(e)(1).
8. *Id.* § 170(e)(1).
9. *Id.* § 170(a)(3).

10. *Id.* §§ 170(b)(1)(A), 170(b)(1)(E).
11. *Id.* § 170(b)(1)(D).
12. *Id.* § 170(b)(1)(B).
13. *Id.* § 170(f)(3)(B)(i).
14. Valuations are determined from IRS Pub. 1457, Actuarial Values Alpha Volume (1989); IRS Pub. 1458, Actuarial Values Beta Volume (1989); IRS Pub. 1459, Actuarial Values Gamma Volume (1989); and use of current interest rates published monthly by the IRS.
15. I.R.C. § 170(f)(3)(B)(iii).
16. *Id.* § 170(h).
17. Rev. Rul. 73-1, 1973-1 C.B. 117.
18. Treas. Reg. § 1.170A-1(d)(2).
19. I.R.C. § 170(f)(3)(B)(ii).
20. *Id.* § 642(c)(5).
21. *Id.* § 664.
22. *Id.* § 664(d).
23. Additional preapproved trust forms based on two life beneficiaries appear in Rev. Proc. 90-30, 1990-1 C.B. 534; Rev. Proc. 90-31, 1990-1 C.B. 539; Rev. Proc. 90-32, 1990-1 C.B. 546; Rev. Proc. 89-20, 1989-1 C.B. 841; Rev. Proc. 89-21, 1989-1 C.B. 842.
24. I.R.C. § 664(d)(1); Treas. Reg. § 1.664-2(b).
25. I.R.C. § 664(d)(2).
26. *Id.* § 664(d)(3).
27. Treas. Reg. § 1.664-3(b).
28. I.R.C. § 664(d).
29. *Id.*
30. I.R.C. § 664(b).
31. *Id.* § 664(b); Treas. Reg. § 1.664-1(d).
32. I.R.C. §§ 2523(g), 2055(a), 2056(b)(8).
33. *Id.* §§ 2522(c)(2)(B), 2055(e)(2)(B).
34. Treas. Reg. § 1.170 A-6 (1), (2).
35. I.R.C. § 408 (d)(8).

Chapter 10

Business Buy-Sell Agreements

10.1 Background
10.2 Redemption and Cross-Purchase Agreements
    10.21 General Considerations
    10.22 Establishing the Sales Price
10.3 Specific Considerations
    10.31 Insurance
    10.32 Income Tax Basis
    10.33 Dividend Problems with Redemption Agreements
        10.331 General Considerations
        10.332 Attribution Rules
    10.34 AMT Problems with Redemption Agreements
    10.35 Partnerships

10.1 Background

The lawyer is frequently faced with advising the owners of closely held businesses. These businesses typically involve family members, but they may involve unrelated owners. Each such business faces a crisis when one of the owners dies, becomes disabled, retires, or simply wants to sell his or her interest in the business. Three additional ABA publications providing in-depth treatment of this area are L. Mezzullo, *An Estate Planner's Guide to Buy-Sell Agreements* (2d ed.; ABA, 2007); L. Mezzullo, *An Estate Planner's Guide to Family Business Entities* (3d ed.; ABA, 2010); and D. Dreux et al., *Business Succession Planning and Beyond* (ABA, 1997).

    The selling owner has a limited market for selling the business interest. The purchasing owner(s) has the cash drain of buying the seller's interest and the loss of the contribution the selling owner made to the success of the business. Both owners have the problem of valuing the business interest. The problems may be compounded when the interest sold is less than 50% of the business, when an estate is involved, or when family members are involved.

In the situation of the death of an owner, the possibility of an inexperienced spouse or child stepping into the business, rather than the deceased owner's interest being sold to the other owner(s), creates a tremendous dilemma for the other owner(s). For this reason, if no other, any closely held business should have a buy-sell agreement. Although the terms are almost always troublesome to resolve, the problems become greater only when not considered and resolved in advance. The two basic types of buy-sell agreements are the redemption agreement and the cross-purchase agreement.

10.2 Redemption and Cross-Purchase Agreements

10.21 General Considerations

The redemption agreement simply involves the entity (whether a corporation, a limited liability company, or a partnership) buying the stockholder's, member's, or partner's interest. For explanatory purposes it will be assumed that a corporation is the entity involved; however, the same considerations apply to partnerships and limited liability companies. Special considerations for partnership and limited liability company buy-sell agreements are discussed in 10.35.

Basically, all that is necessary in a redemption agreement is a contract to be entered into between the corporation and the various stockholders. The agreement should provide for the purchase of stock by the corporation in all possible events. Thus, events of death, disability, retirement, or a stockholder's desire to sell for any reason should be considered. The difficult issues of sales price, terms of payment, and the method of making those payments must be considered.

A cross-purchase agreement involves the same considerations as does a redemption agreement. The primary difference is that the individual stockholders purchase the stock of the deceased or withdrawing owner rather than the entity being the purchaser, as in a redemption agreement. As with a redemption agreement, a contract is entered into among the various owners specifying the terms of sale, such as sales price, terms of payment, and the method of making those payments.

In either type of agreement, various other matters should also be considered. Among them may be covenants not to compete; agreements not to divulge or use business secrets, including client or customer lists; and security for the seller if the sales price is to be paid by the purchaser in installments. In seller-financed sales, a promissory note is essential, and security for the seller may be desired, such as a mortgage on real estate and a security interest in personal property.

Consideration should also be given to prohibiting dividends and large salary increases by the corporation while any balance of the sales price remains unpaid. In addition, an irrevocable proxy can be used to give the selling owner more protection over corporate policy. The proxy could be for only the shares sold or for all corporate shares while the sale is being financed by the selling owner. Admittedly, the use of proxies may tie the hands of the remaining owners, and such a provision may not be desired, but it should be considered.

Further, any agreement should require all stock certificates being surrendered to have typed on the legend of the stock certificate: "Stock transfer subject to Buy-Sell Agreement." The stock certificate then can be returned to the owners because the restriction on the legend will place any purchaser on notice of the preexisting restriction on the sale of stock. (Suggested protective language is found in the buy-sell agreements provided in Chapter 15 at 15.1 and 15.2.)

10.22 Establishing the Sales Price

Establishing the sales price is one of the more difficult aspects of a buy-sell agreement. No matter how difficult, the problem of setting a sales price becomes greater if a determination of sales price is delayed until the death, disability, or retirement of an owner. The business judgment of the owners should be invaluable in setting the sales price. Businesses, even though small, often are relatively easy to value according to known methods of valuation used in the trade or industry. Absent such assistance, there are basically three approaches that can be followed; however, each has its drawbacks.

First, a multiple of earnings can be utilized. For example, the average business earnings (net profit) for the last five years can be multiplied by a factor (number) to arrive at the sales price. The difficulty is in arriving at a factor that is a reliable index; however, in some businesses that is not as difficult as it might seem. The business owners will be the best determiners of the appropriateness of this approach to valuation.

A second approach is to use the book value or some variation of it. Typically, book value can be used with certain adjustments. For example, assets can be appraised to compensate for undervalued and depreciated assets. Accounts receivable may have to be adjusted to better reflect uncollectibles. Goodwill should also be considered and a value placed on it. For many businesses, the book value after adjustments will be a reliable basis for establishing value.

A third approach is for the owners to set the value of the business periodically, such as at 6- or 12-month intervals. This approach is perhaps the best, because it ensures a current value based on the owners' determination of value. Because the value is set without each owner knowing whether the value is one the owner's estate will receive or the owner will pay to the estate of a deceased owner, it represents an arm's-length negotiated value that should correctly reflect fair market value. The major drawback to this approach is the very real possibility that the owners may not remember to adjust the value regularly. The value, after first being set, often becomes outdated and an unrealistic value for the business. A possible solution is to set the value of the business in the initial agreement and, in the event the owners do not adjust the sales price for 12 or more months, have an automatic adjustment for profits or losses that have occurred since the last value was set.

> ### Planning Pointer 1

The value arrived at in the buy-sell agreement will be accepted by the Internal Revenue Service (IRS) for estate tax purposes if several specific criteria are met. If this is done there should be no valuation dispute during estate settlement. The value set in the agreement will settle the issue. Those criteria are as follows:[1]

1. The estate must be obligated to sell the stock at death;
2. The deceased must have been unable to sell the stock during lifetime without first offering it to the other parties to the agreement at the same price as in (1);
3. The agreement must have been entered into for bona fide business reasons and not as a disguise for a gift; and
4. A reasonable price must have been fixed in the agreement, either by dollar amount or formula.

 Caution: The ability of a family business to avail itself of this planning opportunity is limited for buy-sell agreements.[2] The tax code permits the IRS to ignore valuations set at less than fair market value, except when (1) the value is set in a bona fide agreement, (2) the value is not a device to transfer property to family members for less than adequate consideration, and (3) the terms of the agreement are similar to those entered into by persons in arm's-length transactions.[3] A family business may meet the first two requirements, but the third creates difficulties. Objective evidence of comparable agreements will be difficult to obtain; thus, the subjective analysis of the IRS will wreak havoc on many taxpayers.

10.3 Specific Considerations

10.31 Insurance

Life insurance often is used to provide a fund to meet the financial obligation under a buy-sell agreement that arises on the death of an owner. Four factors must be considered. First, with either type of agreement the insurance premiums are not a deductible business expense.[4] Thus, the premiums will be paid with after-tax dollars. The insurance proceeds are not subject to income tax,[5] however; and because the policy is not owned by the decedent, no estate tax is owed on the life insurance proceeds.[6]

Because the insurance premiums are paid with after-tax dollars, the income tax brackets of both the corporation and the owners are a consideration in choosing which type of buy-sell agreement to select. If the corporate bracket is lower, then a redemption may be more appropriate For example, the top individual income tax rate is 37%, whereas the top corporate income tax rate is 21%.[7] This may favor a redemption for some individuals.

Second, a related consideration with a cross-purchase agreement is that the premiums paid by each owner on the insurance policies on the lives of the other owners will vary owing to age differences. The younger owners will be paying a higher premium than the older owners. This disadvantage can possibly be offset by salary adjustments.

A third consideration is the number of life insurance policies required with a cross-purchase agreement. Each owner must carry a policy on the life of each of the other owners; therefore, the number of policies can get rather large. For example, a three-owner business will be purchasing six life insurance policies under a cross-purchase agreement instead of just three policies under a redemption agreement. If there are five owners, the number of policies will be twenty with the cross-purchase agreement rather than just five with the redemption agreement. Although this is not a terribly difficult problem, it does merit consideration.

Fourth, the death of an owner creates an administrative consideration when a cross-purchase agreement is used. The deceased owner's estate will own a life insurance policy on the life of each of the remaining owners. To avoid this problem, the cross-purchase agreement should require the estate to sell all policies subject to the agreement of the other owners. The sales price is the present fair market value of the policies, which is the interpolated terminal reserve value plus the unearned premiums. This value can be obtained from the insurance company, just as is done when valuing a life insurance policy for gift tax purposes. (See Chapter 3, at 3.61, Planning Pointer 6.)

Planning Pointer 2

When a cross-purchase agreement is used, the deceased owner's estate must report and pay an estate tax on the fair market value of each of the policies the decedent owned on the lives of the other owners.[8] If (as suggested earlier) the agreement provides that the estate sell the policies to the other owners, no income tax will be owed because the sales proceeds will be the same as the estate tax value. This is because the estate tax value also establishes the income tax basis in the policies. Because both values are the same, there is no gain on the sale of the policies. An estate tax will be owed or a portion of the unified credit of the decedent's estate will be used, however, because the value of the policies is includable in the decedent's gross estate for federal estate tax purposes. This certainly does not fit in particularly well with other estate planning.

A solution is for the life insurance policies that the decedent owns on the lives of the other owners to name the decedent's surviving spouse as the secondary owner. Another possibility is for the owner to specifically bequeath the policies to his or her surviving spouse. Under either approach, the marital deduction will shield the policies from estate tax, and the subsequent sale will not result in any income tax to the surviving spouse because the basis in the policies will be stepped up to the date-of-death value. Thus, in following this approach there will be no adverse income or estate tax consequences. This suggestion requires that the surviving spouse sign the buy-sell agreement or an addendum to it to bind the surviving spouse to sell the policies to the other surviving owners.

Caution: A problem exists with a cross-purchase agreement involving three or more corporate owners. On the death of the first stockholder, the insurance policies he or she owns on the other stockholders will normally be purchased by the other owners; that is, each surviving stockholder purchases policies insuring the other surviving stockholders (which were owned by the deceased stockholder). The problem is due to an income tax rule known as the "transfer for value" rule.[9] Basically, this rule modifies the normal exemption of life insurance from income taxation. It provides that when a policy has been sold, the death proceeds will be exempt from income taxation only to the extent of the consideration paid for the policy and the premiums subsequently paid by the purchaser. The balance of the death proceeds is subject to income tax.

The only exceptions to this rule are for sales to[10] (1) the insured, (2) a partner of the insured, (3) a partnership in which the insured is a partner, and (4) a corporation in which the insured is a stockholder. The second exception avoids the "transfer for value" rule when a partnership or members of a limited liability company elect to use a cross-purchase agreement. A cross-purchase agreement among stockholders of a corporation creates a problem. Because the life insurance policies are purchased by the stockholders and not the corporation (as in the case of a redemption), none of the exceptions discussed so far applies. Therefore, on the death of the next stockholder, the surviving stockholders will owe income tax on part of the death proceeds received from the policies purchased from the first stockholder's estate. This problem can be avoided if the cross-purchase agreement is converted to a corporate redemption agreement after the first stockholder dies or if the stockholders purchase the policy on their own life.

Example: A, B, and C own equal shares in a "C" corporation, and each owns a $100,000 life insurance policy on the others' lives that funds their stockholder's cross-purchase agreement. Each policy has a value of $25,000 with a $100,000 death benefit. A dies and A's stock is purchased equally by B and C with their respective $100,000 in life insurance death benefits. B buys for $25,000 the policy A owned on C to partially fund B's increased cost to buy C's stock, which now represents a one-half interest in the corporation. C does the same, buying A's policy on B. C dies and B receives the $100,000 death benefit from B's original policy on C's life, for which no income tax is owed. However, the additional $100,000 death benefit B receives from the policy B purchased from A is not excepted from the transfer-for-value rule. Thus, the $100,000 death benefit, less the $25,000 purchase price and any premiums paid by B, is subject to income tax. This harsh result is avoided if the cross-purchase agreement is converted to a redemption agreement after A's death and the corporation purchases the policies A owned on B and C.

10.32 Income Tax Basis

The income tax basis of the deceased owner's stock is stepped up to the value used on the federal estate tax return.[11] This value will be the same as set forth in the buy-sell agreement if that agreement has been properly written. Therefore, there is no taxable gain because the income tax basis and sales price are the same. The result is the same under either type of buy-sell agreement.

The income consequences of a buy-sell agreement on the surviving owners' income tax basis must also be considered. In a cross-purchase agreement, the surviving owners' basis in the purchased stock is the purchase price they pay for the deceased owner's stock. This is the result irrespective of the source of funds; that is, whether paid from life insurance proceeds or other assets. In a redemption agreement, the corporation purchases the stock; thus, the surviving owners retain their same income tax basis in their stock, although their percentage of ownership has now increased. This is a disadvantage of the redemption agreement in the event the surviving owners choose to sell their stock during their lifetimes. If the intent is to hold the stock until death, each owner's estate will receive a stepped-up basis in the stock at that time.

> **Example:** A and B each own 50% of the common stock in XYZ, Inc., with each having an income tax basis in the stock of $30,000. A dies and his 50% interest is valued at $330,000. Whether the buy-sell is a cross-purchase agreement or a redemption agreement, the stock of A will be purchased and B will own 100% of the common stock in the business. B later sells the business for $660,000. If the agreement between A and B was a redemption, B's basis in her stock is $30,000, and she has a taxable gain at sale of $630,000. If a cross-purchase agreement had been utilized, B's basis in the common stock would be her original $30,000 basis, plus a $330,000 basis for the common stock purchased from A. Thus, B's gain would be only $300,000. Assuming that B is in a 20% capital gain tax rate, the redemption agreement results in an added $66,000 in income tax. This issue is usually not a problem for "S" corporations, partnerships, and limited liability companies (unless electing to be taxed as a "C" corporation), as the owners in these type of pass-through entities will receive a basis step-up with both a redemption and a cross-purchase agreement.

10.33 Dividend Problems with Redemption Agreements

10.331 General Considerations

Redemption agreements always involve a consideration of the possible treatment of the corporate redemption as a dividend as opposed to a sale or exchange.[12] It is important for a corporate redemption to be treated as a sale or exchange, because this allows the seller to offset the sales proceeds with his or her income tax basis. If instead the redemption is considered a dividend from the corporation to the stockholder, the entire amount is taxable as income without any offset for the seller's income tax basis in the stock.

There are several rules that, if met, permit the redemption to be treated as a sale or exchange rather than as a dividend.[13] They are relatively simple requirements to meet when the business does not have relatives owning stock in the business. The basic rules are that the redemption will be treated as a sale or exchange if it (1) is not essentially equivalent to a dividend, (2) is substantially disproportionate, (3) completely terminates the stockholder's interest in the corporation, or (4) is of the stock of a corporate stockholder in partial liquidation of the redeeming corporation. Most corporate redemptions in buy-sell agreements are in complete termination of stock ownership, so sale or exchange treatment for income tax purposes is ensured in most cases.

> **Caution:** If the redemption is not in complete termination of the stockholder's interest, then greater care must be exercised by the practitioner in reviewing the finer points of the other exceptions by referring to Section 302 of the Internal Revenue Code and then to the pertinent regulations thereunder.[14]

10.332 Attribution Rules

When the redemption involves family members who will continue to own stock in the corporation, a greater problem exists. The constructive ownership[15] or, as they are sometimes termed, the attribution rules of IRC Section 318 apply and may result in dividend treatment rather than sale or exchange treatment. The attribution rules treat stock owned by related parties as if owned by the redeeming stockholder. This precludes the redeeming stockholder from having a complete termination of his or her interest in the corporation because the stock of the related stockholder is deemed to be owned by the redeeming stockholder. Thus, after the stockholder redeems all of his or her stock in the corporation, the redemption is still not a complete termination in ownership because the relative's stock is deemed to be owned by the redeeming stockholder. Unless one of the other three exceptions applies, the redemption will be treated as a dividend.

The attribution rules can be waived in some situations. The redeeming stockholder who is redeeming his or her entire stock ownership can waive the so-called family attribution rules that treat him or her as owning stock that is owned by his or her spouse, children, grandchildren, and parents.[16] By filing a waiver agreement with the IRS, the redeeming stockholder (1) agrees not to have an interest, including any interest as a stockholder, officer, director, or employee, in the corporation for 10 years following the redemption other than as a creditor or by inheritance; and (2) establishes that none of the redeemed stock was acquired during the 10 years before the redemption from a person whose stock could be deemed to be the distributee's under the attribution rules, in a transaction the primary purpose of which was to avoid income tax. The requirements are obviously rather technical; thus, again, Section 302 of the Internal Revenue Code and the pertinent regulations should be reviewed in planning for this exception to the attribution rules.

Even more tedious are the rules concerning related entities such as estates, trusts, corporations, and partnerships and their beneficiaries, stockholders, and partners, which are also subject to the attribution rules. These entities cannot waive attribution. However, the entity may waive the attribution rule that links family members. This action requires a filing with the IRS under much the same criteria as explained earlier, with the added requirement that both the individual and the entity must agree to be jointly and severally liable for any taxes if a prohibited interest is acquired during the following 10 years.[17] The waiver requires that both the entity and the individual have no ownership. Example 1, following, illustrates a situation in which the entity can waive "family" attribution, and Example 2 illustrates that an entity cannot waive "entity" attribution between it and an individual.

> **Example 1:** A father dies owning 1,000 shares of stock in his family business. His two children own 450 shares each. His wife, who previously owned no stock in the business, inherits her husband's entire estate, which includes the 1,000 shares. During estate administration, the estate redeems the 1,000 shares of stock. Because of attribution, the redemption does not qualify as a complete termination because the estate will be deemed to own the stock of the children: "family" attribution links the children's stock to the wife, and "entity" attribution then links the wife's "linked" stock to the estate. However, "family" attribution can be waived by the estate. This breaks the link between the wife and the children; thus, there is no link between the entity and the wife. The redemption is a complete termination, allowing the payment to be treated as a sale or exchange.

> **Example 2:** A mother owns 50% of the stock in the family business. Her two children are beneficiaries under a trust established by her deceased husband that owns 25% of the business. The balance of the

stock is owned by unrelated parties. A complete redemption by the trust will not qualify as a sale or exchange because "family" attribution links the mother's stock to the children and "entity" attribution then links the children's "linked" stock to the trust; thus, it is not a complete termination. If the trust waives "family" attribution, the redemption will qualify. The link between the mother and children will be broken. If the children owned stock themselves, however, the trust could not waive "entity" attribution between itself and the beneficiaries as to those shares; therefore, the redemption in that situation will not be a complete termination by the trust, thus causing the payment to be treated as a dividend.

 Planning Pointer 3

An obvious planning approach is to use cross-purchase agreements when family members are involved. If this is not possible, a thorough review and analysis of the effects of the attribution rules are essential.

10.34 AMT Problems with Redemption Agreements

The corporate alternative minimum tax (AMT) is a tax on corporations with high accounting income that pay little corporate income tax because they have little taxable income. This tax, which applies to C corporations and not to S corporations, used to cause a corporation receiving life insurance proceeds with which to purchase a deceased stockholder's stock to pay an income tax on the life insurance proceeds. If a corporate redemption was essential, then more life insurance had to be purchased; or if not essential, then the stockholders could enter into a cross-purchase agreement. This is no longer a problem as the corporate AMT has been repealed by the Tax Cuts and Jobs Act passed by Congress in December 2017.

10.35 Partnerships

The purchase by a partnership of the interest of its deceased partner raises several considerations. Payments for fixed assets, investments, and goodwill are capital transactions.[18] To the extent that the sales price consists of such items, the estate will have an income tax basis that has been stepped up to the date-of-death value of such assets. If the sales price is the same as the date-of-death value of these assets, there is no income tax consequence to the sale of the deceased partner's interest by the estate.

If the payment to the estate represents a receivable or salary, it is ordinary income to the estate, not a capital transaction.[19] This is an income tax advantage to the partnership because such items are income tax–deductible expenses of the partnership. In determining the nature of the payment to be received, consideration must be given to these factors. Because the partnership and its remaining partners will be somewhat at odds with the redeeming partner's estate, these differing tax consequences should be considered and addressed in the buy-sell agreement.

Notes

1. Treas. Reg. § 20.2031-2(h).
2. I.R.C. §§ 2701-2704.
3. *Id*. § 2703.
4. Treas. Reg. § 1.264-1(a).
5. I.R.C. § 101(a).
6. *Id*. § 2042.
7. *Id*. §§ 1(a), 11.
8. Treas. Reg. § 20.2031-8.
9. I.R.C. § 101(a)(2); Treas. Reg. § 1.101-1(b)(5) ex. (1).
10. I.R.C. § 101(a)(2)(B).
11. *Id*. § 1014.
12. *Id*. § 301.
13. *Id*. § 302.
14. *Id*. §§ 302(b)(1), (2), (3); 302(e).
15. *Id*. § 302(c).
16. *Id*. § 302(c)(2)(A).
17. *Id*. § 302(c)(2)(B).
18. *Id*. §§ 736, 741.
19. *Id*. §§ 736(b)(2), 751.

Chapter 11

Retirement Plans and Benefits

11.1 Background
11.2 Types of Retirement Plans
    11.21 Pension Plans
    11.22 Profit-Sharing Plans
    11.23 Money-Purchase Plans
    11.24 401(k) Plans
        11.241 Simple 401(k) Plan
    11.25 Self-Employed Persons
    11.26 SEP
    11.27 IRA
        11.271 Roth IRA
        11.272 SIMPLE IRA
11.3 Participation, Vesting, and Nondiscrimination
11.4 Top-Heavy Plans
11.5 Social Security Integration
11.6 Penalty Taxes
    11.61 Premature Distributions
    11.62 Minimum Distributions
11.7 Distributions
    11.71 Distributions during Lifetime
    11.72 Distributions at Death

11.1 Background

The area of pension law and retirement planning is quite complex. This chapter provides an overview. A more detailed treatment of this complex area of the law can be found in the ABA publication, L. Mezzullo, *An Estate Planning Guide to Qualified Retirement Plans* (ABA, 2016). Nonetheless, the practitioner needs a general knowledge of this area of the tax law to advise both individual and business clients. Although there are many types of retirement plans, the reasons for an individual or business to begin a retirement plan are similar and involve both tax and nontax reasons.

A retirement plan helps a business attract and retain competent employees, reward employees for their loyalty to the business, provide the employees a needed supplement to Social Security benefits, and maintain high employee morale, all of which should help the business be more productive and increase its profitability. In closely held businesses, the owner needs to build financial security for the owner's own retirement. The sale of the business in later years may not be possible; even if it is, the sales price may not be sufficient to provide for retirement. Because the owner of a closely held business is usually more highly paid than the other employees, establishing a retirement plan is an ideal solution. It allows a larger contribution for the owner and a potentially large retirement benefit, which then lessens the need to sell the business to provide for retirement.

The income tax advantages make retirement plans most attractive. The employer's contribution to the plan is a tax-deductible business expense in the year of the contribution; however, the employee does not include the contribution in gross income in that year. The contribution remains in the retirement plan, with none of the investment return being currently taxed. The plan is allowed to grow tax free throughout the employee's working years. Only on retirement, when the employee begins receiving the retirement benefit, is an income tax owed. The deferral of income taxes for such a length of time permits a much larger fund to accumulate for retirement than otherwise would be possible.

11.2 Types of Retirement Plans[1]

11.21 Pension Plans

A pension plan, which in the tax law is termed a *defined benefit plan*,[2] is a retirement plan that provides the participant with a fixed benefit. For example, participants may receive an annual retirement benefit equal to 60% of the participant's average annual salary based on the five consecutive years of the highest salary. The annual benefit cannot exceed the lesser of $220,000 per year in 2018, or 100% of the three consecutive years of the highest salary.[3] The benefit cap is indexed annually for cost-of-living increases. The maximum benefit is payable at Social Security retirement age and is actuarily reduced for an earlier retirement.[4]

 Planning Pointer 1

A pension plan is ideally suited for a small business when the owner earns a large salary and is older than most of the other employees because the contributions to a pension plan are not limited in amount. The employer simply contributes annually the actuarially determined amount needed to fund each employee's fixed retirement benefit. Thus, the bulk of the contributions is credited to the owner.

Caution: A disadvantage of a pension plan is that the employer's contribution needed to fund the retirement benefits is required each year, irrespective of the profitability of the business.

11.22 Profit-Sharing Plans

A profit-sharing plan, which in the tax law is one of several types of plans termed *defined contribution plans*,[5] is a plan in which the employer's contribution to the plan is fixed. The benefit to be received by a participant is not fixed. For example, each year after the employer has reviewed year-end profits, a dollar amount is contributed to the plan that is then earmarked to each participant's account on a pro rata basis. Another approach is for the employer to annually contribute a fixed percentage of salary to each participant's account in the plan. The contribution limit is the lesser of 100% of the participant's compensation (not exceeding $275,000 in 2018 as adjusted yearly for inflation) or $55,000.[6] The employer's income tax deduction is limited to 25% of total compensation, thus limiting the usage of the 100% maximum percentage.[7]

Unlike a pension plan, the participant's retirement benefit in a profit-sharing plan is uncertain. It is simply the amount contributed to his or her account plus the growth from the investment of those contributions. Another difference is that annual contributions are not required to be made to a profit-sharing plan. Thus, in years in which profitability is poor, only a small—or even no—contribution may be made.

 Planning Pointer 2

A profit-sharing plan is ideally suited for young, well-paid business owners because they have many years for contributions to be made and for investment growth. For example, a contribution of $10,000 annually for a 25-year-old at 8% growth yields nearly $2.5 million at 65 years of age.

11.23 Money-Purchase Plans

A money-purchase plan is a defined contribution plan; however, the employer's contribution is fixed at a percentage of the participant's salary. Thus, it becomes a hybrid of a pension and a profit-sharing plan. Just as in a pension plan, the employer must make annual contributions, but as in a profit-sharing plan, the participant's benefit is uncertain because it depends on the investment experience. For example, in a money-purchase plan the employer sets an ongoing contribution commitment at a fixed percentage of salary, such as 10% of annual salary. The contribution limit for a money-purchase plan is the lesser of 25% of compensation or $55,000.

 Caution: Because a money-purchase plan sets a fixed and ongoing financial commitment for the employer, future profitability of the business will have no effect on the requirement to fund the annual commitment to the plan. Only an established business with a lengthy history of profitability should consider this type of plan.

> **Planning Pointer 3**
>
> A money-purchase plan is simpler and less costly to implement and administer than a traditional pension plan, yet it assures the employees of a fixed commitment to the future from the business. Just as with a profit-sharing plan, a young, highly paid business owner will reap the greatest benefit from this plan.

11.24 401(k) Plans

There are two types of 401(k) plans: (1) a cash or deferred plan and (2) a salary reduction plan. In the cash or deferred plan, the employer's contribution may be received in cash by the employee and income tax paid on it, or the employee may elect to defer paying income tax on the contribution by having it credited to his or her 401(k) account.[8] The salary reduction plan allows an employee to elect to reduce his or her salary by a set percentage, which amount is deferred from income tax and is credited to the employee's 401(k) plan. The amount deferred is capped in 2018 at $18,500 and is indexed for annual cost-of-living adjustments.[9] An additional $6,000 "catch-up" contribution can be made in 2018 for those age 50 or older. Once a deferral is made, it is treated just like an employer contribution to any other qualified retirement plan; thus, the deferral cannot be withdrawn without tax penalties until retirement. However, a 401(k) plan does allow withdrawals before retirement in the case of some hardships.[10]

A 401(k) plan is not a separate plan; it must be offered in conjunction with a profit-sharing or stock bonus plan.[11] 401(k) plans are sometimes difficult to implement in businesses owing to the nondiscrimination rules. These rules require a reasonable balance in participation between the highly paid and the non-highly paid employees. If this requirement is not met, then a 401(k) plan is not available for any of the employees.¹²

Caution: To avoid running afoul of the nondiscrimination rules, the plan administrator must be aware of these rules and regularly monitor participation to ensure continued qualification.¹³

Planning Pointer 4

To ensure qualification for this benefit for highly paid employees, participation in the plan by the non-highly paid can be encouraged by the employer's matching the employee's deferral, such as at 50 cents per dollar deferred by the employee.

11.241 Simple 401(k) Plan

In 1997, a simplified 401(k) plan was added to the list of tax-favored retirement plans. Basically, a simple 401(k) plan relaxes some of the nondiscrimination requirements of a 401(k) plan. The deferred amount is limited to $12,500 in 2018 (indexed for inflation) rather than the higher amount permissible under a traditional 401(k) plan, plus an additional $3,000 "catch-up" contribution for those age 50 or older. An "eligible employer" is one who (a) employs 100 or fewer employees, each of whom receives at least $5,000 of compensation from the employer during any of the two preceding years; and (b) does not maintain another employer-sponsored retirement plan. An employer's matching contribution can be a nonelective contribution of 2% of compensation, or an elective contribution of 1% to 3% of compensation.

Roth 401(k) plans are also allowed. These plans are similar to a Roth IRA in that contributions are made with after-tax contributions. The amount that may be contributed is the same as the 2018 regular 401(k) limits. As with a Roth IRA, earnings and distributions are income tax free.

11.25 Self-Employed Persons

The retirement planning options available for the self-employed used to differ from those available for all other persons. Changes in this area of the tax law have, with only a few restrictions, created parity between corporate and self-employed retirement plans.¹⁴ Today the same rules that apply to corporate plans, including contribution limits, apply to the self-employed when they seek to adopt a pension, profit-sharing, money-purchase, 401(k), or SEP retirement plan for their business.

Caution: One important difference between corporate and self-employed plans is in the determination of the contribution limit. The contribution limit for the self-employed's account is based on the "earned income" of the self-employed. *Earned income* is defined as net self-employment income (gross income less 50% of self-employment tax) less the contribution made by the self-employed person to his or her own account.[15] In some situations this can create some difficult interrelated mathematical computations. The example that follows demonstrates how this rule reduces the contribution actually available for the self-employed.

Example: A self-employed businessperson wants to make the maximum 25% of compensation contribution to her money-purchase plan. Because she is self-employed, her contribution to the plan is deducted from her compensation to determine her earned income, on which the contribution percentage must then be applied. This rather circular problem is solved by dividing the contribution percentage by 1.0 plus the contribution percentage. The self-employed businessperson can contribute only 20% of compensation (0.25/1.25 = 20%).

11.26 SEP

The SEP is a simplified employee pension plan,[16] or, as it is sometimes referred to, a Super IRA. The SEP is an employer-provided retirement plan, but record-keeping and tax reporting are simplified. As in a profit-sharing plan, annual contributions are not required. The contributions, when made, are placed in each employee's own individual retirement account, and the contributions immediately become the employee's property. A salary deferral feature similar to a 401(k) can be offered as a part of the SEP.[17] The contribution limit to the SEP is the lesser of 25% of compensation (not to exceed $270,000 in 2017 as adjusted annually for inflation) or $54,000.[18] This higher limit makes the SEP just as attractive as a profit-sharing plan, but easier and less costly to administer. The only disadvantage is that the employee immediately owns the contribution in his or her account. Thus, there are no forfeitures of contributions to be redistributed to the other participants' accounts, as there are when an employee terminates employment and has unvested benefits.[19]

11.27 IRA

An IRA is an individual retirement account[20] that can be established by any individual, whether participating in an employer-provided retirement plan or not. The maximum annual contribution to an IRA in 2018 is $5,500.[21] A married couple can each contribute up to $5,500 annually to his or her own IRA even if one of the spouses is not employed.[22] An additional $1,000 "catch-up" contribution may be made for individuals age 50 or older.

The earnings from an IRA are not subject to income tax but are taxed on receipt at retirement.[23] Generally, an individual who contributes to an IRA can deduct the annual IRA contribution from gross income on his or her personal income tax return, provided neither the individual nor his or her spouse is an active participant in an employer-sponsored qualified retirement plan. However, the right to make a deductible contribution on behalf of the nonparticipant spouse when the other spouse participates in an employer-provided retirement plan is phased out for couples who have an adjusted gross income between $189,000 and $199,000 in 2018, adjusted annually for inflation. Further, when an individual is an active participant in a qualified plan, the income tax deduction for a married couple begins phasing out at $101,000 and phases out completely at $121,000.[24] For a single person, the phase-out is from $63,000 to $73,000.

Planning Pointer 5

Even though an individual is not entitled to a deduction from gross income for an IRA contribution, it is still a wise vehicle for savings because the earnings compound income tax free in the account until withdrawn at retirement. This tax-deferred compounding of income normally will yield a larger fund, even after the taxes are ultimately paid during retirement, than if the individual made the same investment outside an IRA with after-tax savings.

11.271 Roth IRA

The Roth IRA,[25] first enacted in 1997, offers a different type of IRA savings. The contributions are nondeductible but qualified distributions are received income tax free. Qualified distributions are those made after age 59-1/2, due to death or disability, or for a first-time home buyer up to a $10,000 lifetime limit. A *first-time home buyer* is one who has not owned a principal residence for two years—but the distribution may be not only to the taxpayer and his or her spouse but also to children, grandchildren, or ancestors. The regular IRA-required minimum distribution rules do not apply. Contributions are limited to $5,500 per year for each spouse, plus an additional $1,000 "catch-up" contribution for individuals 50 years of age or older. The contribution limit is reduced for joint income tax filers with adjusted gross incomes above $189,000 and then eliminated when adjusted gross income exceeds $199,000. The limitations are $120,000 to $135,000 for single taxpayers. These limits are adjusted annually for cost-of-living increases.

11.272 SIMPLE IRA

A significant modification to existing retirement plan law is the addition of the Savings Incentive Match Plan for Employees, known as SIMPLE IRA.[26] Generally, elective employer contributions are made to an IRA on behalf of employees, and the employer makes either a matching contribution or a nonelective contribution. The nondiscrimination rules generally applicable to qualified plans do not apply. The top-heavy plan rules do not apply. There is a simplified reporting procedure. These simple plans are limited to employers with no more than 100 employees, each of whom receives at least $5,000 in compensation, if the employer does not maintain another qualified employee retirement plan. The employee may elect to have up to $12,500 in 2018 (to be adjusted annually for inflation) reduced from compensation. There is an additional $3,000 "catch-up" contribution for those age 50 and older. The employer's matching contribution can be either a nonelective contribution of 2% of compensation or an elective contribution from 1% to 3% of compensation.[27]

11.3 Participation, Vesting, and Nondiscrimination

The concepts of participation, vesting, and nondiscrimination as used in the tax law must be understood. Each of these concepts involves specific statutory requirements that must be met before a retirement plan is qualified for the favorable income tax treatment that is essential under the tax law. *Participation* refers to the time that an employee becomes eligible to participate in the employer's retirement plan. Any employee age 21 with one year of service must be a participant in the plan.[28] To avoid including temporary or part-time employees, anyone who works 1,000 hours or less per year is not required to be a participant in the plan.[29] Participation can be extended to two years if desired, but to do so requires an immediate 100% vesting schedule for all participants.[30]

Even though an employee is a participant in a plan, the employee does not actually own anything until the contributions of the employer have "vested." Vesting for a defined contribution plan occurs under one of three schedules:[31]

1. "Cliff" vesting, which requires 100% vesting after three years of service;
2. "Graded" vesting, which requires 20% vesting after two years and 20% each year thereafter; or
3. 100% immediate vesting if two years of service for eligibility is required.

For defined benefit plans, vesting occurs under either a three- to seven-year graded vesting schedule or a five-year cliff vesting schedule.

Once a vesting schedule is selected for a retirement plan, that schedule will determine when an employee is considered to own the benefits in his or her account. If an employee terminates employment before being 100% vested, the portion of the account that is not vested is forfeited. The forfeitures will either reduce future employer contributions or be an extra allocation for the remaining employees.

Nondiscrimination rules are intended to ensure that the retirement plan is for all employees, not just a few of the highly compensated employees. Retirement plans are not intended to discriminate in coverage, contributions, or benefits in favor of the highly compensated.[32] The retirement plan will qualify as nondiscriminatory if (1) 70% or more of all non-highly compensated employees are covered or (2) the percentage of non-highly compensated employees is at least 70% of the percentage of covered highly compensated employees.[33] If the plan is a defined benefit plan, there is the additional requirement that the plan must cover the lesser of 50 employees or 40% of all employees. The "highly compensated" employees are those who are (1) 5% or more owners or (2) earning more than $120,000 per year and are in the top-paid group of employees.[34] A *top-paid employee* is one who ranks in the top 20% of compensation. The income level for highly compensated employees is adjusted for cost-of-living increases.

11.4 Top-Heavy Plans

Even though a plan meets all of the requirements to be qualified under the Internal Revenue Code, it may still be termed top-heavy, which brings to bear another set of rules. A *top-heavy plan* is one in which more than 60% of the aggregated accumulated benefits or account balances of the plan participants accrue to the benefit of the "key employees." A *key employee* is one who during the current plan year and the four prior years is (1) an officer of the employer having compensation exceeding $175,000 in 2018, subject to cost of living adjustments; (2) a 5% or greater owner; or (3) a 1% or greater owner having a compensation in excess of $150,000.[35]

For any year in which a plan is top-heavy, it must use an accelerated vesting schedule and modify its contribution requirements for the nonkey employees.[36] The vesting schedule must be either a "cliff" vesting reduced to three years or a "graded" vesting requiring 20% vesting after two years and 20% each year thereafter.[37] The contributions in a defined contribution plan must be at least 3% of compensation for nonkey employees, or if less than 3%, the percentage for the key employees. If the plan is a defined benefit plan (pension plan), the fixed benefit for the nonkey employees must be at least 2% of the highest five-year average compensation of service for each year in which the plan is top-heavy, or a maximum of 20% of average compensation.[38]

11.5 Social Security Integration

Every employer provides a retirement plan for its employees through the employer's Social Security contribution. An employer-provided qualified retirement plan is actually a second retirement plan being provided by the employer.

Because Social Security covers a minimum wage base amount, many employers want their retirement plan to apply to compensation in excess of the wage base, which is already provided by the employer through its Social Security contribution. Within certain IRS-permitted guidelines, the integration of Social Security benefits into the retirement plan is permissible.[39] The effect of Social Security integration is to cause greater employer contributions to be paid to the higher paid employees, which, of course, will normally include the owners.

11.6 Penalty Taxes

There are two tax penalties that can have an effect on a participant in a retirement plan. The practitioner must be aware of these penalties because they must be considered in making decisions about the distribution of benefits during lifetime or at death. The taxes are a penalty (1) on premature distributions and are (2) due to the failure to make required minimum withdrawals from the plan.

11.61 Premature Distributions

Any distribution from a qualified retirement plan, 401(k), IRA, or SEP before the participant reaches 59-1/2 years of age is subject to a 10% premature distribution penalty.[40] The distribution also is subject to income tax. The tax does not apply if the distribution is made owing to the participant's death, disability, divorce, if pursuant to a qualified domestic relations order, or for medical expenses that exceed the 72% of adjusted gross income floor.[41] The distribution also is not subject to the 10% penalty if made to the participant after age 55 pursuant to early retirement, or earlier if made in equal periodic payments over the life expectancy of the participant or the participant and his or her beneficiary. Payments for medical expenses also are excluded.[42] Further, most distributions from qualified retirement plans that are rolled over into an IRA within 60 days from distribution are not taxed as premature distributions.[43]

> **Caution:** A 20% mandatory income tax withholding is required, even though the 60-day rollover requirement is met, unless the transfer is directly from trustee to trustee.[44]

11.62 Minimum Distributions

Distributions from all qualified retirement plans and IRAs must begin no later than April 1 following the year in which the participant reaches 70-1/2 years of age and must be distributed over (a) the participant's life; (b) his life and the life of a designated beneficiary; (c) a period of not more than his life expectancy; or (d) a period of not more than his life expectancy and that of a designated beneficiary.[45] The minimum distribution rules were simplified beginning on January 1, 2003, eliminating the need to elect recalculation of life expectancy, determine a designated beneficiary by the required beginning date, or satisfy a separate incidental death benefit rule. The IRS regulations now provide a single table that any recipient can use to calculate the annual required minimum distribution.[46] The recipient simply plugs in her age as of her birthday in the relevant distribution year and the prior year-end balance of her retirement account or IRA. The regulations specify the applicable distribution period for required minimum distributions during the participant's lifetime and after the participant's death.[47] If distribution is not made in the minimum amount required, a penalty of 50% is imposed on the difference between the minimum required and the actual distribution. The penalty can be waived by the IRS if reasonable cause is established for the error and if steps are taken to ensure that the error will be remedied.[48]

11.7 Distributions

11.71 Distributions during Lifetime

The tax consequences of a distribution from a qualified retirement plan, 401(k), IRA, SEP, or any of the other tax-deferred retirement plans is relatively simple. The distributions are taxed when received.[49] Thus, a participant who is receiving periodic installments pays income tax on those installments in the year received. In the situation in which the participant's installments include both employer and employee contributions, the employee's contribution is returned tax free, as it was made with after-tax contributions, and the remainder of the installments are subject to income tax. Because most retirement plans do not permit after-tax employee contributions, this complication is seldom a factor.

In some situations, an individual elects a lump-sum distribution. This alternative was more appealing under earlier tax law provisions, which at one time permitted a favorable 10-year income averaging. Generally, those rules no longer apply.[50]

> ### Planning Pointer 6

A lump-sum distribution from a qualified plan can be rolled into an IRA within 60 days of the distribution.[51] When this is done, the income tax continues to be deferred and the premature distribution penalty is avoided.

 Caution: The distribution must be a trustee-to-trustee transfer to avoid the imposition of a 20% income tax withholding.[52]

The determination of whether to receive a lump sum or installment payment of benefits is not the difficult choice it used to be. The current minimum distribution rules permit a longer payout term, thus increasing the possibility that the tax-deferred earnings on the retirement account will continue to increase the size of the account that is available to be distributed at the individual's death to his or her beneficiaries. As there is no income tax advantage to a lump-sum distribution, there seems little incentive to receive a lump-sum distribution. About the only reason to receive a lump-sum distribution is if the individual desires to pay the income tax to reduce the individual's own estate, following a plan of lessening his or her federal estate tax; or desires to be certain the beneficiary does not have to pay income taxes on future distributions from the retirement plan. Because an individual can withdraw any amount from his or her retirement account after age 59-1/2 without penalty, there seems little reason to take a lump-sum distribution of the entire account, although distributions of any size may be taken if there appear to be overall tax advantages in doing so.

> **Caution:** The spouse of the participant has certain guaranteed rights that must be considered. In a pension or money-purchase plan, the retirement benefit must be payable in a joint and survivor's annuity, unless this option is waived by the spouse. Generally, this is not required in profit-sharing plans; however, the spouse must be designated as the beneficiary of the benefits in the event of death.[53]

11.72 Distributions at Death

Distributions following the death of the participant are subject to estate tax.[54] They are included in the gross estate if (1) before death the annuity was payable to the decedent or to the decedent and another and (2) after death any payment is made to a beneficiary who has survived the decedent. In other words if, because of a contractual obligation owed to the decedent, payment is made to a beneficiary who survived the decedent, the payment is included in the gross estate. This includes not only commercial annuities and private annuities but also the various types of qualified employee benefit plans, such as pension plans, profit-sharing plans, 401(k) plans, SEPs, and IRAs.

Frequently, the beneficiary of an annuity has the payment option of receiving a lump sum, in which event the lump-sum payment is included in the gross estate. If payment is receivable as a periodic payment instead, then the present value of the income right of the beneficiary is included in the gross estate of the decedent. This computation is made according to the IRS valuation tables in Treasury Regulation 20.2031-11. In those rare situations in which someone other than the decedent and his or her employer contributed to the annuity, a proportionate reduction is allowed for those third-party contributions to the purchase of the annuity when valuing the annuity.

Example 1: The decedent was receiving $30,000 per year from his retirement plan, and after his death payment continues for the benefit of his wife. The wife is 60 at the decedent's death. Thus, the gross estate must include $305,886 for the value of the retirement annuity (10.1962 annuity factor - $30,000). This computation is based on a 6.4% interest factor. Current Treasury Regulations and Notices must be consulted in making calculations due to monthly changes in the interest rate factor.[55]

Example 2: If in the preceding example the decedent and his wife had purchased an annuity paying $30,000 per year for their joint lifetimes, with each spouse paying one-half of the purchase price for the annuity, then the decedent's gross estate would include only $152,943, which represents his proportionate part of the annuity.

Planning Pointer 7

Purely voluntary employer payments to a beneficiary such as a surviving spouse, which are not made pursuant to a contractual obligation, are not included in the gross estate and are not subject to the federal estate tax.

 Caution: Before 1983, death benefits under a qualified retirement plan were fully excluded from the estate tax. The exclusion then was reduced to $100,000. Since 1985 such benefits have been fully taxable, except for estates of decedents who were in pay status (retired) on December 31, 1984, and before July 19, 1984, had irrevocably elected the form for paying the remaining benefits. In this limited situation, the first $100,000 of plan proceeds is exempt from the federal estate tax. It appears that this exemption will be of little benefit because the decedent's election must be irrevocable. Most elections would be revocable, but this fine point should not be overlooked.

Notes

1. This discussion includes only the more common types of plans.
2. I.R.C. § 414(j).
3. *Id.* § 415(b)(1).
4. *Id.* § 415(b)(2)(C).
5. *Id.* § 414(i).
6. *Id.* § 415(c)(1).
7. *Id.* § 404(a)(3).
8. *Id.* § 401(k)(2).
9. *Id.* § 402(g).
10. *Id.* § 401(k)(2)(B).
11. *Id.* § 401(k)(2).
12. *Id.* § 401(k)(3).
13. *Id.* § 401(k)(4).

14. *Id.* § 401(c).
15. *Id.* § 401(c)(2).
16. *Id.* § 408(k).
17. *Id.* § 408(k)(6).
18. *Id.* § 402(h).
19. See 11.3 in this chapter.
20. I.R.C. § 408.
21. *Id.* § 219(b).
22. *Id.* § 219(c).
23. *Id.* § 408(e).
24. *Id.* § 219(g).
25. *Id.* § 408(A).
26. *Id.* § 408(p).
27. *Id.* § 401(k)(11).
28. *Id.* § 410(a)(1).
29. *Id.* § 410(a)(3).
30. *Id.* § 410(a)(1)(B).
31. *Id.* § 411(a)(2).
32. *Id.* §§ 401(a)(4), (5).
33. *Id.* § 410(b)(1).
34. *Id.* § 414(q).
35. *Id.* §§ 416(g), (i).
36. *Id.* § 416(a).
37. *Id.* § 416(b).
38. *Id.* §§ 416(c)(1), (2).
39. *Id.* § 401(1).
40. *Id.* § 72(t).
41. I.R.C. §§ 401(a)(9), 414(p). An IRA transferred incident to a divorce is governed by I.R.C. § 408(d)(6).
42. I.R.C. § 72(t)(2).
43. *Id.* §§ 401(a)(5), 408(d)(3).
44. *Id.* § 3405(c).
45. *Id.* §§ 401(a)(9)(A), (C).
46. *Id.* § 1.401(a)(9)-9, Uniform Lifetime Table in A-2.
47. *Id.* § 1.401(a)(9).
48. *Id.* § 4974(c).
49. *Id.* §§ 402, 1.402(a)-1(a)(1).
50. *Id.* § 401(d)(4).
51. *Id.* § 401(a)(5).
52. *Id.* § 3405(c).
53. *Id.* § 401(a)(11).
54. *Id.* § 2039.
55. This calculation is based on life expectancy and interest factors in effect at the time of writing. Current factors should be consulted when making calculations.

Chapter 12

Valuation of Assets

12.1 Background
12.2 Real Estate
    12.21 Cost Method
    12.22 Market Data Approach
    12.23 Income Approach
    12.24 Special-Use Valuation
12.3 Tangible Personal Property
12.4 Intangible Personal Property
    12.41 Valuation of Closely Held Stock
        12.411 Book-Value Approach
        12.412 Capitalization-of-Income Approach
        12.413 Discounts
        12.414 Buy-Sell Agreements

12.1 Background

The valuation of property for the purpose of imposing the estate or gift tax can be a complex task. In this chapter only the general principles are considered, and the focus will be on the estate tax, although the principles stated are equally applicable to the gift tax.

Valuation, as the term is used in estate tax law, means the fair market value of the particular asset that passes from the decedent to the beneficiary, valued at the date of the decedent's death. The federal estate tax regulations provide the following classic definition of the term *fair market value*: "The fair market value is the price at which the property would change hands between a willing buyer and a willing seller, neither being under any compulsion to buy or to sell and both having reasonable knowledge of relevant facts."[1]

Valuation problems often are present in the administration of an estate, but such questions are seldom litigated. Normally the taxpayer and the Internal Revenue Service (IRS) are able to compromise in a valuation dispute. The general principles of valuation used in valuing property are considered in this chapter.

⚠ **Caution:** IRC Section 6662 imposes a 20% penalty on the amount of any underpayment due to undervaluation of assets for estate or gift tax purposes. The understatement penalty applies if the valuation of the property on the tax return is 65% or less of the amount determined to be the correct valuation. No penalty is imposed unless the underpayment attributable to the undervaluation results in additional taxes in excess of $5,000. The 20% penalty is increased to 40% if the undervaluation is attributable to a gross valuation misstatement. A *gross valuation misstatement* is one in which the estate or gift tax valuation understatement claimed on the return is 40% or less of the amount determined to be the correct valuation.

12.2 Real Estate

Generally, to determine the value of real estate, one or more of the following three methods of valuation are used: (1) cost method, (2) market data method, and (3) income method. The estimates of value obtained from each approach are not averaged. Rather, they are reviewed to determine the applicability of each of the three approaches. For example, an apartment building, because of its income-producing nature, might be valued more properly by the income approach, whereas the market data approach might be more accurate for a residence and the cost approach more accurate for a factory.

12.21 Cost Method

In the cost approach, the value of the land is estimated (normally by the market data or income approach) and the depreciated reproduction cost of the building and other improvements is added to this value. The cost approach may be performed in the following steps: (1) estimate the value of the land as if vacant, (2) estimate the current cost of reproducing or replacing the existing improvements, (3) estimate the accrued depreciation from all causes, (4) deduct the accrued depreciation from the cost of reproducing the improvements to arrive at the indicated value of the improvements, and (5) add the value of the land to the value of the indicated improvements. For most types of property this method is less satisfactory than the other two methods; however, for some properties it is appropriate. The type of property will dictate the best method of appraisal.[2]

12.22 Market Data Approach

The market data or comparable sales approach is essential to almost every appraisal of real estate. This approach produces an estimate of value for a property by comparing it with similar properties that have been sold recently in the same or a similar area. The market data approach consists of the following steps: (1) locate similar properties for which sales, listings, offerings, or rental data are available; (2) determine the nature and conditions of the sale, including sales price, terms, and motivating forces; (3) analyze each of the similar property's important characteristics and compare with the corresponding ones of the property being appraised; (4) consider the dissimilarities in terms of the probable effect on sales price; and (5) formulate, in light of these comparisons, an opinion on the value of the subject property. This method is usually the most satisfactory, especially if there are a sufficient number of similar properties sold within a relatively recent period of time.[3]

12.23 Income Approach

The income approach places more emphasis on the present value of the future benefits of property ownership. Generally, this is indicated by the net income a fully informed person may assume the property will produce during its remaining useful life. After comparing interest yields for similar investments, the income is capitalized to an estimated value. For example, if the property produced an annual net income of $12,000 and the capitalization rate is 10%, the value of the property would be $120,000. The steps involved in this approach are as follows: (1) obtain the rent schedules and the percentage of occupancy for the subject property and for comparable properties for the current year and for several past years; (2) compare these data and adjust them to an effective estimate of gross income that the subject property may reasonably be expected to produce; (3) obtain expense data such as taxes, insurance, and operating costs being paid by the subject property and by comparable properties; (4) estimate the remaining economic life of the property to establish the probable duration of its income; and (5) select the appropriate capitalization method and the applicable technique and appropriate rate for projecting the net income. Obviously, the income approach is especially useful in the valuation of income-producing property because the average investor in such property purchases it to receive income.[4]

12.24 Special-Use Valuation

Although real estate is valued at its fair market value, a special exception is available for real estate owned by farms and other closely held businesses. The exception allows qualifying real estate to be valued at its actual use rather than its highest and best use, which is the usual standard in arriving at fair market value. The exception is made because the real estate owned by farms and closely held businesses is often encroached on by commercial and residential developments. This causes the highest and best use to be other than the actual use of the real estate and thus greatly increases the fair market value of the real estate; however, its productivity has not increased because its present use is not commercial or residential. The special-use valuation allows the fair market value of such real estate to be reduced by a maximum of $1,140,000 for 2018, which amount is adjusted for inflation.[5]

The special-use valuation for farm real estate is determined based on the following formula:

Average Gross Cash Rental—Average State and Local Property Tax
Effective Interest Rate for New Farm Credit Bank Loans in the Decedent's District

The averages used in this formula are based on the five-year average of cash rentals for comparable land, state and local real estate property taxes, and Farm Credit Bank loans. The interest rate for Farm Credit Bank loans is published by the IRS.[6]

Real estate in closely held businesses, farms for which there is no comparable land from which to obtain cash rental comparisons, and farms for which the executor so elects are valued at actual use after considering the following factors:

1. Capitalization of the income that the property can be expected to yield;

2. Capitalization of the fair rental value of the land;

3. State or local property valuation in states that assess such land at actual-use value;

4. Comparable sales of land removed from encroaching developments that distort valuation; and

5. Any other factors that fairly value the land.

To be entitled to the special-use valuation, a number of requirements must be met. Initially, the following requirements are essential:

1. The value of the real and personal property used in the farm or business must be at least 50% of the adjusted gross estate;

2. The farm or business real estate must represent at least 25% of the adjusted gross estate;

3. The decedent or a family member must have owned the real estate and have been using it for a qualified purpose (including cash rental to a member of the lineal descendent's family) for at least five of the eight years preceding the decedent's death;

4. The decedent or a family member must have materially participated in the operation of the farm or business; and

5. The real estate must pass to qualified heirs who are ancestors, lineal descendants, and spouses.

Additionally, the real estate must continue to be used for the same purpose for the following 10 years. If the qualifying use ceases or if the property is sold, then additional estate taxes will be owed.

12.3 Tangible Personal Property

Tangible personal property creates fewer problems in valuation. Automobiles, jewelry, household furniture and furnishings, and other tangible personal property are valued by the market data approach. The IRS prefers a room-by-room itemization, with each article that has a value of $100 or more listed separately. Those items having values of less than $100 may be grouped together for valuation. In lieu of a detailed listing, the executor can have the property professionally appraised and file with the estate tax return a written statement declaring under penalties of perjury that the value listed is based on the appraisal.

The greater problem arises in valuing artworks, oriental rugs, valuable antiques, and other unique items. Items such as these that have "artistic or intrinsic" value in excess of $5,000 should be professionally appraised and the appraisal filed with the estate tax return. The appraiser should be reputable and of recognized competency to appraise the particular type of property involved.[7]

12.4 Intangible Personal Property

The principal types of intangible personal property consist of stocks, bonds, and similar securities.[8] For valuation purposes, securities can be classified as actively traded securities and inactive or closely held securities. The value of securities listed on a stock exchange is easily obtainable by referring to the trading prices on the date of death, then valuing the security at the average of the highest and lowest quoted selling prices on such date.[9] If the decedent dies on a day when the security was not traded, the value of the stock is determined by taking the average of the highest and lowest selling prices on the nearest dates before and after the date of death. These mean prices for the two days closest to the valuation date are then averaged, but the average must be weighted inversely by the number of days between the two selling dates and the date of death. For example, assume that the sales of stock nearest the date of death occurred two trading days before and three trading days after such date, and on these days the mean sales prices were $10 and $15, respectively. The price of $12 represents the fair market value on the date of death, computed as follows:[10]

(3 x $10) + (2 x $15) / 5 = $12

Dividends sometime create a problem in valuation. For example, dividends on common stock are included in the gross estate if the decedent was the owner of record of the stock on the date of his or her death, even though the dividend was not payable until after death.[11] Similarly, if the dividend was declared before the decedent's death and was payable to stockholders of record after the decedent's death, the stock is selling "ex-dividend" at the decedent's death. In this situation the amount of the dividend is added to the ex-dividend stock quotation to determine the value of the stock at the date of death.[12]

Bonds are valued much the same as stock when the bonds are actively traded. Many highly marketable bonds, such as municipal bonds, do not have generally accepted published trading values. Valuation for a particular bond issue is usually easily obtainable from a brokerage house or bank that is familiar with the bond market.[13] The value should include the accrued interest on the bond to the date of the decedent's death.

12.41 Valuation of Closely Held Stock

Valuation of closely held or inactively traded securities is more difficult. Because of the lack of an established market for this type of stock, different criteria must be used. Although there are numerous factors that have a bearing on valuation, the following offer a good general guideline: (a) the nature of the business and its history; (b) the economic outlook in general, and the condition and outlook of the industry in particular; (c) the book value of the stock; (d) the company's earning capacity; (e) the company's dividend-paying capacity; (f) goodwill and other intangible values; (g) the relative size of the block of stock to be valued; and (h) sales of similar stocks.[14]

Although these criteria are helpful, they provide only guidelines and do little to arrive at a valuation for a particular closely held stock. There are several different approaches to valuation, but two of these approaches are most frequently used and will be the most helpful. They are (1) the book-value approach and (2) the capitalization-of-income approach. When using these approaches to arrive at valuation, certain information must be furnished to the IRS, including complete financial and other data used to determine value, recent balance sheets, and income statements for the five years immediately before the valuation date.

Planning Pointer 1

A frequent estate planning technique is the estate freeze, whereby the owner tries to freeze the present value of the business and shift future growth to the successors, typically the owner's children. This technique involves the owner's receiving voting preferred stock with a fixed liquidation value and creating common stock that is nonvoting. Future growth in the business will benefit the common stockholders, with the owner's value frozen at the liquidation value of the preferred stock. This technique has been codified in Internal Revenue Code Sections 2701-2704. The tax code has sought to limit overzealous use of this planning technique and in the process has greatly complicated its use. One seeking to use this technique should carefully review the pertinent statutes and regulations.

12.411 Book-Value Approach

Book value is a good beginning point in valuing a business. It will not always be the best measure of value; however, in individual cases it may provide the best measure of value. For example, a business involved primarily in the holding of investments such as real estate or other investment assets may best be valued at book value. A business that is successful because of one individual may have little value except its value on liquidation, once that person is deceased. A new business often can be valued only at book value, as can a business that has low profits or is operating at a loss. Similarly, a business with a low profit margin in a highly competitive industry may be more appropriately valued by the book-value approach. Obviously, a business that is soon to liquidate also will be more properly valued at book value.

In contrast, a business that has a small amount of capital but maintains a good profit margin should be valued under another approach. The book-value approach provides a good beginning point, but it is unlikely that a business that does not require much capital could be properly valued at book value. This certainly would be the case in some professional practices, such as an accounting, law, or medical practice.

In the simplest application of the book-value approach, all that is initially required is to determine the total value of assets, then subtract the outstanding liabilities. The remaining equity then is divided by the number of outstanding shares of common stock to determine the per-share value of the common stock. Several adjustments are necessary to adjust this initial determination to have a more accurate adjusted book-value computation in arriving at fair market value.

If the assets of the business are valued at cost, an adjustment to fair market value should be made. For example, many businesses value land and capital investments at their initial cost, which provides a historical value but is inaccurate for purposes of determining fair market value. Therefore, assets should be adjusted to their fair market value. Additionally, many assets will be partially or fully depreciated. Even though depreciated, the assets may have a value in excess of that reflected on the books. Therefore, any fully depreciated asset should be valued at its present value and any partially depreciated asset should be adjusted to reflect the market value of those assets. Many businesses carry a low value, or no value, for goodwill. Normally, some adjustment should be made to recognize the goodwill value of the business.

Several other factors may indicate necessary adjustments due to overvaluations of assets as carried on the books of the company. Accounts receivable should be reviewed to make adjustments for possible uncollectible accounts receivable. Inventories often include obsolete items, and values should be reduced for such items. Of course, it is possible that inventories may be grossly undervalued, in which case there will be an upward adjustment for the inventory. There may be lawsuits threatened or pending, as well as other potential problems that should be considered in reducing the book value. Examples include long-term leases that have unfavorable terms, a financial burden to the company due to long-term indebtedness that may have large payments ballooning in the future, a poor liquidity position, and poor recent earnings and profits even though accumulated savings may be high.

With these various factors taken into consideration, the book value of the business should then be adjusted to arrive at an adjusted book value for the entire business. The number of outstanding shares of common stock are then divided into the adjusted book value for the entire business to arrive at the adjusted book value per share of common stock, which should then reflect the fair market value.

12.412 Capitalization-of-Income Approach

The capitalization-of-income approach simply requires taking the projected income flow from the business and converting it into a present value for the entire business. Several subjective factors are involved in making this determination; in many cases, however, this is a realistic way to value a closely held business. The beginning point is determining the income flow from the business.

In arriving at the income from the business, typically the beginning point is the average annual after-tax profits over the past five years. Then any excessive payments to the business owners, such as large bonuses, excessively large salaries, or high rents paid to the stockholders for rental of the building or other properties rented by the business from the stockholders are added to the profits. In some cases income may have been overstated by the corporation because of unusually low salaries. Obviously, if this is the case, a reduction in profits is required. Adjustments should also be made for any nonrecurring income items or expense items during this five-year period. If excessive depreciation was taken, an upward adjustment should be made. If any changes in accounting practices are a factor in unusually large increases or decreases in earnings, then offsetting adjustments should be made. An adjustment should also be made if the earnings trend for the past five years has been unusually strong or weak.

With the earnings as adjusted now determined, a capitalization rate must be determined. The capitalization rate simply is the rate of return that investors would demand if they were purchasing the business. The same risk-reward concept present in the purchase of any stocks also is present in selecting a capitalization rate. Basically, an investor who is purchasing a risky business investment will demand a much higher rate of return than would an investor of a less risky business investment. Therefore, the consideration in arriving at the capitalization rate is: What rate of return will an investor demand for an investment in this type of business? It will obviously be higher than could be received by the investor with no-risk investments such as U.S. government treasury bonds or certificates of deposit; how much higher the return must be, however, depends on the risk involved in the particular business. For example, the risk for an established accounting firm is much less than for a coal-mining business. Once the capitalization rate is determined, it is divided into the adjusted earnings to arrive at a value for the business.

12.413 Discounts

When a minority interest in a business is being valued, a discount frequently is necessary in recognition of the lack of marketability of a minority interest in a closely held corporation. Factors that will support the need for a minority discount are if the minority stockholders have no power to (1) force a dividend, (2) affect corporate policy and decisions, or (3) cause a liquidation of the corporation. These factors affect marketability of the minority ownership, and a discount must be made.

If the decedent is a key employee of the corporation, then a discount normally should be given for the loss of this key employee. In a typical closely held corporation, the business will lose significant profits owing to the death of the key employee. A discount is thus appropriate. As with the minority discount, there are no formulas or rules of thumb to apply. Serious consideration must be given to determine how long it will take the business to replace the key employee, the possible losses of profits during this interim, the probable effect of competitors during this interim, and any other pertinent factors.

Discounts for lack of marketability and a minority interest are often the subject of litigation with the IRS, but the courts often favor the taxpayer. In *Estate of Ford v. Commissioner,*[15] the courts allowed a 10% discount for lack of marketability and a 20% discount for a minority interest. A 40% discount for lack of marketability was allowed in *Estate of Joseph H. Lauder;*[16] and in *Estate of Anthony J. Frank,*[17] the court allowed a 40% lack-of-marketability discount and a 20% minority interest discount, which cumulatively represented a 44% discount. Taxpayers have also been successful in obtaining a discount from fair market value for built-in capital gains under the theory that a willing buyer will pay less for a corporation because of the capital gains tax that must be paid when the corporation is liquidated. This tax problem was created after the repeal of the *General Utilities* doctrine in 1986. Several courts have upheld this reduction under the theory that the built-in capital gains reduce marketability.[18]

> **Caution:** Although courts have frequently allowed discounts because of minority ownership and lack of marketability, the IRS puts the taxpayer to the test of establishing such discounts by competent expert evidence. Competent, certified appraisers should be used. It is preferable that the stock be valued by a national or regional stock brokerage firm that regularly provides such service or by certified appraisers with experience in valuing business interests.

12.414 Buy-Sell Agreements

The IRS generally recognizes the price set in a buy-sell agreement as binding in establishing valuation for estate tax purposes. The basic requirement for a binding and valid agreement is (1) the agreement must represent an arm's-length transaction, (2) the agreement must be binding both during the lifetime of the stockholders and at death, and (3) the agreement must be binding on the executor of the decedent.[19] If these requirements are met, the value of the business as set in the buy-sell agreement will be accepted by the IRS as the fair market value of the business.[20]

Caution: The ability of a family business to avail itself of this planning opportunity is limited for buy-sell agreements entered into or modified after October 8, 1990, the effective date of certain tax laws that negatively affect family businesses.[21] The tax code permits the IRS to ignore valuations set at less than fair market value, except when (1) the value is set in a bona fide agreement, (2) the value is not a device to transfer property to family members for less than adequate consideration, and (3) the terms of the agreement are similar to those entered into by persons in arm's-length transactions.[22] A family business may meet the first two requirements, but the third creates difficulties. Objective evidence of comparable agreements will be difficult to obtain; thus, the subjective analysis of the IRS can wreak havoc on many taxpayers.

Notes

1. Treas. Reg. § 20.2031-1(b).
2. THE APPRAISAL OF REAL ESTATE, 312-23 (10th ed., American Institute of Real Estate Appraisers 1992).
3. *Id.*, 367-407.
4. *Id.*, 408-27.
5. I.R.C. § 2032A. See also Chapter 13, at 13.43.
6. Treas. Reg. § 20.2032A-4. *See also* Rev. Rul. 93-28, 1993-15 I.R.B. 7, for the current rates.
7. Treas. Reg. § 20.2031-6.
8. The valuation of other intangible property, such as life insurance and annuities, is discussed in Chapter 2, at 2.23 and 2.26.
9. Treas. Reg. § 20.2031-2(b).
10. *Id.* § 20.2031-2(b)(3), Ex. 1.
11. *Id.* § 20.2033-1(b).
12. *Id.* § 20.2031-2(i).
13. *See also Id.* §§ 20.2031-2(b), (e).
14. Treas. Reg. § 20.2031-2(f); Rev. Rul. 59-60, 1959-1 C.B. 273.
15. Estate of Ford v. Commissioner, 53 F.3d 924 (8th Cir. 1995).
16. Estate of Joseph H. Lauder, T.C.M. 1994-527.
17. Estate of Anthony J. Frank, T.C.M. 1995-132.
18. Eisenberg v. Commissioner, 155 F.3d 50 (2d Cir. 1998); Estate of Welch v. Commissioner, 85 A.F.T.R.2d 2000-534 (6th Cir. 2000).
19. See Chapter 10, at 10.22, Planning Pointer; and the forms in Chapter 15, at 15.1 and 15.2.
20. Treas. Reg. § 20.2031-2(h); May v. McGowan, 194 F.2d 396 (2d Cir. 1952).
21. I.R.C. §§ 2701-2704, Treas. Reg. § 25.2703.
22. I.R.C. § 2703.

Chapter 13

Postmortem Estate Planning

13.1 Background
13.2 Qualified Disclaimers
13.3 Will and Estate Litigation
13.4 Considerations Affecting the Estate Taxes
    13.41 Alternate Valuation Date
    13.42 Section 303 Stock Redemption
    13.43 Special-Use Valuation
    13.44 Deferred Payment of Estate Taxes
13.5 Considerations Affecting Income Taxes
    13.51 Medical Expenses
    13.52 Series E and EE U.S. Savings Bonds
    13.53 Selection of Estate's Tax Year
    13.54 Filing Joint Returns
    13.55 Administrative Expenses
    13.56 Termination of the Estate
    13.57 Waiver of Executor's Fee

13.1 Background

In addition to the numerous estate-planning considerations during lifetime, there are a number of planning ideas to be considered by the decedent's executor or other beneficiaries. These planning considerations are loosely combined under the heading of postmortem estate planning ideas. The ideas include such diverse areas as (1) renunciations or disclaimers of inherited property, (2) considerations in estate litigation, (3) estate tax elections available to the executor, and (4) income tax considerations for the executor.

13.2 Qualified Disclaimers

An individual may refuse to accept a bequest, devise, or other property interest passing to him or her from the decedent. This refusal is often termed a *renunciation* in estate and property law, but it is termed a *disclaimer* in federal estate tax law. If the disclaimer meets both the state law requirements of the decedent's place of domicile and the federal tax law requirements, it is termed a *qualified disclaimer* and is effective for federal estate, gift, income, and generation-skipping tax purposes.

Assuming the disclaimer meets state law requirements, it must also meet the following requirements to be qualified for federal tax purposes:[1]

1. It must be an irrevocable and unqualified refusal to accept an interest in the property.
2. The refusal must be in writing.
3. The writing must be received by the transferor of the interest, his or her legal representative, or the holder of the legal title to the property to which the interest relates not later than the date that is nine months after the later of (a) the day on which the transfer creating the interest in such person is made or (b) the day on which such person reaches age 21.
4. The disclaimant must not have accepted the interest or any of its benefits.
5. As a result of such person's refusal, and without any direction from the disclaimant, the interest must pass to either (a) the decedent's spouse or (b) to a person other than the person making the disclaimer.

> **Planning Pointer 1**

When the decedent's will contains a specific bequest that the beneficiary does not need and thus plans to give the bequest to his or her children, a disclaimer will accomplish the same purpose, but it will save a gift tax or the use of part of the beneficiary's unified credit.

Example: A mother bequeaths $100,000 to her son, who is financially secure. The son intends to give the $100,000 to his daughter. If the son makes a gift of the bequest to his daughter, a gift of $85,000 after using the annual gift tax exclusion occurs, thus reducing the son's 2018 exclusion amount by this amount (assuming that no prior taxable gifts have been made). If the son has already used his entire exclusion amount, a gift tax of $34,000 will be owed. If the son disclaims the bequest, his daughter will receive the $100,000 (assuming a per stirpes distribution is applicable under either the will or state intestacy law) and no gift tax will be owed, nor will a reduction in the son's exclusion amount be required.

 Caution: There are two considerations that give rise to caution. First, no disclaimer should be filed until a clear determination has been made as to the effect of the disclaimer. The terms of the will or state intestacy law must be considered to determine who will receive the disclaimed property. The second consideration is that a disclaimer may involve a generation-skipping transfer tax if the effect of the disclaimer is to skip a generation. The preceding example clearly involves a direct skip, and the generation-skipping transfer tax will be applicable. In many situations the GST exemption will be sufficient to avoid any tax; however, consideration must be given to the GST tax before a disclaimer is made.[2]

 Planning Pointer 2

The use of a disclaimer can be anticipated by the decedent, and a provision can be inserted in his or her will providing for what is sometimes termed a *disclaimer trust*. Advance planning for a disclaimer trust can add greater flexibility to the use of a disclaimer, as seen in the following example.

Example: The husband's estate is $11,200,000 and the wife's estate is also $11,200,000. The husband's and the wife's wills make full use of the marital deduction;[3] thus, no federal estate tax will be owed at either the husband's death or the wife's death due to the marital deduction and portability of the exclusion amounts for each spouse. This favorable result occurs only if the estate assets do not increase significantly during the lifetime of the survivor. If the survivor anticipates a growth in the value of the assets inherited from the deceased spouse in excess of the anticipated inflation-adjusted exclusion amount, a disclaimer of these assets into a trust may be wise. The trust can provide income and principal distributions to the survivor. With proper drafting, the survivor can serve as trustee of the trust. At death, the trust assets can pass to the ultimate estate beneficiaries without an estate tax. For example, assume the husband's assets double in value while the wife's assets are invested in fixed income investments that do not appreciate in value. Assuming for purposes of illustration that the trust assets that initially equaled the exclusion amount increase over the years following the husband's death by $1,000,000, there will be a possible estate tax savings of $400,000 by using the trust. The disclaimer trust offers great flexibility, as the survivor can decide if the trust makes economic sense at the first spouse's death rather than the estate planning documents locking the couple into a trust that may not be needed. A will making use of this planning technique appears in Chapter 15 at 15.4.[4]

13.3 Will and Estate Litigation

On occasion an estate becomes involved in litigation. This sometimes occurs when the surviving spouse is bequeathed less than the statutory share or dower interest allowed under state law. In other situations, heirs who are omitted from the will or are granted an unusually small share may claim that the will was the result of undue influence or that the decedent was mentally incompetent at the time of writing the will. The decision to litigate is quite obviously a postmortem decision, which may alter the testator's testamentary plan.

Planning Pointer 3

Though not a controlling factor in making a decision to litigate, the estate tax ramifications should be considered. This is especially important when a settlement of the litigation is possible. Generally, if the settlement is entered into in good faith, is the result of an arm's-length negotiation, and is based on a bona fide claim, the terms of the settlement will be followed by the Internal Revenue Service (IRS) in computing the federal estate tax. If one of the litigants is a surviving spouse, this becomes important because the interest passing to the surviving spouse will be entitled to the marital deduction and will pass estate tax free. This causes a settlement to be less costly when property passes to the surviving spouse. For example, an estate in the 40% estate tax bracket can pass property to the surviving spouse in a settlement that will cost the estate and its other beneficiaries only 60% of the settlement amount.

Example: John and Jane were both married before their present marriage. Jane's separate estate is $12,000,000 and John's is $5,000,000. Before marriage they executed a premarital agreement in which each waived all rights to the estate of the other. Jane predeceases John in 2018, and in her will she devises her entire estate to her two children from her first marriage. Jane's will was written shortly before her death, but in an earlier will she bequeathed $1,000,000 to John. John renounces the present will, claiming it is invalid because of undue influence and lack of testamentary capacity, thus seeking to revive the prior will. Alternatively, he claims that the premarital agreement is invalid, and he should be entitled to his statutory share under state property law, which in his state is one-half of the estate. Even if John is unsuccessful in the litigation, Jane's children will owe $320,000 in estate taxes. If they settle the litigation by paying John $800,000, they will owe no federal estate taxes. The settlement thus costs them only $480,000 because John's $800,000 settlement qualifies for the estate tax marital deduction.

13.4 Considerations Affecting the Estate Taxes

13.41 Alternate Valuation Date

The normal date for valuing assets of a decedent's estate is the date of death of the decedent.[5] The executor has the option, however, of electing to value all assets six months after the date of death.[6] This date is referred to as the *alternate valuation date*. The only assets that cannot be valued on the alternate valuation date are assets sold before the six-month date (which are valued at the date of sale) and assets the value of which is affected by the passing of time, such as patents, which are valued at the date of death.[7] The election to use the alternate valuation date is made on a timely filed federal estate tax return or on one filed no more than one year after the date of death; interestingly, the election cannot be made on an amended return. Once the election is made, it is irrevocable.[8]

The alternate valuation date has importance for both estate tax and income tax planning. The more normal and obvious use of the election is to reduce the amount of estate taxes owed when estate assets have lost value during the first six months of estate administration. A less obvious use of the election is to increase the income tax basis of estate assets to lessen the income taxes that will be owed on a subsequent sale of the assets.

 Caution: The alternate valuation date cannot be used when no federal estate tax is owed. The election must decrease both the total value of the gross estate and the federal estate tax liability.[9] This rule is intended to lessen the ability to use the election to increase the income tax basis in estate assets.

This precludes use of the election for estates passing to the surviving spouse in which the unified credit and marital deduction have been used to defer the payment of any estate tax because there is no estate tax liability in such estates.

Planning Pointer 4

The surviving spouse can disclaim enough of the estate to create a small tax liability, thus complying with part of this rule. In an appropriate situation, the alternate valuation requirements can be met with an overall tax savings.

13.42 Section 303 Stock Redemption

Section 303 of the Internal Revenue Code permits stockholders of a corporation to redeem stock included in the decedent's gross estate to pay death taxes, funeral expenses, and administrative expenses. The redemption will be treated for income tax purposes as a sale or exchange rather than as a dividend. This is a significant benefit. A dividend is ordinary income to the recipient. A sale also results in ordinary income to the seller, but only to the extent the sales price exceeds the income tax basis of the stock. Normally, a redemption occurs shortly after the date of the decedent's death, in which event there will be little, if any, gain because the decedent's stock will receive a stepped-up income tax basis equal to its estate tax value.

> **Example:** The decedent owned 750 shares of common stock in a closely held business that had a date-of-death value of $1,000 per share, for a total value of $750,000. The estate redeems 100 shares to pay the estate taxes, funeral expenses, and administrative costs, all of which total $100,000. Because the basis in the stock is $1,000 per share and that is the

price paid for the redeemed stock, there is no gain from the redemption of the stock and no income tax owed because of the redemption.

To qualify for the redemption, all of the stock of the corporation that is included in the decedent's estate must exceed 35% of the decedent's adjusted gross estate. Further, the amount of stock redeemed that qualifies for a Section 303 redemption may not exceed the sum of all estate, inheritance, or other death taxes, plus interest owed thereon (if any) and the funeral and administrative expenses, which are allowable as deductions on the federal estate tax return.[10] If administrative expenses are deducted on the fiduciary income tax return, this does not affect the election because the expenses are "allowable" estate tax deductions, even though not deducted on the federal estate tax return.[11]

 Caution: The typical debt and estate tax payment clause in a will can cause a problem because one of the requirements of Section 303 is that the redemption can be used only by beneficiaries who actually bear the burden of paying the death taxes and the funeral and administrative expenses.[12] Thus, if the debt and tax payment clause in the will provides for payment of these costs from the residue of the estate, then only the residuary legatees can use the Section 303 redemption election. For example, if the decedent bequeaths his stock to a beneficiary who does not receive a residuary legacy and the decedent's will provides for the estate expenses and death taxes to be paid from the residue, then a Section 303 redemption is not available.

Planning Pointer 5

To ensure qualification for a Section 303 redemption, an individual should periodically determine during his or her lifetime whether the 35% of adjusted gross estate requirement is going to be met. If it is not, then the individual can make gifts of other estate assets to reduce the estate size to meet the 35% requirement. Transfers for this purpose made within three years of the individual's death will be added back to the gross estate in determining whether the 35% requirement is met.[13] Thus, last-minute planning will not be successful.

13.43 Special-Use Valuation

Special-use valuation is intended to assist owners of farms and other closely held businesses whose real property is located in an area where its highest and best use is other than as a farm or in the decedent's business.[14] For example, a farm located near a commercial shopping area is more valuable as commercial property than as a farm. Because the estate tax is imposed on the fair market value of property, the farm real estate must be valued based on its higher commercial value. The special-use valuation is an election available to the executor to value the real estate at its customary use, rather than at its highest and best use. Obviously, in some situations this can be a significant savings.

A number of requirements must be met to qualify for this election. If they are met, the value of the real estate in 2018 can be reduced by up to $1,140,000 of this highest-and-best-use valuation, with a resultant reduction in the federal estate tax that otherwise would be owed.[15] This amount is indexed yearly for inflation. The basic requirements are:[16]

- The adjusted value of the real and personal property (gross value less mortgages and liens) must equal or exceed 50% of the adjusted gross estate;
- The adjusted value of the real property must equal or exceed 25% of the adjusted gross estate;
- The decedent or a member of his or her family must have owned and materially participated in the operation of the farm or business during five of the last eight years preceding the decedent's date of death;
- All qualified heirs must agree in writing to the election, which must be filed by the executor; and
- The property must continue to be used as a farm or closely held business for 10 years; if it is not, the tax that otherwise would have been owed must be paid.[17]

13.44 Deferred Payment of Estate Taxes

The federal estate tax is due on the filing of the estate tax return, which is due nine months after the date of the decedent's death. Although the estate tax must be paid in full, there are three situations in which the estate tax payment may be deferred. The IRS may grant extensions to pay from 1 to 10 years when the estate can establish reasonable cause for the delay.[18] Reasonable cause is not defined, but the regulations provide examples of situations that qualify, such as if the estate is illiquid and there will be a loss of value to the estate if assets have to be sold at a loss to pay the estate tax.[19] A similar situation that qualifies is when an estate asset that could be used to pay the tax will not be received by the estate until a future date. The deferral is discretionary with the IRS. A second deferral is available for reversionary or remainder interests that were not created by the decedent but are included in his or her estate.[20] The extension may be granted for up to six months after the termination of the reversionary or remainder interest and is automatic if elected by the executor. A discretionary extension of time to pay may be allowed for reasonable cause for additional periods not to exceed three years.

The third deferral is for 5 years from the due date of the return followed by an additional 10 years of installment payments for estates that consist of farms or closely held businesses.[21] The entities qualifying for this deferral now include qualifying lending and financial businesses. The basic requirement for farms and closely held business apply for these type of businesses also; however, the term for the installment payments is reduced to five years. The ensuing discussion refers to farms and closely held businesses but does also apply (with certain limitations) to the qualifying lending and financial businesses. The basic requirement for this deferral is that the value of the farm or closely held business must exceed 35% of the decedent's adjusted gross estate. A closely held business includes[22] (1) a proprietorship or (2) a partnership or corporation, provided (a) the decedent's interest included in his or her gross estate is 20% or more of the value of the partnership or corporation or (b) the partnership or corporation has 45 or fewer partners or stockholders. Any passive assets of the business will also be excluded in arriving at the percentage limitations. Thus, the election is intended for active businesses, not investment businesses.

This third deferral election is made by the executor on a timely filed return, including any extensions. It may not be elected on a late or amended return. Interestingly, the election also can be made after the estate is closed if all the beneficiaries enter into an agreement to pay the tax and interest and file that agreement with the final settlement.[23] The election will remain effective unless there is a disposition of 50% or more of the decedent's interest in the closely held business.[24]

Planning Pointer 6

The election must be made on a timely filed return and not on an amended return, so it is a wise practice to file a protective election, even though the estate does not meet the 35% requirement. A subsequent audit of the estate tax return could result in the value of the closely held business being increased and the estate then meeting the percentage requirement. If the protective election is made, the estate then will qualify for the election, but if the election is not made, it cannot qualify later by filing an amended return.

Once the estate qualifies for the election, no payment on the estate tax liability is required for five years and nine months from the date of the decedent's death. Thereafter, the estate tax is paid in 10 equal annual installments.[25] Interest on the deferred amount will be owed annually, but the rate is reduced to only 2% on the deferred estate tax attributed to the first $1,520,000 in taxable value.[26] So, for decedents dying in 2018, the estate tax to which the 2% rate applies is $608,000. This amount is indexed annually for inflation. The interest rate on the balance is 45% of the rate imposed by the IRS on tax delinquencies.

Caution: Interest is paid each year on the deferred amount. The interest may not be deducted as an administrative expense on the estate tax return or as an interest expense on the estate's fiduciary income tax return. This is a change from prior tax law.

13.5 Considerations Affecting Income Taxes

13.51 Medical Expenses

Expenses for the decedent's medical care paid by his or her estate during the 12-month period following the date of death can be deducted on either the decedent's final income tax return or the estate tax return.[27] To determine whether the deduction should be taken on the final income tax return or on the estate tax return, one must compare the marginal tax rates applicable to each return. Current income tax rates range from 10% to 39.6%, whereas estate tax rates are 40%.

 Caution: In estates greater in amount than the exclusion amount ($11,200,000 in 2018), the estate should not automatically take the deduction because the estate may owe no estate tax due to the exclusion amount and the marital deduction for the surviving spouse. Obviously, if the estate will owe no estate tax, the deduction should be made on the decedent's final income tax return.

> **Planning Pointer 7**

If possible, the medical expenses should be paid before death. Then an income tax deduction is still available for the decedent's final income tax return, but the gross estate has been reduced by the medical expense payment, which then reduces the amount of estate tax.

13.52 Series E and EE U.S. Savings Bonds

Individuals owning Series E and EE U.S. Savings Bonds may elect to recognize currently the annual increase in the redemption value of their bonds; however, most individuals defer recognizing the increase (interest income) until the bonds are redeemed.[28] When an individual dies owning bonds with untaxed income accrued on them, there are three options available to the estate.

First, an election can be made to pay the income tax on all previously deferred income from the bonds on the decedent's final income tax return. If this election is made and the bonds are not redeemed, annual income recognition will be required thereafter. This may be a good option if the decedent died early in the tax year and has little other income. Also, the increase in the income tax liability resulting from the inclusion of this income on the decedent's final income tax return will increase the deduction for estate debts on the estate tax return, thus reducing the estate tax liability.

Second, if the election is not made on the decedent's final income tax return, it can be made on the estate's fiduciary income tax return. The income tax can even be deferred until the filing of the final fiduciary income tax return. The income accrued up to the date of the decedent's death will be deemed income in respect of a decedent. This permits a deduction on the fiduciary return for the estate tax attributable to the accrued income.

A third alternative is to distribute the bonds to the beneficiaries of the estate. No tax is then paid until the beneficiaries redeem the bonds. When the beneficiaries redeem the bonds, then the income tax will be paid.

> **Planning Pointer 8**

The determination of which option to follow can best be made only after the executor determines the income tax brackets of the estate, the decedent, and the beneficiaries. An analysis of the overall tax can then be computed and a decision made.

13.53 Selection of Estate's Tax Year

The estate may select any tax year it desires, thus permitting the estate to have a tax year other than a calendar year.[29] This may offer some income tax planning advantages. Because the length of the estate's first tax year can be shorter than a 12-month period, income can be split between two tax years, thereby reducing the marginal tax rate applicable to the estate income.

> **Example:** The decedent dies on February 1, 2018. The estate receives a large income payment on April 1, 2018. The first tax year of the estate can end on April 30, 2018, thus trapping the large income payment in the first tax year with income later in the year being taxed in the following fiscal year.

> **Caution:** Estates are now required to file quarterly estimated fiduciary income tax payments for tax years ending two or more years after the date of death of the decedent. Failure to make estimated payments results in a tax penalty.[30]

13.54 Filing Joint Returns

The decedent's executor and the surviving spouse can file a joint income tax return for the year in which the decedent died. This normally will result in a lower income tax liability because the joint rates for married couples are the most favorable income tax rate schedule. The surviving spouse can file a joint return only if agreed to by the executor, unless no executor has been appointed or the executor has failed to file an income tax return.[31]

13.55 Administrative Expenses

The expenses incurred during estate settlement for administrative expenses and losses during administration may be deducted from the gross estate in determining the federal estate taxes owed. These expenses may be deducted instead on the fiduciary income tax return. If the expenses are deducted on the fiduciary income tax return, the executor must file a statement with the return stating that no deduction will be made for these expenses on the estate tax return.[32] Administrative expenses include executor's fees, legal fees, and other administrative expenses such as court costs, accounting fees, appraiser's fees, and certain sales expenses when estate assets must be sold.

The decision whether to use the deduction on the fiduciary income tax return or on the estate tax return depends on the marginal tax rates of each. The effect on the beneficiaries of the estate should also be considered, especially when the estate passes into trust. For example, a deduction claimed on the fiduciary income tax return will cause the estate tax to be increased. This is a disadvantage to the remaindermen of a trust because the estate tax will be paid from the principal of the estate, thus reducing the amount passing into the trust and available for distribution to the remaindermen. Although the conflict cannot be resolved, the executor's task is simplified when the decedent's will grants the executor broad discretionary powers and exonerates the executor from liability in making the decision about which return should take the deduction.

Will Form: Executor's Discretion on Tax Decisions

The executor may make such elections under the tax laws applicable to my estate as my executor determines should be made, and no compensating adjustments between principal and income, nor with respect to any bequest or devise, shall be made, even though the elections so made may affect (beneficially or adversely) the interests of the beneficiaries. In determining the federal estate and income tax liabilities of my estate, my executor shall have sole discretion to determine whether to deduct administrative expenses of my estate on the estate tax or income tax returns. Further, my executor may join with my spouse in filing income tax returns, or to consent for gift tax purposes to having gifts made by either of us during my lifetime considered as made one-half by each of us. The action of my executor in making any decisions concerning tax decisions affecting my estate shall be final and binding upon all beneficiaries and shall not be subject to question by any individual or court.

13.56 Termination of the Estate

There are several income tax considerations in determining when to terminate an estate. The existence of the estate as an additional taxable entity permits greater spreading of income and the possibility of lessening the amount of overall income tax owed. An estate may remain in existence for a reasonable period of administration. Thus, income-splitting between the estate and the beneficiaries can produce income tax savings during a reasonably extended period of administration. In timing the conclusion of the administration of an estate, there is sometimes the opportunity to lessen the income taxes of the beneficiaries. For example, if the estate for its last taxable year has deductions in excess of gross income, the excess is allowed as a deduction to the beneficiaries who receive the estate property.

13.57 Waiver of Executor's Fee

A simple planning consideration is whether the executor should charge the normal executor fee or waive the fee. If the executor is the sole beneficiary, the decision is simply a question of which produces the better estate and income tax result. The executor's fee is taxable to the executor as ordinary income but is deductible for estate or fiduciary income tax purposes. If the fee is not charged, the estate will pay a higher estate or fiduciary income tax, but the executor will not realize ordinary income on his or her individual income tax return. If the executor is one of several beneficiaries, the waiver may still be of value in shifting more estate value from one beneficiary to another. As with most postmortem planning ideas, the best decisions can be made after doing trial computations.

Notes

1. I.R.C. §§ 2046, 2518.
2. See Chapter 4 on the generation-skipping transfer tax and the discussion of direct skips at 4.25.
3. See Chapter 6, at 6.3.
4. Treas. Reg. § 20.2056(e)-2(d)(2); Rev. Rul. 83-107, 1983-2 C.B. 159.
5. I.R.C. § 2031.
6. *Id.* § 2032.
7. *Id.* §§ 2032(a)(1), (3).
8. *Id.* § 2032(d).
9. *Id.* § 2032(c).
10. *Id.* § 303(a).
11. *Id.* § 303(a)(2).
12. *Id.* § 303(b)(3).
13. *Id.* § 2035(d)(3)(A).
14. *Id.* § 2032A. (See also Chapter 12, at 12.24.)
15. *Id.* § 2032A(a)(2).
16. *Id.* § 2032A(b). This election is made on Schedule A-7 of IRS Form 706.
17. *Id.* § 2032A(c).
18. *Id.* § 6161. IRS Form 4768 is used when filing for an extension to pay.
19. Treas. Reg. § 20.6161-1.
20. I.R.C. § 6163.
21. *Id.* § 6166.
22. *Id.* § 6166(b).
23. Ltr. Rul. 8304033.
24. I.R.C. § 6161(g).
25. *Id.* § 6166(a)(3).

26. *Id.* §§ 6166(a), 6601(j).
27. *Id.* §§ 2053, 213(c).
28. *Id.* § 454(a).
29. *Id.* § 441(b).
30. *Id.* § 6654(1).
31. *Id.* § 6013(a)(3).
32. *Id.* § 642(g).

Chapter 14

Choosing Executors and Trustees

14.1 Choosing an Executor
14.2 Choosing a Trustee
14.3 Trustee Removal
14.4 Individual Trustees
    14.41 Powers over Principal
    14.42 Power to Discharge Trustee's Obligation of Support
    14.43 Power to Sprinkle Income
    14.44 Life Insurance on Trustee's Life

14.1 Choosing an Executor

The selection of an executor for the estate is often given little consideration. Rather routinely, each spouse names the other as executor, with the oldest child or the child who lives in the same community as the parents named as the alternate executor. Occasionally, two or more of the children are named as alternate coexecutors when the parents begin to struggle with fear of favoring one child over the other. Typically, a corporate executor is used only when the children live far from the parents' home or are too busy to handle the task. Also, if the relationship between the children is not harmonious or if the estate administration is expected to be complicated and time consuming, the parents then may consider naming a corporate executor.

    The practitioner should urge his or her clients to consider more carefully the nature of their estate and what will be required to properly settle the estate. State and federal death tax returns, estate and fiduciary income tax returns, and final income tax returns for the decedent must be prepared. The preparation of these tax returns often requires much time and expertise to be properly filed. Decisions as to which estate investments should be sold and the proper time for selling them must be considered. Collecting and inventorying estate assets, filing the necessary court reports and reports to the beneficiaries, determining and paying estate debts, and myriad other activities involved in estate settlement require a more thorough discussion of this important function with the clients than simply asking whom they would like to name as executor.

Often the handling of the distribution of family keepsakes and other items of sentimental value by a brother or sister who serves as executor can cause hurt feelings and hostile reactions, the wounds from which may never heal. The use of a corporate executor may avoid such potential problems. Even in harmonious family situations, the presence of a corporate executor assures fairness among all of the beneficiaries.

Although the surviving spouse is the usual choice for executor, that may not always be appropriate. The widow or widower may lack the background, time, interest, or desire to become concerned with all of the details involved in settling an estate. If death is later in life, the survivor may be unable to properly handle this important and technical task. Further, the emotional strain the survivor faces after the loss of his or her mate may cause the administration of the estate to be a strain that the survivor would prefer to delegate to a corporate executor. The surviving spouse can receive regular reports from the corporate executor and be kept advised of all the activities in the estate-settlement process without having to become involved with the details of carrying out the various tasks of estate settlement.

Certainly, many clients still will prefer to use family members as the executors of their estates. This practice is not to be discouraged, but neither should it be encouraged. Rather, the practitioner should make the client aware of the possible complexities of the estate settlement process. Experience teaches that the size of an estate is no measure of the difficulty of its settlement. Thus, a thorough discussion with the client of the function of the executor is very important. If a corporate executor is desired, the practitioner should assist the client to select a corporate executor that is well versed in estate and trust administration. This may not be the same institution the client uses for personal banking. Also, the practitioner should discuss the fee schedule with the proposed fiduciary. There may be certain factors that justify a reduction in the normal fee. Also, if agreed on by the corporate executor, its fee can be set in advance in the will or in a separate instrument. The outline that follows gives some idea of the scope and complexity of an executor's duties.

Outline of Executor's Duties[1]

I. Take Preliminary Steps
   A. Locate and review will.
   B. Help with funeral arrangements if requested; meet with family and others properly interested in the estate.
   C. Confer with lawyer who drafted the will.

D. Hire a lawyer to handle all legal matters, prepare petition, be ready to defend the will.

II. Arrange for Probate of Will and Appointment of Executor
   A. Locate witnesses, if will is not self-proved.
   B. Notify creditors.
   C. Arrange for bond if necessary.
   D. File petition to probate will and appoint executor.

III. Assemble, Inventory, and Protect Assets
   A. If not previously done, contact financial institutions to open all safe-deposit boxes; list contents of all safe-deposit boxes.
   B. Analyze business interests; decide whether to continue, liquidate, or sell; arrange interim management.
   C. Prepare and file inventory of estate with the court, if required.
   D. Locate all of decedent's property, real and personal.
   E. Consider supervision for decedent's business.
   F. Ascertain if decedent owned property in another state.
   G. Examine insurance policies on real estate and personal property. Have policies endorsed to estate and increase coverage if needed.

IV. Study Financial Records of Decedent
   A. Send notification of death to concerned insurance companies.
   B. Decide whether jointly owned property is includable in decedent's gross estate for federal estate purposes.
   C. Obtain all canceled checks and brokerage records for past several years; secure reproductions of insurance policies that are owned by others, or that are deductible items for marital deduction purposes.
   D. Collect life insurance proceeds payable to the estate; assist other beneficiaries with claims for life insurance proceeds.
   E. Make comprehensive study of decedent's financial and business interests for years immediately preceding the decedent's death.
   F. Study available employment contract or any deferred compensation plan decedent may have had and determine whether payments are due to estate.

V. Administer the Estate
   A. Request post office to forward mail.
   B. Have appropriate assets appraised by qualified appraiser.
   C. Transfer assets to estate.
   D. Constantly observe market and investment conditions in reference to estate securities and keep a record of all transactions, income, and expenses.

E. Pay just claims against estate and reject improper ones.

F. Ascertain whether trustee under life insurance trust is authorized to lend part of cash proceeds to estate or to buy estate assets to provide cash to pay taxes or settlement costs.

G. Determine whether to retain or sell securities, depending on the powers granted in the will, market conditions, and the need for cash to pay taxes, bequests, and costs.

H. Obtain waivers and releases as needed for transfer of securities and bank accounts.

I. Keep beneficiaries and others with proper interest informed of progress of estate settlement.

J. Notify banks, investment brokers, and others of appointment as executor.

K. Inspect real estate, leases, and mortgages.

L. File claim for Social Security or veteran's benefits that may be due.

M. Collect income, accounts receivable, and other funds owed decedent or estate.

N. Distribute household and personal effects according to will provisions.

O. Pay support for surviving spouse and children as required by law or will.

P. Supervise real estate or sell if required to do so.

Q. Make appropriate partial distributions as estate administration progresses.

R. Decide whether to include accrued interest on U.S. savings bonds in income.

S. Follow closely the management and finances of any business enterprise and real estate owned by decedent.

VI. Determine Personal and Estate Tax Liability

A. Estimate cash needed to pay taxes, legacies, and other costs of estate settlement; select assets for sale to provide needed cash, being mindful of tax considerations.

B. File income tax return for decedent. Prepare for audit of income tax returns previously filed by decedent.

C. File fiduciary tax returns on estate during administration.

D. Determine whether beneficiaries who receive property outside the will shall be required to pay their proportional share of the death taxes.

E. See that supplemental and supporting documents are filed with return, such as copies of trusts established by decedent or financial statements of the decedent's business.

F. Ascertain lifetime gifts.

G. File state inheritance tax return; collect death taxes from beneficiaries if law requires.

H. Ascertain income tax basis of estate assets and furnish such information to the beneficiaries.

I. Determine whether any insurance policies on decedent's life, trusts in which the decedent had an interest, or trusts over which the decedent held any powers are includable in the estate for tax purposes.

J. Determine availability of certain tax relief provisions applicable to closely held business or farmland.

K. Determine whether administration costs are to be deducted against the federal income or estate tax.

L. Decide whether any trusts made by decedent during his or her life or gifts made by the decedent shall be included in the taxable estate.

M. File federal estate tax return; arrange for valuation of the estate and determine whether estate is to be valued as of date of death or six months later.

N. Secure federal estate tax release so that distributions may be made as promptly as possible.

VII. Distribute Estate and Make Final Settlement

A. Ascertain if any assignments are on file, pay legacies, and deliver specific bequests according to will.

B. Secure releases for beneficiaries and discharge from the court.

C. In distributing assets from residuary estate, choose date that will result in income tax economy for the beneficiaries as well as for the estate.

D. Prepare information for final accounting, including all assets, income, and disbursements.

E. Set up trusts created by will, arrange for payment of any income due trust funds for regular remittances to beneficiaries.

14.2 Choosing a Trustee

The choice of a trustee is significantly different from the choice of an executor. The executor function is short term, whereas the trustee may act in that capacity for many years. Because the trustee is handling the trust assets for the benefit of another, the competency of the trustee in handling investments is quite important. Equally important is the integrity of the trustee, because it is handling the money of others. The need for efficient receipt of investment income, payment of expenses, and reporting of its activities to the income and remainder beneficiaries is important.

Typically, clients name corporate trustees more often than individual trustees for this function, with the exception of estates that consist largely of a farm or family business. All corporate trustees are not the same. A corporate trustee should not be selected simply because that is the bank where the client financed his or her home.

The practitioner should be familiar with the administrative capabilities of the trustee. For example, what type of report is provided to the client and with what frequency? How long have the trust officers been employed at that particular bank? What is the educational background and experience of the trust officers who handle the administration of the trust? What are the number of trust accounts for which each trust officer has oversight?

The investment capabilities of the trustee are critically important. For example, to what extent will the trustee utilize its own common stock or bond funds rather than individualizing the investment portfolio? What are the average rates of return since inception on these common trust funds? Many trustees have these funds rated by independent rating firms, thus providing a good basis for reviewing the trustee's investment performance compared with other money managers. Most trustees have cash swept daily into a high-yield money market account. Does the trustee of the client's choice do this? Does the trustee buy investments, such as bonds, in large blocks, thus gaining the client a better yield than would be possible with an individual trustee buying the same investment? The educational and professional background of investment officers for the trust department and the number of years they have been employed at that particular bank are also very important.

This discussion is certainly not exhaustive. It is simply intended to provide ideas for thought. The point is simply that the practitioner should assist the client in choosing a trustee. The question to be asked is not simply, "Who do you want as trustee?" This is not practicing law. The client needs the practitioner's assistance in making a wise choice of trustee. If the choice is a corporate trustee, then the trustee's fee must be considered. Again, as with the executor's fee, the fee can be set in the agreement, if appropriate, or it may simply be whatever the fee schedule is when the trust services are rendered. If there are special circumstances that justify a reduced fee, those should be considered, discussed, and agreed on in advance.

14.3 Trustee Removal

If a corporate trustee is selected, consideration should be given to whether the beneficiaries of the trust should have the right to remove the trustee and name a successor trustee. If the beneficiaries are spendthrifts, this right should not be granted to them. They will simply shop around until they find a corporate trustee whom they expect to be lenient in distributing income and principal and then remove the current trustee and appoint the more lenient trustee as successor. In most other situations it will be appropriate to grant the surviving spouse or current income beneficiaries the right to remove the current trustee and appoint a successor trustee. This right should give rise to no adverse tax consequences if the successor trustee is also a corporate trustee, but caution must be exercised.

If the successor trustee can be an individual, including a beneficiary who has the right of removal, the right (even if never exercised) could result in the trust being included in the beneficiary's estate.[2] Thus, a right of removal should only permit another corporate trustee to be appointed, unless the trust has been carefully drafted to avoid the tax traps to individual trustees, as discussed in 14.4. Even when the successor is a corporate trustee, there used to be some concern that the IRS may consider such a right to result in the inclusion of the trust property in the beneficiary's estate under two Revenue Rulings. This position seems absurd and has been routinely criticized. Fortunately, the tax court has now ruled against the IRS and it has softened its position. There are legitimate reasons to permit a beneficiary to be able to remove a trustee: Investment performance may be poor. Change in personnel or ownership may have an adverse effect on both investment performance and administrative service. The beneficiaries may have moved to another community or area of the country, thus causing them an inconvenience if they must continue to use the same trustee. These and other practicalities favor providing for the right both to remove an acting trustee and to appoint a successor. The form that follows should be sufficient to satisfy the concerns of the IRS, especially in light of its 1993 private letter ruling approving 13 specific causes for removal of a trustee.[3]

Form: Removal of Trustee

1.1 After the Settlor's death, the Settlor's wife may name a successor Trustee, which shall be a bank or trust company qualified to do business under state or federal law, by delivering to the Trustee herein a notice naming the successor Trustee and indicating its willingness to serve. Upon receipt of such notice, the Trustee shall transfer to such successor Trustee the trust property and make a full accounting to the Settlor's wife and other beneficiaries under this trust agreement, whereupon the Trustee shall be discharged and have no further responsibility under this trust agreement. The right of the Settlor's wife to remove an acting trustee and name a successor Trustee shall be limited to the following circumstances: (a) the Settlor's wife moving to a new locality and desiring to name a corporate Trustee in that locality; (b) a change in ownership of the Trustee, whether through corporate merger, acquisition, or otherwise; (c) a trust officer being assigned to this trust account whose office is in a locality other than the locality in which the Settlor's wife resides; (d) investment performance on investments in this trust for any eighteen-month period has underperformed the S&P 500 stock index in the case of stock investments, or the Salomon Brothers bond index in the case of bond investments; and (e) an increase in total Trustee fees in excess of those charged by the Trustee at the time this trust was first funded.

1.2 The Trustee may resign by giving the current adult income beneficiary or beneficiaries thirty (30) days notice in writing delivered to such beneficiary or beneficiaries in person or mailed to their last known address, the resignation to become effective as hereinafter provided. Upon receipt of such notice, the majority of the current adult beneficiaries shall appoint a successor Trustee, which shall be a bank or trust company qualified to do business under state or federal law. In the event of failure to appoint a successor Trustee who accepts the trust within thirty (30) days from the date the notice was given, the Trustee may resign to the district court in the Settlor's domicile, which court may, if it deems advisable, accept the resignation and appoint a successor Trustee, which shall be a bank or trust company qualified to do business in the state of the Settlor's domicile. Upon the appointment of and acceptance by the successor Trustee, the original Trustee shall transfer to such successor Trustee the trust property and make a full and proper accounting to the current beneficiary or beneficiaries, whereupon its resignation shall become effective.

1.3 The successor Trustee upon acceptance of this trust and the trust property shall succeed to and possess all the rights, powers and duties, authority and responsibilities conferred upon the Trustee originally named herein, and shall have no duty to inquire into the prior acts of any prior Trustee.

14.4 Individual Trustees

Frequently it is desired that individuals serve as trustees. Typically, the choice is for the surviving spouse or the children to act as trustee. The use of family members as trustees can create possible estate, gift, and income tax problems; however, most of these problems can be solved with careful drafting and without the loss of too much flexibility. The discussion that follows focuses on the use of an individual trustee for both a testamentary and a revocable inter vivos trust. The use of an individual trustee for an irrevocable trust is not considered because normally a corporate trustee should be used in those situations. For a limited discussion of irrevocable life insurance trusts and the use of a corporate trustee, see the illustration and trust agreement in Chapter 15, at 15.6.

14.41 Powers over Principal

An individual trustee who is also beneficiary of the trust should not be given broad power (whether held as fiduciary or beneficiary) to distribute principal from the trust for his or her own benefit. This power of distribution is a general power of appointment and will result in inclusion of the trust property in his or her estate.[4] This may become important if the trust assets appreciate in value during the survivor's lifetime and the trust has been drafted to avoid inclusion in the survivor's estate.

Planning Pointer 1

This problem can be solved by limiting the trustee's power to distribute principal to an ascertainable standard, such as the health, education, and support of the surviving spouse.[5] For a discussion of the use of this type of standard, see Chapter 6, at 6.32. Also, a "5 or 5" power can be granted to the beneficiary without any adverse estate or gift tax consequences.[6] A discussion of this type of power is presented in Chapter 6, at 6.33.

Trust Form: Power Limited to Ascertainable Standard

The Trustee is authorized to distribute to the Settlor's wife or apply for her benefit from the principal of Fund __ such amounts as are necessary to provide for her reasonable health, maintenance, and support, taking into consideration such other income and other resources as the Settlor's wife may have available to her.

Trust Form: 5 or 5 Power

During the lifetime of the Settlor's wife, she shall have the right during the last month of any calendar year to withdraw from the principal of Fund __ an amount not to exceed the greater of Five Thousand Dollars ($5,000) or five percent (5%) of the market value of the principal of the trust valued on the last day of the calendar year in which such withdrawal is requested. This right of withdrawal shall be noncumulative.

Caution: Even these two planning alternatives have drawbacks. Either the limited standard or the 5 and 5 power will result in the capital gains being taxed to the beneficiary who possesses this power rather than being taxed to the trust, as would normally be the situation when the trustee is independent.[7]

14.42 Power to Discharge Trustee's Obligation of Support

If the individual trustee has the power (whether or not exercised) to distribute principal to discharge a legal support obligation of the trustee, the power will constitute a general power of appointment.[8] This will result in the trust property's being included in the trustee's own estate. Similarly, a power to distribute income in discharge of the trustee's duty of support will result in the income's being taxed to the trustee personally to the extent the income is so distributed.[9]

 Planning Pointer 2

Obviously, an individual trustee should not be granted either of these powers. If this flexibility is needed, an independent cotrustee, such as a corporate trustee, can be named, and the trust can specify that such powers can only be exercised by the independent cotrustee. The form that follows prohibits such powers over income and principal and permits their exercise only by the independent cotrustee.

Trust Form: Limiting Individual Trustee's Power over Distributions for Support

No Trustee shall participate in the exercise of any discretion with respect to the distribution of income or principal of any portion of the trust property in which any person such Trustee is obligated to support has a beneficial interest. Such discretion shall be exercised only the by remaining Trustee.

14.43 Power to Sprinkle Income

A common trust provision is to allow the trustee to distribute income among a group of beneficiaries as needed rather than distributions being equal. In this manner each beneficiary's income tax bracket can be considered before making distributions or accumulations of income. With prior planning, income taxes often can be saved when a trust permits sprinkling of income. This is an excellent income tax planning tool; however, it should be used only when the trustee is a corporate or independent trustee. This power should not be used when the trustee is also a beneficiary, because such right will cause all trust income to be taxed to the trustee personally, irrespective of who actually receives the income.[10] The exercise of this power also constitutes a taxable gift.[11] If the power to sprinkle income applies to principal, the earlier discussed problem exists of the capital gains being taxed to the trustee individually and the trust property being included in the trustee's estate, because this power constitutes a general power of appointment when it applies to principal.[12]

 Planning Pointer 3

The same planning approach must be used as discussed in the preceding Planning Pointer. The power must not be permitted. If flexibility in sprinkling income is needed, then a corporate trustee should be used rather than an individual. If an individual trustee who is also a beneficiary must be used, then a corporate or independent cotrustee must be given this discretionary sprinkling power. The individual trustee who is also a beneficiary cannot be granted this discretionary power.

Trust Form: Limiting Individual Trustee's Power to Sprinkle Income

No individual Trustee who is also a beneficiary hereunder shall have any right to make or participate in making any decision regarding the distribution or accumulation of trust income among the beneficiaries of this trust, and all such decisions shall be made by the remaining Trustee.

14.44 Life Insurance on Trustee's Life

A difficult problem exists when the trust owns life insurance on the life of the trustee. This can occur when the settlor owns a life insurance policy on the life of the trustee and the settlor's will passes this asset into the trust at the settlor's death. This also could occur if the trustee were to imprudently transfer a life insurance policy on his or her life to the trust. Because a trustee normally has broad administrative powers, the trustee will be considered to possess incidents of ownership in the life insurance.[13] This will result in the proceeds payable to the trust on the trustee's death being taxable in the trustee's own estate.

Planning Pointer 4

Obviously, the problem is most easily solved if the trustee is a corporate or independent trustee. If this is not possible, the trust instrument should provide that the individual trustee has no power over life insurance, and it should name a corporate or independent cotrustee to handle all administration of such property.

Trust Form: Limiting Trustee's Power over Insurance

No Trustee who is also the insured of any life insurance policy that is owned by this trust shall have any rights in regard to such policy or policies, including in the capacity as a fiduciary, and all such rights shall be exercised solely by the remaining Trustee.

Caution: If a beneficiary has the power to remove the trustee and has the right to name himself or herself, each of the problems discussed concerning individual trustees exists, irrespective of whether the power is exercised. The problem is solvable by drafting the trust with consideration for each of the problem areas discussed throughout 14.4: that is, the trust is simply drafted as if the beneficiary were the trustee. If this right of removal is not needed, then the removal power can be limited to a corporate or independent trustee, as discussed at 14.3.

Notes

1. Based on a chart from Citizens Bank of Kentucky and used with permission.
2. I.R.C. § 2041; Treas. Reg. § 20.2041-1(b)(1).
3. Priv. Ltr. Rul. 9303018.
4. I.R.C. § 2041; Treas. Reg. § 20.2041-1(b)(1).
5. I.R.C. § 2041(b)(1)(A); Treas. Reg. § 20.2041-1(c)(2).
5. I.R.C. §§ 2041(b)(2), 2514(e).
7. Id. § 678.
8. Id. § 2041; Treas. Reg. § 20.2041-1(c).
9. I.R.C. §§ 678(a)(1), (c).
10. I.R.C. § 678; Treas. Reg. § 678(a)-1.
11. Treas. Reg. § 25.2511-1(g)(2).
12. I.R.C. § 2041; Treas. Reg. § 20.2041-1(b).
13. Treas. Reg. § 20.2041(c)(4).

Chapter 15

Sample Forms

15.1 Corporate Redemption Agreement

15.2 Stockholder Cross-Purchase Agreement

15.3 A-B Trust Planning Approach: Equalization of Estate between Husband and Wife

15.4 Marital Deduction Planning with Disclaimer Trust

15.5 Minor's or Educational Trust

15.6 Irrevocable Life Insurance Trust

15.7 Will, Trust, and Premarital Agreement

15.8 Special Needs Trust for Handicapped Child

15.9 Income-Only Trust

15.10 Charitable Remainder Trusts

15.11 Standby Trust

15.12 Living Trust

Caution: Use of these forms requires adaptation to the user's own state law. The forms are offered only to aid the user in the development of his or her own forms. For additional forms, these two ABA publications will be helpful: R. Hunt, *Estate Planning Forms* (ABA, 2009); and J. Horn, *Flexible Trusts and Estates for Uncertain Times* (5th ed.; ABA, 2014).

15.1 Corporate Redemption Agreement

Three business persons who are unrelated want to enter into a buy-sell agreement for their business that will provide for a buyout in the event of death, or one of them wanting to sell his or her interest. The comments that follow explain some of the considerations involved in using this type of agreement rather than a cross-purchase agreement. When using the corporate redemption agreement, consideration must be given to the alternative minimum tax. See Chapter 10 and the discussion at 10.34. There is a complete discussion of buy-sell agreements in Chapter 10. Three additional ABA publications providing in-depth treatment of buy-sell agreements are L. Mezzullo, *An Estate Planner's Guide to Buy-Sell Agreements* (2d ed.; ABA, 2007); L. Mezzullo, *An Estate Planner's Guide to Family Business Entities* (3d ed.; ABA, 2010); and D. Dreux et al., *Business Succession Planning and Beyond* (ABA, 1997).

AGREEMENT

THIS AGREEMENT is entered into this ____ day of _____, 20__, by XYZ Company, Inc., a Kentucky corporation, hereinafter referred to as "Corporation," and John A. Roe, Frank B. Doe, and Jane C. Moe, hereinafter referred to as "Stockholders."

WHEREAS, the Stockholders presently own all of the issued and outstanding capital stock of the Corporation, and

WHEREAS, the parties desire to make their stock subject to certain restrictions and obligations;

NOW THEREFORE, in consideration of the mutual promises herein contained, the parties agree as follows:

1. Sale During Lifetime. If a Stockholder during lifetime desires to sell his or her stock in the Corporation, the selling Stockholder shall first give written notice to the Corporation of the Stockholder's offer to sell all of his or her stock in the Corporation for a value per share as determined in paragraph three. The Corporation shall have thirty days after receipt of the written offer to accept the offer to sell such stock. If the Corporation does not accept the offer to sell all of the stock within thirty days of receipt of such offer, then the stock shall be offered to the other Stockholders at the same price. The Stockholders shall have thirty days after the Corporation's right has expired to accept the offer to sell such stock. The purchasing Stockholders shall purchase the stock based upon their respective pro rata ownership in the Corporation. If a Stockholder does not desire to purchase his or her pro rata share of such stock, then the other Stockholder shall have the right to purchase such stock. If the offer to sell is not accepted by the Stockholders within thirty days, then the selling Stockholder may sell his or her stock to any other person or entity; however, such sale shall not be for an amount less than determined under this Agreement without first offering to sell the stock to the Corporation and other Stockholders as provided in this Agreement at such lesser price.

> ▶ **Comment:** For the redemption agreement to establish a value of the stock that is binding on the IRS for estate tax purposes, not only must the value at death be established but also the sale price of the stock during lifetime must be subject to a right of first refusal at the price specified in the agreement. See the discussion at 10.22.

2. Purchase of Decedent's Stock. Upon the death of a Stockholder and within sixty days after the appointment of a Personal Representative of the deceased Stockholder's estate, the Corporation shall purchase and the Personal Representative of the deceased Stockholder shall sell all of his or her stock for the value determined in paragraph three.

> ▶ **Comment:** A redemption must be treated as a sale or exchange to avoid taxation as a dividend. Sales or exchange treatment will allow the seller's income tax basis in the stock to be offset against the sales price, whereas if treated as a dividend, the entire

amount received is subject to income tax. A complete termination of the seller's interest in the corporation will normally result in sale or exchange treatment. When the other stockholders are relatives, a problem may be encountered. The attribution rules of I.R.C. Section 318 may cause the redemption to be treated as a dividend. The discussion at 10.33 and the examples should be helpful.

> **Comment:** The income tax basis of the remaining stockholders in their stock creates an income tax disadvantage with the redemption agreement. Following the death of the first stockholder, the corporation will purchase his or her stock. Each of the remaining stockholders will then own a proportionately larger interest in the corporation; however, their income tax basis remains the same. A subsequent sale will cause a higher income tax cost to them than if a cross-purchase agreement had been used. See the discussion at 10.32.

3. Purchase Price. Subject to the right to modify the value of the stock, the purchase price of the stock shall be $_____ per share.

The Corporation and Stockholders may from time to time revalue the stock, which value shall be noted on Exhibit A and be signed by all parties. In the event the parties fail to redetermine the value of the stock for a period in excess of twenty-four months, then the value shall be redetermined by the Corporation naming an appraiser to establish the value of the stock, the Stockholders naming an appraiser to value the stock, and the two appointed appraisers naming a third appraiser to value the stock. The majority decision of these three appraisers as to value shall establish the value of the stock. This procedure does not preclude the appraisers or Stockholders from accepting the last stipulated value as controlling.

> **Comment:** The formula used in this form requires the periodic resetting of the sales price. The use of appraisers is not essential, but it is used to set value when the stockholders have failed to do so. See the discussion at 10.22. Also, a review of approaches to valuation of closely held businesses at 12.41 will be helpful.

4. Manner of Payment. The purchase price shall be paid in cash or certified check at the closing, which date shall be selected by mutual agreement, but in no event later than thirty days after notice of acceptance of the offer to sell is given.

> **Comment:** If any portion of the sales price is to be financed by the seller, appropriate modifications should be made to the form. A promissory note should be added to the redemption agreement as an exhibit. Also, the redemption agreement may have to include added security for the seller, such as a security interest in corporation assets, an irrevocable proxy for the seller's stock so he or she can continue to vote it until the sales price is paid, and restrictions on bonuses or other large payments being made to the remaining stockholders while the sale is being financed. Further, some formula should be set for the interest rate to be charged for a financed sale. The rate cannot be too low or it will violate the imputed interest rules in IRC Section 483, which should be considered in setting an interest rate in the agreement.

5. Insurance Policies. In order to meet its obligation under this Agreement, the Corporation has purchased and is both owner and beneficiary of the following life insurance policies on each of the Stockholders:

Name of Insured	Policy Number	Insurance Company	Face Amount
John A. Roe			$
Frank B. Doe			$
Jane C. Moe			$

In the event a Stockholder sells his or her stock in the Corporation during his or her lifetime, the selling Stockholder shall have the option for a period of sixty days following the sale of the Stockholder's stock to purchase from the Corporation any life insurance owned by the Corporation on the life of the selling Stockholder. The purchase price shall be the sum of any unearned premiums plus the total cash value of the policy, if any, less any indebtednesses owed thereon.

▶ **Comment:** The value of the life insurance policy can be obtained from the insurance company.

6. Restrictions and Endorsement. Each Stockholder agrees not to dispose of the stock presently owned by the Stockholder except in accordance with the terms of this Agreement and further shall not encumber this stock. All stock certificates shall have the following endorsement:

The transfer, pledge, or sale of this stock certificate is subject to a Stock Redemption Agreement dated the _____ day of _____, 20__.

7. Amendments and Termination. This Agreement can be voluntarily terminated by agreement of the parties hereto, and shall also be terminated in the event of the bankruptcy, receivership, or dissolution of the Corporation.

8. Binding Effect. This Agreement shall be binding upon the parties hereto and their respective heirs, executors, administrators, successors, and assigns.

9. Interpretation. Any references to "stock" shall include not only the stock presently owned by any Stockholder in the Corporation, but also any shares of stock hereafter acquired by any of the Stockholders, whether by stock dividend, purchase, recapitalization, or otherwise.

10. Choice of Law. This Agreement shall be governed and construed by the laws of the State of Kentucky.

IN WITNESS WHEREOF, the parties hereto have executed this Agreement on the day and year first above written.

Attest:

XYZ Corporation

_____
President

Stockholders:

_____
_____
Secretary

John A. Roe

_____
Frank B. Doe

_____
Jane C. Moe

EXHIBIT A

_____, 20_____

Pursuant to Paragraph 3 of this Agreement, the parties do hereby determine that the total value of the stock of this business as of this date is $_____ per share.

XYZ Corporation

Attest: **Stockholders:**

_____
President

_____
John A. Roe

_____   _____
Secretary   Frank B. Doe

_____
Jane C. Mac

EXHIBIT B: Insurance Policies on the Lives of the Stockholders

Name of Insured	Policy Number	Name of Issuing Company	Face Amount of Policy	Owner
John A. Roe			$	XYZ Company, Inc.
Frank B. Doe			$	XYZ Company, Inc.
Jane C. Moe			$	XYZ Company, Inc.

15.2 Stockholder Cross-Purchase Agreement

Two brothers own a family business and desire to enter into a buy-sell agreement. The following agreement funds the buyout at death with life insurance. A purchase during lifetime is restricted with a right of first refusal, although no price is set for a purchase during lifetime. This form can easily be modified for a partnership. A complete discussion of buy-sell agreements appears in Chapter 10.

AGREEMENT

THIS AGREEMENT, made and entered into between Richard R. Roe, hereinafter referred to as First Party; and James J. Roe, hereinafter referred to as Second Party;

First and Second Parties are the Stockholders in a corporation known as XYZ Company, Inc., 1000 Main Street, Madisonville, Kentucky. The interest of each of the Stockholders in the corporation is as follows:

Richard R. Roe   500 shares
James J. Roe   500 shares

> **Comment:** If a stockholder cross-purchase agreement (unlike a partnership cross-purchase or corporate redemption agreement) that is funded by life insurance involves three or more stockholders, the transfer-for-value rule will cause a disastrous income tax result. After the death of the first stockholder, consideration must be given to this rule, and a decision may have to be made to switch to a redemption agreement. See the discussion at 10.31.

The purpose of this Agreement is threefold: (a) to provide for the purchase by the survivor of the decedent's interest in the corporation; (b) to provide the funds necessary to carry out such purchase; and (c) to restrict the sale of stock during the lifetime of the Stockholders.

> **Comment:** A cross-purchase agreement is often preferable to a redemption agreement because the sale or exchange versus dividend income tax problem does not exist for this type of agreement. This will make a cross purchase preferable, particularly when the buy-sell involves family members.

It is, therefore, mutually agreed by First Party and Second Party as follows:

1. Neither First Party nor Second Party shall assign, encumber, or dispose of any portion of their respective interest in XYZ Company, Inc., by sale or otherwise, without complying with the terms of this Agreement and without the prior written consent of the other Stockholder.

2. First Party is insured under Policy 123,456, issued by ABC Life Insurance Company, for $200,000, and Second Party is the applicant, owner, and beneficiary thereof.

Second Party is insured under Policy 654,321, issued by ABC Life Insurance Company, for $200,000, and First Party is the applicant, owner, and beneficiary thereof.

> **Comment:** Because each stockholder owns life insurance policies on the life of the other stockholders, a cross-purchase agreement can involve a large number of policies when there are very many stockholders. Also, if there is a very great age disparity between stockholders, the younger stockholders will be paying more in insurance premiums than the older stockholders. See the discussion at 10.31.

During the lifetime of both Stockholders and the continuance in force of this Agreement, each Stockholder shall pay the premiums on the policy owned by him as they become due, but neither Stockholder shall exercise any of the rights, privileges, and benefits accruing under the policy owned by him, except as otherwise provided herein, or assign, encumber, borrow against, or otherwise dispose of the policy, without the prior written consent of the other Stockholder. All dividends shall be applied on account of premiums or loan interest, if any. ABC Life Insurance Company is hereby authorized and directed to give the insured, upon his written request, any information with respect to the status of the policy on his life. Each Stockholder shall give proof of payment to the other Stockholder within twenty (20) days after the due date of each premium. If any premium is not paid within twenty (20) days after its due date, the insured Stockholder shall have the right to pay such premium and be reimbursed by the other Stockholder.

3. This Agreement shall extend to and shall include all additional policies issued pursuant hereto, such additional policies to be listed in Schedule A, attached hereto.

4. Upon the death of either Stockholder, the survivor shall purchase, and the estate of the decedent shall sell, the interest then owned by the Stockholder who is the first to die. The purchase price of such interest shall be computed in accordance with the provisions of Paragraph 5 of this Agreement.

> **Comment:** A cross-purchase agreement will allow for an increase in the income tax basis of the surviving stockholders on their purchase of the decedent's stock. This is important if the surviving stockholders anticipate selling their interest at a later date because it will lessen the income tax they will owe. See the discussion at 10.32.

5. Unless and until changed as hereinafter provided, the value of each Stockholder's respective interest in the corporation shall be as follows:

| Richard R. Roe | $ 250,000 |
| James J. Roe | $ 250,000 |

Within thirty (30) days following the end of each fiscal year, First and Second Parties shall redetermine the value of the corporation and their respective interests therein. Such values shall be endorsed on Schedule B, attached hereto. If First and Second Parties fail to redetermine such values for a particular year, the last previously stipulated values shall control, except that if no valuation is agreed upon for two consecutive years, the value of a Stockholder's interest shall be determined by the independent certified public accountant regularly retained by the Corporation for the auditing of its books. If there is no such certified public accountant available, or if that accountant fails to make a determination of such valuation, then the value shall be determined by any other certified public accountant who may be selected by mutual agreement of the surviving Stockholder and the personal representative of the deceased Stockholder. In the event no agreement can be reached as to a certified public accountant, then the surviving Stockholder and the personal representative shall each select a certified public accountant to determine the value. The two certified public accountants shall select a third certified public accountant and the valuation decision of the three shall be binding.

> **Comment:** The formula for setting the sales price in this form is based on the stockholders regularly setting the price. If they fail to set a price, the earlier sales price will be adjusted by an independent third party. If that is not workable, the price will be set by arbitration.

6. Each Stockholder agrees that the proceeds of the policies owned by him for the purposes of this Agreement shall be applied toward the purchase price set forth above. If the purchase price exceeds the proceeds of the life insurance, the balance of the purchase price shall be paid in twenty-four (24) consecutive monthly payments beginning three (3) months after the date of the decedent's death. The unpaid balance of the purchase price shall be evidenced by a series of negotiable promissory notes made by the surviving Stockholder to the order of the estate of the deceased with interest at the rate then charged by financial institutions in the area to preferred business customers. Such notes shall provide for the acceleration of the due date of all unpaid notes in the series on default in the payment of any note or interest thereon and shall give the maker thereof the option of prepayment in whole or in part at any time.

> **Comment:** A reasonable rate of interest must be charged; otherwise, the agreement will run afoul of the imputed interest rules in IRC Section 483.

7. Upon the death of either Stockholder, the surviving Stockholder shall have the right to purchase from the estate of the decedent any or all of the policies insuring the life of the surviving Stockholder, for a price equal to the interpolated terminal reserve value as of the date of death of the Stockholder, less any existing indebtedness charged against the policy, plus the proportionate part of the gross premium last paid before the date of death which covers the period extending beyond that date. This right may be exercised at any time within sixty (60) days after the qualification of the legal representative of the deceased Stockholder by the payment of such price and, if the right is not so exercised within the time allowed, it shall lapse.

> **Comment:** This provision is needed so the surviving stockholders can purchase the policies that the decedent owned on their lives. This is particularly important when there are two or more surviving stockholders. Each will have an increased financial obligation to the other's estate, which he or she will need to fund with the insurance. A related consideration is that the value of the insurance owned by the decedent on the other stockholders is an asset subject to estate tax in the decedent's estate. The only way to avoid this result is for each stockholder's spouse to be a secondary owner of the policies and be bound by signing the agreement. Then the marital deduction will shield the value of the policies from the estate tax. See the discussion at 10.31.

8. Upon the payment of the purchase price to the estate of the deceased Stockholder, in cash or in cash notes, the estate shall execute and deliver to the surviving Stockholder all documents reasonably required to evidence the purchase; and all rights of the estate in the Corporation and in its business and assets shall thereafter belong to the surviving Stockholder. Simultaneously, the surviving Stockholder shall deliver to the estate of the deceased Stockholder an agreement indemnifying the estate against all liabilities of the Corporation.

9. If a Stockholder during his lifetime desires to sell his interest in the Corporation, he shall give written notice to the other Stockholder, which notice shall specify the price at which the withdrawing Stockholder shall sell his entire stock ownership. The other Stockholder shall have thirty (30) days within which to accept or reject the offer to sell. If accepted, the closing for the sale shall be held within forty-five (45) days following receipt of the acceptance. If rejected, the withdrawing Stockholder may sell his entire stock ownership to anyone without restriction; provided, however, this right of first refusal shall exist for any future offers to sell made by the withdrawing Stockholder which are at a price below the price offered to the other Stockholder.

> **Comment:** For the value set in the buy-sell agreement to be binding on the IRS for estate tax valuation purposes, the right to sell during lifetime must also be restricted and the sales price must be the same as set in the agreement for purchase in the event of death. This paragraph does not do that; however, the value may still satisfy the IRS if it otherwise appears to be reasonable. The form is drafted in this manner because many times stockholders will not want to reach a decision on the value for a sale of their interests during their lifetimes. Nonetheless, a buy-sell agreement is important to establish a sales price and a way of payment, as well as to avoid family members being involved in the running of the business. If it is desired that the agreement also set the estate tax value, see the prior form, 15.1, at paragraph 5. For further discussion see Chapter 10, at 10.22.

10. This Agreement may be altered, amended, or terminated by a writing signed by both Stockholders. In the event of a termination of this Agreement before the death of

either Stockholder, each shall be entitled to an assignment to him of any policy on his life upon payment by him to the owner within sixty (60) days of such termination, of a sum equal to the interpolated terminal reserve value as of the date of transfer, less any existing indebtedness charged against the policy, plus the proportionate part of the gross premium last paid before the date of transfer that covers the period extending beyond that date.

11. This Agreement shall terminate on the occurrence of any of the following events:

    (a) Cessation of the corporation business.

    (b) Bankruptcy, receivership, or dissolution of the corporation.

    (c) Bankruptcy or insolvency of either Stockholder.

    (d) Mutual agreement of the Stockholders.

12. This Agreement shall be binding upon the Stockholders, their heirs, legal representatives, successors, and assigns.

13. This Agreement shall be subject to and governed by the laws of the Commonwealth of Kentucky.

IN TESTIMONY WHEREOF, witness the signatures of the parties hereto on this the _____ day of _____, 20_____.

_____
Richard R. Roe

_____
James J. Roe

SCHEDULE A

Schedule of Life Insurance Policies

Name of Company	Policy No.	Amount	Insured Owner
ABC Life Insurance Company	123,456	$200,000	Richard R. Roe
ABC Life Insurance Company	654, 321	$200,000	James J. Roe

SCHEDULE B

Pursuant to Paragraph 5 of this Agreement, the parties do hereby determine on this the _____ day of _____, 20___, that the value of each Stockholder's respective interest is:

Richard R. Roe $

James J. Roe $

_____
Richard R. Roe

_____
James J. Roe

15.3 A-B Trust Planning Approach: Equalization of Estate between Husband and Wife

The last will and testament and trust agreement that follow are based on the discussion in Chapter 7 and in particular 7.3. The basic planning concept is quite simple. This trust will be used when the couple's estate may equal or exceed their combined estate tax exclusion amount ($10,980,000 in 2017), and the estate values are expected to increase between the death of the first spouse to die and the death of the second spouse to die. When possible, the estate will be divided equally between the two spouses. Each should own property in his or her individual name, rather than jointly with right of survivorship. If it is not possible or appropriate to divide the estate equally between the spouses, survivorship ownership should be limited because such property will pass directly to the survivor rather than into the trust. The intent is to trap assets in Trust B in the amount of the exclusion amount so that future increases in Trust B asset values will not be taxed in the estate of the survivor. Any insurance should be made payable to the insured's trust, not to the other spouse. An additional ABA publication that deals extensively with drafting is J. Horn, *Flexible Trusts and Estates for Uncertain Times* (5th ed.; ABA, 2014).

In some situations the estate should not be divided equally between the husband and wife; an example is a second marriage in which the spouses do not have common heirs. The estate may be largely held in the ownership of one spouse. In this situation, the same will and trust used in the prior illustration is appropriate for the spouse with the larger estate. The will and trust of the spouse with the smaller estate need not be the same.

Assuming the husband's estate is the larger one, the will and trust set forth in 15.3 may be used for his estate. The wife's will could be a simple will that passes the entire estate to the husband if she predeceases him, or she may will her assets to other beneficiaries.

The forms that follow and the accompanying comments are based on the husband's will and trust. A similar will and trust agreement should be used for the wife. When using these forms, be sure to make appropriate changes as needed for such terms as *wife, he, she, his,* or *hers*.

The Trust Agreement that follows has a number of options, not all of which are essential. The comments clarify what paragraphs are needed. There are two basic approaches to follow: (1) a trust for the survivor with a general power of appointment over Trust A or (2) a trust for the survivor that qualifies as a QTIP trust. The first approach would use the following paragraphs: 1, 2.1 or 2.1A, 3, 4.1, 4.2, 4.3, 4.4, 4.5; such paragraphs in Article 5 as are appropriate; and generally all of the remaining paragraphs. The second approach (QTIP) would use paragraphs 1, 2.1 or 2.1A, 3, 4.1A, 4.2, 4.3A, 4.5, 4.6, 4.7; such paragraphs in Article 5 as are appropriate; and generally all of the remaining paragraphs. For a complete discussion of marital deduction planning, see Chapter 7. Chapter 6, on the use of powers of appointment, will also be helpful.

LAST WILL AND TESTAMENT OF RICHARD HENRY ROE

I, Richard Henry Roe, a resident of Madisonville, Hopkins County, Kentucky, make this my Last Will and Testament, hereby revoking all prior wills and codicils.

ARTICLE I

I direct that my just debts, funeral expenses, costs of administration, and all estate, inheritance, succession, and transfer taxes imposed by the United States or any state, which become payable by reason of my death, be paid out of my residuary estate as soon as practicable after my death.

ARTICLE II

I direct that, after the payment of all administration expenses and death taxes as hereinabove provided, my Personal Representative shall deliver and convey all the remainder of my residuary estate wheresoever situated, including all the property which I may acquire or become entitled to after the execution of this Will, including all lapsed legacies and devises, but expressly excluding any property over or concerning which I may have any power of appointment, to the Trustee of the Richard Henry Roe Trust, to be held, administered, and distributed pursuant to the terms of a trust agreement I entered into on the _____ day of _____, 20__, including any amendments thereto.

> ▶ **Comment:** This will simply pours over the entire estate after the payment of death taxes and the various estate settlement-related expenses into the trust, which then makes all of the necessary provisions for the distribution of the estate. If specific bequests are desired, they should be inserted as a separate article preceding this article.

ARTICLE III

I nominate and appoint my wife, Mary Jane Roe, to be the Personal Representative of my estate. If my wife fails to qualify as Personal Representative, or having qualified, she dies, resigns, or declines to serve, then and in such event, I nominate and appoint _____, to serve as Successor Personal Representative. Neither my wife nor the Successor Personal Representative shall be required to furnish any surety upon their bond as my Personal Representative.

> ▶ **Comment:** The wife is named as personal representative, with either an individual or a corporate fiduciary acting as a successor. If the wife does not wish to serve in this capacity, or if the estate is large or contains assets that may require skilled oversight, it may be better to name only the corporate fiduciary.

ARTICLE IV

My Personal Representative shall have the following powers in addition to any other powers expressly or impliedly granted by law:

A. To retain any property owned by me at the time of my death and no sale thereof shall be required;

B. To sell, lease, transfer, and convey any estate property, real or personal, at public or private sale, and at such price and upon such terms as my Personal Representative deems proper. A lease of real estate shall be binding for the full time thereof, even though it may extend beyond the duration of the settlement of my estate;

C. To invest and reinvest in any investments my Personal Representative deems proper without diversification and without restriction of any law or regulation limiting the investment authority of a fiduciary;

D. To borrow money (from the Personal Representative or from others) upon such terms and conditions as my Personal Representative deems proper, and when required to mortgage or pledge estate assets as collateral;

E. To divide and distribute my estate, in cash or in kind or partly in cash and partly in kind, without regard to the income tax basis of any in-kind property allocated to any beneficiary;

F. To compromise and settle any claim by or against my estate;

G. To employ accountants, attorneys, or other advisors and when relying upon their recommendations to do so without any liability.

ARTICLE V

In the event that my wife predeceases me, I nominate and appoint _____ as guardian of any of my children during their minority. I direct that no surety shall be required of my guardian in the event it shall be necessary for _____ to be appointed by order of any court.

> ▶ **Comment:** This article is only needed if the couple have minor children. The precise wording may have to be modified to conform to unique state law.

ARTICLE VI

In the event that my wife and I die simultaneously or under such circumstances as to render it impossible or difficult to determine which predeceased the other, I direct that it shall be deemed that I predeceased my wife, and that this Will and any and all of its provisions shall be constructed on that assumption and basis.

> ▶ **Comment:** This provision should not be used when the separate estates of the spouses are equal. It is only needed when the estates of the spouses are significantly unequal. If it is needed, the spouse with the larger estate should be presumed to have died first. For example, if the husband's estate is the larger, then the husband's will should state that he is presumed to predecease his wife and the wife's will should state that it is presumed that she survives her husband. See Chapter 7, at 7.21.

IN TESTIMONY WHEREOF, I have hereunto set my hand on this the _____ day of _____, 20_____.

_____
Testator

We, whose names are hereto signed as subscribing witnesses, have, at the request of the Testator, _____, witnessed the execution of this Will, consisting of this page and the _____ (_____) pages, and each has signed as subscribing witness in the presence of the Testator and in the presence of each other, on this the _____ day of _____, 20_____.

_____   _____
Witness   Address

_____   _____
Witness   Address

[ADD SELF-PROVING NOTARIZATION AS PROVIDED BY STATE LAW]

TRUST AGREEMENT

THIS TRUST AGREEMENT is entered into by me, Richard Henry Roe, of Madisonville, Kentucky, as both Settlor and Trustee.

▶ **Comment:** This introductory paragraph simply names the parties to the agreement. This trust names the husband as both Settlor (grantor) and Trustee, rather than naming a third party, such as a bank, as the Trustee. If a third party acts as Trustee, an appropriate modification is necessary. Also, this trust is written in the first person, as that wording is more client-friendly than traditional third-party legalese. This form is for a Settlor who is the husband. Obviously, when the Settlor is the wife, the various gendered terms, such as *wife* and *she*, must be changed to *husband* and *he*.

WITNESSETH

In consideration of the promises and the covenants hereinafter contained, I own certain insurance policies on my life listed in Schedule "A," attached hereto, and have named this trust as beneficiary under said policies to receive the proceeds thereof. I may, at any time and from time to time, deposit with the Trustee other insurance policies on my life in which the trust is named as beneficiary, as well as other assets all of which shall be held and administered in accordance with the following terms and provisions:

▶ **Comment:** This is a revocable life insurance trust. The policies will continue to be owned by the settlor; however, the trustee will be named as beneficiary of all current policies and any future policies. An appropriate beneficiary designation is as follows: "The proceeds shall be payable to the Insured's Trustee, pursuant to a trust agreement executed by the Insured on January 3, 20___, including any amendments thereto." The settlor can add other property to the trust during lifetime, as specified in Article VI, at 6.1. If no life insurance is payable to the trustee, the portion of this paragraph referring to life insurance should be deleted, as should Article IX and a portion of 2.1. If there is no life insurance payable to the trust, or other assets titled in the trust, some attorneys insert on Schedule A the words "Ten Dollars ($10.00)" and tape a 10-dollar bill to the trust to avoid a later legal challenge that the trust had no trust corpus at creation, thus it is not a valid document. Your own state law determines the need for this additional drafting.

ARTICLE I

Identification of Beneficiaries

1.1 The term "wife" shall be understood to mean Mary Jane Roe. The term "children" shall be understood to mean the children of my marriage to my wife, whose names are _____. If subsequent to the execution of this Trust Agreement, there shall be an additional child or children born to me, such child or children (or issue thereof) shall share in the benefits hereunder the same as my children hereinabove named. Further, adopted children of mine, and their issue whether or not adopted, and adopted children, and their issue whether or not adopted of any descendent of the mine shall be treated in all respects the same as children born to me.

▶ **Comment:** The identification of the beneficiaries both provides clarity and avoids naming the beneficiaries subsequently in the trust. If the settlor has children other than by marriage to his current wife, such as from a prior marriage, the phrase "the children of my marriage to my wife" should be deleted. Instead, "my children" should be substituted.

This article ensures that afterborn children are treated the same as the named children. Adopted children of the settlor and later generations are treated the same as natural children. If this is not desired, limiting wording should be added, such as "only children adopted while under age 18 shall be treated as natural children." If the settlor does not want children born out of wedlock to inherit, as would be the case at the termination of the trust if one of the settlor's children was deceased and that child's share was passing to his or her issue, the word "legitimate" should be added before "child" and "issue."

ARTICLE II

Establishing Trust Funds

2.1 After my death, the net proceeds payable to the Trustee under all insurance policies owned by me on my life shall be added to the other property, if any, which was transferred to the trust during my lifetime, or transferred after my death; and if my wife survives me, the Trustee shall divide the aforesaid property into two (2) parts: One part shall be known as Trust A and the other part shall be known as Trust B. The amount placed in each trust shall be determined as follows:

The Trustee shall allocate to Trust A (undiminished by any estate or inheritance taxes), an amount, if any, which is equal to the maximum marital deduction allowable to my estate for Federal estate tax purposes, less (i) the value of all other property interests included in my gross estate for Federal estate tax purposes which pass or have passed to or for the benefit of my wife under my Will or otherwise in such manner as to qualify for the marital deduction, and (ii) an amount, if any, needed to increase my taxable estate to the largest amount that will result in the smallest, if any, Federal estate tax being imposed on my estate after allowing for the unified credit against the Federal estate tax. The remaining trust property, or all of the trust property if my wife does not survive me, shall constitute Trust B hereunder.

▶ **Comment:** This is a pecuniary share formula clause that provides for Trust B to receive an amount, including cash and specific property, equal to the amount needed to result in the smallest federal estate tax. This will be an increasing amount which in 2018 is up to $11,200,000, but will increase each year as the exclusion amount is indexed for future inflation.

Trust A will include the balance of the estate after funding Trust B less (1) nonprobate property that passes directly to the wife, such as property owned jointly with right of survivorship, retirement benefits, or life insurance payable to the wife; and (2) property specifically bequeathed to the wife, such as household furniture, jewelry, and vehicles.

2.1A After my death, the net proceeds payable to the Trustee under all insurance policies owned by me on my life shall be added to the other property, if any, which was transferred to the trust by me during my lifetime, or transferred after my death; and if my wife survives me, the Trustee shall divide the aforesaid property into two (2) parts: One part shall be known as Trust A and the other part shall be known as Trust B. The amount placed in each trust shall be determined as follows:

The Trustee shall allocate to Trust A that fraction of my trust estate (undiminished by any estate or inheritance taxes) determined as follows: The numerator of the fraction shall be the maximum marital deduction allowable to my estate for Federal estate tax purposes, less (i) the value of all property interests included in my gross estate for Federal estate tax purposes which pass or have passed to or for the benefit of my wife under my Will or otherwise in such manner as to qualify for the marital deduction, and (ii) an amount, if any, needed to increase my taxable estate to the largest amount that will result in the smallest, if any, Federal estate tax being imposed on my estate after allowing for the unified credit against the Federal estate tax. The denominator of the fraction shall be my trust estate based upon the values as determined for Federal estate tax purposes. The remaining trust property, or all of the trust property if my wife does not survive me, shall constitute Trust B hereunder.

> ▶ **Comment:** This is a fractional share formula clause. Although there is considerable discussion as to whether or not to use a fractional share or pecuniary formula, this type of formula is particularly useful in estates largely comprising a single asset, such as a farm or closely held business. This formula places a fraction of each asset in the two trusts. The pecuniary formula permits specific assets to be placed in each trust. For an excellent discussion of formula clauses, see Richard B. Covey, *Marital Deduction and Credit Shelter Dispositions* (New York: U.S. Trust Co. of New York, 1997).

ARTICLE III

Technical Directions and Definitions

3.1 The words "gross estate," "taxable estate," "marital deduction," "pass," "qualified terminable interest property," and "unified credit" shall have the same meaning as these words have in the Internal Revenue Code of 1986, as amended.

> ▶ **Comment:** This clarifies the meaning of various technical terms of the federal estate tax law and includes the meanings of these terms as they may be modified by future legislative changes.

3.2 In making the computations to determine the amount of property to be set aside as Trust A, the final determinations for Federal estate tax purposes shall control, and only property that qualifies for the marital deduction shall be allocated to Trust A.

▶ **Comment:** Setting values based on final estate tax values is needed for administrative convenience in making allocation between the two trusts. If the estate may be less than the exclusion amount ($11,200,000 in 2018), which is also the estate tax filing limit in 2017, a slight ambiguity exists. If this situation is anticipated, the following sentence could be added: "If no Federal estate tax return is required to be filed, my trust estate shall pass into Trust B." Also, this sentence is designed to avoid the tainted asset rule in IRC Section 2056(b)(2). For further illustrations, see Treas. Reg. Section 20.2056(b)-2.

The Trustee may allocate to Trust A money or property in kind, or partly in money and partly in kind; provided, however, that any property transferred in kind shall be valued at its fair market value determined as of the date or dates it is allocated to Trust A. Allocations of property may be made to Trusts A and B without regard to the income tax basis of the property so transferred, irrespective of the fact that the Trustee's decision may affect a beneficiary's interest in the trust estate.

▶ **Comment:** This clause is required to satisfy Revenue Procedure 64-19, which applies to pecuniary bequests as in 2.1. Without this clause, Rev. Proc. 64-19 may disallow the marital deduction. This clause will cause any appreciation after the date of death (or alternate valuation date) to be a taxable income gain to the estate at the time of distribution. The final sentence affords the trustee some liability protection when allocating assets between the two trust funds. These two sentences can be omitted when using a fractional share formula.

3.3 The Trustee may estimate the amount of property to be allocated to Trusts A and B, and may make a tentative allocation in satisfaction thereof; making any final adjustments as may be necessary to preserve the deductibility of Trust A as the marital deduction trust in determining my taxable estate. Trusts A and B shall carry with them (as income and not as principal) their proportionate part of the income received by the Trustee until such Trusts are fully funded.

▶ **Comment:** This clause is administrative and permits an early funding of the two trusts pending final adjustment on settlement of the estate and the estate tax audit.

3.4 It is expressly intended that Trust A be available for the Federal estate tax marital deduction and all questions applicable to the creation and funding of Trust A shall be resolved so as to achieve such deduction for my estate. Any provision of this instrument which cannot be so interpreted or limited, or which is inconsistent with such intent, shall be void. The powers, duties, and discretions given to the Trustee with respect to Trust A and with respect to its administration shall not be exercised or exercisable except in a manner to preserve the deductibility of Trust A as the marital deduction.

▶ **Comment:** A savings clause is commonly used in an effort to save the marital deduction if some power or act of the trustee could jeopardize the entitlement to the marital deduction.

3.5 Any property transferred to the Trustee under the terms of my Will or my wife's Will shall be added to Trust A and Trust B as provided by my or my wife's Will. Further, the Trustee may accept that property delivered to it by my or my wife's Personal Representative as all the property it is entitled to receive without having to examine the records and accounts of the Personal Representatives.

▶ **Comment:** This paragraph is largely administrative. If the trustee and personal representative are the same, the second sentence can be deleted.

ARTICLE IV

Marital Trust—Trust A

4.1 The net income of Trust A shall be paid to my wife in quarterly or more frequent installments, or used for her benefit if she is disabled.

4.1A The net income of Trust A shall be paid to my wife in quarterly or more frequent installments, or used for her benefit if she is disabled. Any income accrued and undistributed at the death of my wife shall be paid to her Personal Representative.

▶ **Comment:** There are two approaches to qualifying Trust A for the marital deduction. One approach (shown in 4.1 here) involves Trust A with a general power of appointment for the wife. The other approach (4.1A here) is Trust A, which is a terminable interest but which still qualifies for the marital deduction when the personal representative makes a QTIP election. See Chapter 7, at 7.241. The option of an outright bequest of Trust A to the spouse is not considered in these forms, but it can be accomplished very easily by making Trust A a Share A and then specifying that it is to be distributed outright to the settlor's wife.

4.2 If the net income from Trust A is not sufficient to provide for the maintenance and support of my wife in accordance with the standard of living to which she became accustomed during my life, or if by reason of illness, emergency, or any extraordinary or unusual circumstances, she should need additional funds, the Trustee shall pay to or use for the benefit of my wife such amounts from the principal of Trust A as may be needed to meet her said requirements.

▶ **Comment:** If the invasion of principal for the wife has to be limited, this paragraph can be used with 4.1; however, 4.3 (following), which is a general power of appointment, must be used. If the wife is to be given the lifetime right to withdraw principal as she desires, then 4.2A can be used, and the use of 4.3 is optional. If 4.1A is used, thus creating a QTIP trust, this paragraph (4.2) should be used if there is the desire to allow some invasion of principal for the wife's benefit in the event of extraordinary circumstances. If there is not, then this paragraph can be omitted in estate plans that make use of the QTIP approach.

4.2A During her lifetime, my wife shall have the right to withdraw from the principal of the trust, at any time and from time to time, such part or all of the principal of the trust fund as she may desire for herself or any person, corporation, or other entity. The right of withdrawal of my wife shall be exercisable by my wife exclusively and in all events; however, she shall be required to give the Trustee adequate notice of her desire to make withdrawals from the principal. For any such withdrawals the Trustee shall have full acquittance. Further, such payments shall not be subject to questions by any person or any court.

▶ **Comment:** The wife's right to withdraw principal can be this broad if desired when using a general power of appointment to qualify for the marital deduction (4.1 and 4.2A). If this paragraph (4.2A) is used, then 4.3 is not necessary, although it can still be used. Another option is to give the wife a limited lifetime power to withdraw from principal, such as the greater of $10,000 or 10% of trust principal; however, if such a restriction is used, 4.3 is essential.

4.3 At the time of her death, my wife may appoint, by specifically referring to this power in her Will, part or all of the principal of Trust A to her estate or to any person or corporation. To the extent this power is not effectively exercised, the principal of Trust A shall be added to the principal of Trust B and shall be administered and distributed in accordance with Article V.

> ▶ **Comment:** This power is essential if 4.1 and 4.2 are used or if only 4.1 is used, because it creates a general power of appointment, which is needed to qualify for the marital deduction. It is also needed if a right of withdrawal less broad than that shown in 4.2A is used. Paragraph 4.3 would not be used if the QTIP approach were used (4.1A with 4.2 optional).

4.3A My wife may at any time, by written notice, require the Trustee to make any nonproductive property of Trust A productive or to convert such nonproductive property to productive property within a reasonable time.

> ▶ **Comment:** Paragraph 4.3A is essential for the QTIP approach to qualify for the marital deduction.

4.4 The Trustee may consider any writing probated in a proper court as the Will of my wife and shall not be liable for its actions in reliance thereon. Likewise, if no writing purporting to be her Will is duly offered for probate within three months of her death, the Trustee may conclusively presume that she left no Will and shall not be liable for its actions in reliance thereon. However, this provision shall not limit or qualify a donee of the power of appointment conferred upon my wife to pursue any funds affected by the exercise of it, irrespective of the place of probate or time of discovery of her Will.

> ▶ **Comment:** Paragraph 4.4 is for administrative clarity and is only used with the general power of appointment approach when 4.3 is used.

4.5 Unless my wife by her Will specifically provides that the estate, inheritance, death, or similar taxes assessed with respect to the assets of Trustee A be paid otherwise, the Trustee shall pay to the Personal Representative of the estate of my wife for the purpose of paying such taxes, the amount by which such taxes assessed by reason of the death of my wife shall be increased as a result of the inclusion of the assets of Trust A in her estate for such tax purposes.

> ▶ **Comment:** Paragraph 4.5 could be used in either option for administrative flexibility in paying death taxes assessed at the wife's death because of the Trust A assets being taxed in her estate. The tax payment clause in the wife's will should be coordinated with this paragraph.

4.6 At the time of the death of my wife, Trust A shall be added to the principal of Trust B and shall be administered and distributed in accordance with Article V.

> ▶ **Comment:** Paragraph 4.6 will be used with the QTIP approach but is not needed with the general power of appointment approach if 4.3 is used.

4.7 It is intended to qualify Trust A as qualified terminable interest property for which the marital deduction is allowable under the Internal Revenue Code and any amendments thereto, and this instrument is to be construed accordingly. Notwithstanding any provision of this instrument, the Trustee shall have:

1. No discretion or power in the administration of this trust the existence or exercise of which would disqualify it for the marital deduction.
2. No discretion or power to so allocate receipts and disbursements as between principal and income so as to deny to my wife all the net income of the trust.

> **Comment:** This tax savings clause is needed only when the QTIP approach is used (4.1A with 4.2 optional).

ARTICLE V

Residuary Trust—Trust B

After my death, the Trustee shall hold and dispose of the trust property as follows:

> **Comment:** There is great flexibility in the utilization of Trust B. Generally, as long as the wife is given no general power of appointment over the principal of Trust B, such as in 4.2A or 4.3, this trust will not be subject to estate tax in her estate on her subsequent death. The following paragraphs illustrate several frequently used options, any of which are permissible under the two approaches followed in Article IV.

5.1 The net income of Trust B shall be paid to my wife in quarterly or more frequent installments, or used for her benefit if she is disabled.

> **Comment:** If desired, all of the income can be paid to the wife.

5.1A The Trustee is authorized to accumulate the net income or to pay or apply so much of such income and principal to the use of one or more, all, or none, of the following persons: (a) my wife, (b) my children, and (c) the then-living issue of my children, whether the parents of such issue are living or dead, in such amounts and proportions as my Trustee deems advisable from time to time, without regard to equality of distribution.

> **Comment:** The income can be distributed among a group of beneficiaries, which will have an income tax savings potential because the distributed income will be taxed to the beneficiaries. This will be particularly beneficial when the income distributions are to beneficiaries who are in a lower income tax bracket than is the wife. Care must be exercised not to pay income that is then used to discharge a parent's obligation of support for his or her own children, because this will cause the income to be taxed to the parent under IRC Sections 677 and 678. Also, if the surviving spouse becomes the trustee, 5.1A will cause all trust income to be taxed to the survivor and the trust assets will be taxed in the survivor's estate. Thus, this 5.1A should not be used. Further, an income payment that skips a generation, such as to a grandchild of the wife, is a "direct skip" under the generation-skipping transfer tax and should not be made without first determining the effect of this tax. This provision is not appropriate if the wife is the trustee: In that event 5.1 and 5.2 should be used. See Chapter 6, at 6.32.

5.2 The Trustee is authorized at any time and from time to time to distribute to my wife or apply to her benefit from the principal of Trust B (even to the point of completely exhausting the same) such amounts as the Trustee deems necessary to provide for her reasonable health, maintenance, and support. In determining the amounts of principal to be so disbursed, the Trustee may take into consideration any other income that my wife may have from any other source, and also her capital resources other than household goods, residence, and personal effects.

▶ **Comment:** Paragraph 5.2 will follow 5.1 and permit the principal to be expended for the wife, if needed. Though not required, this flexibility is normally desired. This paragraph does not result in adverse tax consequences to the survivor who serves as trustee.

5.2A It is my desire, however, that the income and principal be used primarily for the support, health, and maintenance of my wife. This expression of desire is to be considered merely as a guide to the Trustee and not as a binding obligation of trust. Any accumulated income shall be periodically, at least annually, incorporated into the principal of the trust fund as an integral part thereof to be held, administered, and distributed in accordance with all the terms, conditions, and limitations applying thereto.

▶ **Comment:** Paragraph 5.2A may be desired if 5.1A is used, but it is not essential. This paragraph will be used with 5.1A when the trustee is not the surviving spouse.

5.3 During the lifetime of my wife, she shall have the right in any calendar year (including the year of my death) to withdraw from the principal of Trust B an amount or specific assets that are not in excess of the greater of the following: Five thousand dollars ($5,000) or five percent (5%) of the market value of the principal of the trust on the last day of the calendar year in which such withdrawal is requested. Such right of withdrawal shall be exercised in each case by my wife notifying the Trustee in writing to that effect, specifying the cash or assets at current market value that she desires to withdraw; and promptly thereafter the Trustee shall make such distribution to her. Such right of withdrawal shall be noncumulative.

▶ **Comment:** If greater flexibility is desired so the wife can have a right during lifetime to invade trust principal without the trustee's approval, paragraph 5.3 can be used; however, she can be given no greater right of withdrawal. There is little reason for this provision if the wife is the trustee.

5.4 Upon the death of my wife after my death or upon my death if my wife does not survive me, the remaining trust fund and any property transferred to the Trustee under the Will of my wife shall be held, administered, and distributed by the Trustee in accordance with the terms and conditions hereinafter set out.

▶ **Comment:** Paragraph 5.4 would be used if the settlor's children are young and the trust is to continue for some period of time for their benefit following the death of the wife.

5.4A Upon the death of my wife after my death or upon my death if my wife does not survive me, the remaining trust fund and any property transferred to the Trustee under the Will of my wife shall be distributed by the Trustee to my children outright and per stirpes.

▶ **Comment:** If the children are of sufficient maturity, the trust can terminate at the wife's death and be distributed to the children. Paragraph 5.4A reflects distribution equally among the children and can be modified if a different distribution is desired. There may also be a need to provide for contingent beneficiaries if the children and their issue do not survive the wife.

5.4B Upon the death of my wife after my death, the remaining trust fund shall be distributed, in trust or otherwise, among my children, their spouses, or more remote descendants and their spouses, and charities as defined in I.R.C. Section 2055, in such proportions as my wife may direct by specific reference to this power in her last will and testament. The Trustee may rely upon an instrument admitted to probate in any jurisdiction as the last will of my wife and if no such instrument is offered for probate within three months after her death, the Trustee may presume that she died intestate. In default of the exercise of this limited power of appointment, the trust estate shall be distributed to my children outright and per stirpes.

> **Comment:** The wife can be given a limited power of appointment without Trust B being taxed in her estate. This adds greater flexibility, which may be, but is not always, needed. A limited power of appointment is one that cannot be exercised in favor of the donee, his or her estate, and the creditors of either. This power is more limited than required but is used because it includes most normal needs. See Chapter 6, at 6.31.

5.5 The trust shall be divided into trusts of equal value, one for each of my children then living, and one for the issue of any deceased child of mine. After division of the trust into separate shares, the Trustee shall expend or use all, part, or none of the net income of a child's trust, as may be necessary to provide for the maintenance, health, education, or advancement in life of my children (or their issue if a separate trust exists due to the death of a child). Such expenditures shall be made by the Trustee, with or without regard to the duty of anyone to support such children (or their issue if a separate trust exists due to the death of a child), or his or her ability to be self-supporting, and with or without regard to any other income or property of my children which may be applicable or available for any such purposes. Any net income not so expended during any calendar year shall be accumulated and added to the principal of the trust estate. Further, in regard to any trust for the issue of a deceased child, distributions of income shall not be taken into account in the final distribution of assets.

> **Comment:** This paragraph divides the trust into separate shares, each of which is a discretionary trust used for the support of the settlor's children or their issue if a child predeceases the settlor and his wife. If the settlor prefers that other income sources be considered in deciding whether to distribute income, modification of paragraph 5.5 will be needed.

5.6 When each child attains _____ years of age, the Trustee shall distribute _____ of the trust estate to such child; when such child attains _____ years of age, the Trustee shall likewise distribute _____ of the trust estate as then constituted to such child; and when such child attains _____ years of age, the trust shall terminate and the Trustee shall distribute the entire remaining principal of the trust estate to such child. Any trust for the issue of a deceased child shall be distributed equally among such issue upon the youngest attaining _____ years of age.

> **Comment:** Paragraph 5.6 is used together with 5.5 to provide for the distribution of each child's separate trust. If distribution is to be in three equal shares, one-third would be inserted in the first blank space relating to distribution, then one-half in the second blank space. If other distributions are preferred, slight modifications will be necessary. The last sentence provides for a different distribution when a trust exists for the issue

of a deceased child. This approach is for administrative convenience because such a trust might be small in size if divided into separate trusts for each issue. If desired, however, it can be handled the same as for the settlor's children, with only minor drafting modifications.

5.7 If any of my children (or their issue if a separate trust exists due to the death of a child) shall need additional funds for maintenance, support, education, or advancement in life, or by reason of illness, emergency, or any extraordinary or unusual circumstances, the Trustee shall use such amounts from the principal of a child's or issue's trust estate as may be needed to meet said requirements of such beneficiary. Any payment or use of any portion of the principal of such trust estate for such purposes shall not be subject to question by any person or in any court.

> ▶ **Comment:** Paragraph 5.7 permits flexibility to spend principal for specific needs of the children or issue.

5.8 After each child reaches the age of twenty-one years, the Trustee may advance to such child an amount to enable the child to enter into a trade, business, or profession, or to buy a home.

> ▶ **Comment:** Paragraph 5.8 adds flexibility and may be needed if the trust withholds distribution of the principal for a number of years. It does not refer to the issue of a deceased child; thus, modification is needed if the desire is for this flexibility also to apply to the issue of the deceased child.

5.9 If any child dies prior to the complete distribution of his or her trust estate, such trust estate shall be paid, outright and per stirpes, to such child's then living issue, or in default of such issue, to my then living issue, outright and per stirpes; subject to 5.10.

> ▶ **Comment:** If a child of the settlor dies before complete distribution of his or her trust, the issue of that child will receive the trust, subject to 5.10.

5.10 If any beneficiary to whom the Trustee is directed under 5.9 of this Article to distribute any share of trust principal is under the age of twenty-one years when the distribution is made and if no other trust is then to be held under this instrument for such beneficiary's primary benefit, such beneficiary's share shall vest in interest in such beneficiary indefeasibly, but the Trustee may, in the Trustee's sole discretion, withhold possession of it under the provisions of this instrument for such beneficiary's benefit until such beneficiary attains the age of twenty-one years (or dies prior thereto), at which time such beneficiary's portion shall be distributed to such beneficiary (or to such beneficiary's Personal Representative as the case may be). In the meantime, the Trustee shall disburse so much of the net income and principal of such beneficiary's portion as, in the Trustee's sole discretion, may be necessary to provide for the support, comfort, and education of such beneficiary. For all sums so disbursed the Trustee shall have full acquittance. Any net income not so disbursed shall be annually accumulated by the Trustee and added to the portion from which it was derived.

> ▶ **Comment:** If the beneficiary in paragraph 5.9 is under age 21, then the share can be held in trust until he or she reaches age 21. The trust does not extend beyond age 21 owing to possible violations of the rule against perpetuities.

ARTICLE VI

Right During Lifetime to Fund Trust

6.1 Subject to the willingness of the Trustee to accept any such assets, I, or any other person, shall have the right to add property to the principal of this trust. All additions shall be held, administered, and distributed in accordance with the provisions of this Agreement.

> ▶ **Comment:** The entire Article VI permits the trust to be funded during the settlor's lifetime and, if funded, for the trust to be administered as directed by the settlor. There are no income tax advantages to this approach; however, if funded during the settlor's lifetime, his or her estate will avoid probate and the incident expenses, which can be substantial. Article VI also enables the trustee to care for the settlor's financial needs during periods of disability or poor health. Article VI is written as if the children were still being supported, at least in part, by the settlor. If the children are older, the part of Article VI referring to the children should be deleted.

6.2 During my lifetime, all or such part of the net income and principal of the trust as I may direct shall be paid to me or to such person or persons as I may designate from time to time. Net income not so distributed shall be accumulated and added to the principal of the trust.

6.3 Should I become incapacitated and unable to act for myself (which determination shall be made by my then-treating physician), then the Trustee shall use or expend so much of the income and principal of the trust for my benefit, or for the benefit of my wife and children as the Trustee deems advisable from time to time for their health, maintenance, support, and education.

6.4 During my lifetime, the Trustee shall follow my written directions, if they are given, with regard to the management and control of the trust estate. If I give no instructions as to the management and control of the trust estate by the Trustee, the Trustee may act in accordance with the powers granted herein in Article VIII.

6.5 When acting at my direction, or with my consent, the Trustee shall be relieved from any liability arising out of such action except such liability as may arise from the Trustee's own gross negligence or intentional misconduct.

6.6 Upon my death, the Trustee shall divide any funds then held under this Article in the same manner as provided with other property under Article II, et seq.

ARTICLE VII

Maximum Duration of Trust

7.1 Notwithstanding anything herein to the contrary, the trusts under this instrument shall terminate not later than twenty-one years after the death of the last survivor of me, my wife, and my descendants living on the date of my death, at the end of which period the Trustee shall distribute each remaining portion of the trust property to the beneficiary or beneficiaries, at that time, of the current income thereof, and if there is more than one beneficiary, in the proportions in which they are beneficiaries.

> **Comment:** This provision is inserted to guard against an inadvertent violation of the rule against perpetuities. The practitioner must review this paragraph with his or her own state law and make any necessary modifications.

ARTICLE VIII

Powers of Trustee

8.1 With reference to the trust estate created herein and every part thereof, the Trustee shall have the following rights and powers without limitation and in addition to power conferred by law:

> **Comment:** A trustee is held to a very high standard of care under fiduciary law. The powers stated in this article do not lessen that standard, but do assure the trustee of sufficient flexibility to carry out its duty. If the trustee is a corporate fiduciary, the protection is even greater because its activity is backed by the financial strength of the institution, liability insurance, in-house auditing, and regular state and federal examinations.

8.2 The Trustee may sell publicly or privately, for cash or on time, without an order of court, upon such terms and conditions as to it shall seem best, any property of the trust estates; and no person dealing with the Trustee shall have any obligation to look to the application of the purchase money therefor.

8.3 The Trustee may invest and reinvest all or any part of the principal of the trust estates in any stocks, bonds, mortgages, shares, or interests in common trust funds, mutual funds, or other securities or property, real, personal, or mixed, and of any kind or nature whatsoever, as the Trustee may deem advisable, and without diversification if the Trustee deems it advisable, irrespective of whether or not such securities or property are eligible for trust investment under state or any other law, and may change any investment received or made by the Trustee, and may hold cash if the Trustee deems it advisable.

8.4 The Trustee may exercise broad discretion as to diversification of trust property, and shall not be required to reduce any concentrated holdings merely because of such concentration, and shall have full discretion as to the percentage to be invested in fixed income securities, and is specifically relieved from any requirements, legal or otherwise, as to the percentage of the trust estate to be invested in fixed income securities, and may invest and retain invested any trust estate wholly in common stocks.

8.5 The Trustee shall have full power to sell, convey, lease or mortgage, repair and improve, and take any and all other steps with regard to any real estate that may at any time be a part of the principal of the trust estates; and any lease of such real property or contract with regard thereto made by the Trustee shall be binding for the full period of the lease or contract, though said period shall extend beyond the termination of the trust.

8.6 The Trustee shall have the power to vote shares of stock held in the trust estates at stockholders' meetings in person or by special, limited, or general proxy, with or without power of substitution, as to the Trustee shall seem best.

8.7 The Trustee shall have the power to participate in the liquidation, reorganization, consolidation, incorporation and reincorporation, or any other financial readjustment of any corporation or business in which the trust estates are or shall be financially interested.

8.8 The Trustee shall have full power to borrow money from any source for any purpose connected with the protection, preservation, improvement, or development of the trust hereunder, whenever in the Trustee's judgment the Trustee deems it advisable, and as security to mortgage or pledge any real estate or personal property forming a part of the trust estate upon such terms and conditions as the Trustee may deem advisable.

8.9 The Trustee shall have authority to hold any and all securities in bearer form, in the Trustee's own name, or the name of some other person, partnership, or corporation, or in the name of a duly appointed nominee, with or without disclosing the fiduciary ownership thereof.

8.10 Whenever the Trustee is required, pursuant to a provision hereof, to divide the principal of the trust estate into parts or shares and to distribute or allot same, the Trustee is authorized to make such division in cash or in kind or both; and for the purpose of such division or allotment, the judgment of the Trustee concerning the propriety thereof and relative value of property so distributed or allotted shall be binding and conclusive with respect to all persons interested herein.

8.11 During the minority or incapacity of any beneficiary to whom income is herein directed to be paid, or for whose benefit income and principal may be expended, the Trustee may pay such income and principal in any one or more of the following ways: (1) directly to said beneficiary; (2) to the legal guardian or committee of said beneficiary; (3) to a relative of said beneficiary to be expended by such relative for the maintenance, health, and education of said beneficiary; (4) by expending the same directly for the maintenance, health, and education of said beneficiary. The Trustee shall not be obliged to see to the application of the funds so paid, but the receipt by such person shall be full acquittance to the Trustee.

8.12 The Trustee may pay to the Personal Representative of my estate, from the principal of Trust B, such sum or sums as the Personal Representative may certify to be due and payable as the proportionate share of any trust estate herein created of all inheritance and estate taxes (including interest and penalties thereon, if any) due from or assessed against my estate. The certificate of the Personal Representative of my estate as to the amount of such proportionate share shall be sufficient authority to the Trustee to pay the same and shall be binding and conclusive upon all persons.

8.13 In determining whether or not I am incapacitated, the Trustee may rely upon the findings of my personal physician, if any, and if none, the Trustee may rely upon the findings of the physician or physicians the Trustee may employ, and the Trustee shall not be liable to anyone for so acting.

8.14 The Trustee may, in the Trustee's discretion, use the principal of the trust estate, or as much thereof as may be necessary, for the purpose of buying at private sale, any securities or other property belonging to my general estate, although such property may not be income producing or may not be of the character prescribed by law for the investment of trust funds and regardless of the diversification or nondiversification thereof. Such purchase is to be at the prevailing market price or fair and reasonable market value at the time of such purchase; provided, however, the Trustee shall not purchase for Trust A any asset that does not qualify for the Federal estate tax marital deduction.

8.15 To continue and operate any business owned by me at my death and to do any and all things deemed appropriate by the Trustee, including the power to incorporate the business and to put additional capital into the business, for such time as the Trustee shall deem advisable, without liability for loss resulting from the continuance or operation of the business except for the Trustee's own negligence; and to close out, liquidate, or sell the business at such time and upon such terms as the Trustee shall deem proper.

8.16 In general, the Trustee shall have the same powers, authorities, and discretions in the management of the trust estate as I would have in the management and control of my own personal estate. The Trustee may continue to exercise any powers and discretions hereunder for a reasonable period after the termination of any trust estate or estates, but only for so long as no rule of law relating to perpetuities would be violated.

ARTICLE IX

Rights and Duties Relating to Insurance Policies

9.1 I shall pay all premiums, assessments, and other charges necessary to keep all insurance policies in force. The Trustee shall be under no duty or obligation to pay any such premiums or charges or to see that said policies are renewed or kept in force; and until my death, the Trustee shall not have any duty with respect to such policies (except to hold same in safekeeping).

> ▶ **Comment:** Article IX contains various administrative provisions that are needed when the trust is an unfunded life insurance trust. In an unfunded life insurance trust, the settlor names the trustee as beneficiary of various life insurance policies on his or her life, but the settlor continues to own them and pay the premiums. The trust owns no present assets and is only funded at death when the insurance is paid into the trust. At that time the probate estate also is transferred into the trust. Of course, if the trust was funded during the settlor's lifetime under Article VI, those assets will also be added to the life insurance proceeds. If no life insurance is payable to the trust, this should be omitted.

9.2 In the event this trust is funded or partly funded prior to my death, the Trustee shall be obligated to pay premiums on policies on which the Trustee has consented in writing to pay, but only to the extent of funds in the Trustee's possession at the time any such premiums become due.

9.3 I reserve the right and power to withdraw any policy or policies and to exercise, without the consent of the Trustee or any beneficiary hereunder, or under any of said policies, any and all options, elections, rights, and privileges given to me under the terms of said policies or any of them, including the right to change the beneficiaries as often as I may elect to do so, to receive the dividends and make loans thereon, to convert the same into other forms of insurance, to collect the cash values thereof, or to permit the same to lapse. If I shall exercise any such options, elections, rights, or privileges, or shall alter, amend, or revoke this Agreement as hereinafter provided, the Trustee shall execute such releases and other papers as may be required therefor, without liability to anyone for so doing.

9.4 After my death when the policies hereunder shall become payable, the Trustee shall promptly furnish to the insurance companies proof of loss, and shall collect and receive the proceeds of the policies; to that end, the Trustee shall have power to execute and deliver receipts and other instruments and to take such action as is appropriate for the collection thereof; provided, however, that if payment of any policy is contested, the Trustee shall be under no obligation to institute legal action for the collection thereof unless and until the Trustee has been indemnified to the Trustee's satisfaction for all costs including attorneys' fees. In the event that the Trustee is not so indemnified, the Trustee shall deliver the policy (or policies) in question to the beneficiaries of this trust as hereinafter set forth as their interests may appear. The Trustee may out of the trust repay any advances made to the Trustee or reimburse the Trustee for any advances made by the Trustee for expenses incurred in collecting or attempting to collect any sum from any insurance company by suit or otherwise.

9.5 No insurance company under any policy of insurance deposited with the Trustee hereunder shall be responsible for the application or disposition of the proceeds of such policy by the Trustee. Payment to and receipt by the Trustee of such proceeds shall be a full discharge of the liability of such insurance company under such policy.

9.6 The Trustee may accept any of the optional modes of payment provided in any of such policies where such modes of payment are permitted to the Trustee by the insurance companies.

ARTICLE X

Compensation of Trustee

10.1 As compensation for the Trustee's services hereunder, any corporate Trustee shall receive the fees set forth in the Trustee's then current Schedule of Trust Fees.

> ▶ **Comment:** This is a standard provision. Some trustees will agree to set the fee at a specified amount. If desired, this can be done by modifying this provision to insert the exact commission to be received. If an individual trustee is used, minor modifications are obviously needed.

ARTICLE XI

Right to Amend or Revoke

11.1 I reserve the right and power to alter, amend, or revoke this Agreement, at any time and from time to time, either in whole or in part, without the consent of the Trustee or any beneficiary hereunder, by written notice to the Trustee to that effect; provided, however, that the duties, responsibilities, and compensation of the Trustee shall not be altered or modified without the Trustee's written consent.

> ▶ **Comment:** Article XI clarifies that the trust is revocable.

ARTICLE XII

Spendthrift Restriction

12.1 This trust and the benefits hereunder, both income and principal, which are payable to any beneficiary shall not be subject to assignment, alienation, pledge, attachment, or the claims of creditors.

▶ **Comment:** A spendthrift provision is generally enforceable and should be used in almost any trust. More protective language can be used, but this has not been done in this article because the wife is also a beneficiary and this provision also applies to her. Treas. Reg. Section 20.2056(b)-5(f)(7) specifically allows this wording without loss of the marital deduction; thus, no more restrictive wording has been used.

ARTICLE XIII

Law Applicable

13.1 This Agreement shall be construed and regulated in all respects by the laws of the State of Kentucky.

▶ **Comment:** It is traditional to specify the law that applies in a trust just as is often done in a contract. A consideration is that if the trust is moved to another state, questions of interpretation and administration might be complicated by this provision. If this is a possibility, a modification in wording could be made to specify that the trust situs can be moved to another state by the trustee and that the law of the state of the trust situs shall apply.

ARTICLE XIV

Audit

14.1 My Trustee shall be under no duty to examine, verify, question, or audit the books, records, or accounts or transactions of my or my wife's Executor, Administrator, Trustee, or other Personal Representative, nor shall my Trustee have any responsibility for any act or omission of any such Executor, Administrator, Trustee, or other Personal Representative.

▶ **Comment:** Article XIV is helpful in clarifying the extent of the duties of a trustee to inquire into the handling of the estate or trust administration when it did not act as executor or was not acting as a trustee. It is an important provision.

ARTICLE XV

Presumption of Survivorship

15.1 If my wife and I die under circumstances creating any doubt as to which of us survived the other, my wife shall be presumed to have survived me and the trusts created herein shall be administered accordingly.

▶ **Comment:** This presumption is used when the estate of one spouse is larger than the other and Trust B will be underutilized if death is simultaneous. If this clause is needed, then a reverse clause is used in the wife's will and trust. When the estates are similar in size, the presumption may not be needed. This provision should not be used without determining its effect. See Chapter 7, at 7.21.

ARTICLE XVI

Removal of and Resignation by Trustee

16.1 After my death, incompetency, or resignation, XYZ Bank and Trust Company of Louisville, Kentucky, shall be my successor Trustee. In this event, my wife may remove any acting Trustee and name a successor Trustee which shall be a bank or trust company qualified to do business under state or federal law, by delivering to the Trustee herein a notice naming the successor Trustee and indicating its willingness to serve. Upon receipt of such notice, the Trustee shall transfer to such successor Trustee the trust property and make a full accounting to my wife and other beneficiaries under this trust agreement, whereupon the Trustee shall be discharged and have no further responsibility under this trust agreement. The right of my wife to remove an acting Trustee and name a successor Trustee shall be limited to the following circumstances: (a) my wife moving to a new locality and desiring to name a corporate Trustee in that locality; (b) a change in ownership of the Trustee, whether through corporate merger, acquisition, or otherwise; (c) a trust officer being assigned to this trust account whose office is in a locality other than the locality in which my wife resides; (d) investment performance on investments in this trust for any eighteen month period has underperformed the S&P 500 stock index in the case of stock investments, or the Salomon Brothers bond index in the case of bond investments; and (e) an increase in total Trustee fees in excess of those charged by the Trustee at the time this trust was first funded.

16.2 The Trustee may resign by giving the current adult income beneficiary or beneficiaries thirty (30) days notice in writing delivered to such beneficiary or beneficiaries in person or mailed to their last known address, the resignation to become effective as hereinafter provided. Upon receipt of such notice, the majority of the current adult beneficiaries shall appoint a successor Trustee which shall be a bank or trust company qualified to do business under state or federal law. In the event of failure to appoint a successor Trustee who accepts the trust within thirty (30) days from the date the notice was given, the Trustee may resign to the district court of my domicile. Upon the appointment of and acceptance by the successor Trustee, the original Trustee shall transfer to such successor Trustee the trust property and make a full and proper accounting to the current beneficiary or beneficiaries, whereupon its resignation shall become effective.

16.3 The successor Trustee, upon acceptance of this trust and the trust property, shall succeed to and possess all the rights, powers and duties, authority, and responsibilities conferred upon the Trustee originally named herein, and shall have no duty to inquire into the prior acts of any prior Trustee.

> ▶ **Comment:** It is often important to retain for the beneficiary the right to change trustees. Often a trust beneficiary may move from the area where the trustee is located and prefer a trustee closer to home. Also, this right can ensure a better business relationship between the beneficiary and the trustee because the trustee must provide good service and investment performance to retain the right to act as trustee. The criteria listed in 16.1 are not essential and may be omitted. If the beneficiaries are classic "spendthrifts," it will be better not to grant the beneficiaries the right to change the trustee, because they may "shop" for a trustee who will make unwise distributions of principal and then change to that trustee. Also, see Chapter 14, at 14.41 to 14.45. If a corporate trustee is not used, then drafting changes are needed. For example, there may be no need for a right to remove a trustee, thus most of 16.1 and 16.2 can be eliminated. Be certain to limit the surviving spouse's discretion over trust distribution if he or she is named as the successor trustee. See the discussion under Trust B.

ARTICLE XVII

Acceptance of Trust

17.1 The Trustee hereby accepts the trust herein created.

IN WITNESS WHEREOF, the undersigned has executed this instrument on this the _____ day of _____, 20_____.

_____
Richard Henry Roe, Settlor and Trustee

SCHEDULE A

ASSETS   DATE TRANSFERRED

15.4 Marital Deduction Planning with Disclaimer Trust

With the disclaimer trust approach, each spouse gives to the survivor the estate outright. The marital deduction eliminates all estate taxes. The combined exclusion amounts eliminate all estate taxes at the second death. (This is due to portability, which is discussed at 7.3.) There is a cost-basis increase for all estate assets at the second death resulting in the best income tax result. If it appears at the first death that asset values may exceed the combined exclusion amount, the survivor can disclaim sufficient assets to eliminate this possibility. The disclaimed assets pass into trust for the surviving spouse, who gets the use of the assets, but those assets are not taxable assets in the survivor's estate. The following form uses a testamentary trust rather than a separate inter vivos trust. The approach is up to the lawyer. Also, this form is admittedly a "bare-bones" form, so the lawyer should feel free to modify it.

LAST WILL AND TESTAMENT OF MARY JANE ROE

I, Mary Jane Roe, a resident of Madisonville, Hopkins County, Kentucky, do make this to be my Last Will and Testament, hereby revoking all prior wills and codicils.

ARTICLE I

Identification of Husband and Children

A. My Husband's name is Richard Henry Roe, and all references in this instrument to "my Husband" or to "my Spouse" are to him only.

B. My children are Delores Lynn Roe, Carol Rae Roe, and Kent Allen Roe, and all references in this instrument to "my children" are to them only.

ARTICLE II

Payment of Debts and Funeral Expenses

I direct that all of my just debts, my funeral expenses, and costs of estate administration be paid as soon as practicable after my death.

ARTICLE III

Payment of Taxes

All inheritance, estate, and succession taxes, including interest and penalties payable by reason of my death, shall be paid from my residuary estate.

ARTICLE IV

Disposition of Tangible Personal Property

All of my clothing, jewelry, personal effects, automobiles, and all other similar tangible personal property not otherwise specifically bequeathed that are owned by me at the time of my death, I bequeath to my Husband. If my Husband shall not survive me, I bequeath in equal shares to my children who survive me all of such tangible personal property.

ARTICLE V

Bequest to Husband

I bequeath in fee simple my entire residuary estate to my Husband, Richard Henry Roe, and if he should disclaim all or any part of this bequest, such disclaimed property shall pass under Article VI hereunder. If my Husband does not survive me, I bequeath my residuary estate in equal shares among my children. If any child shall be deceased at the time of distribution, then such child's share shall be distributed per stirpes and absolutely to such child's then-living issue, if any, and if none, then in like manner unto my other children and their issue, per stirpes.

> ▶ **Comment:** The wife's will simply passes the entire estate to her husband. If the assets are needed by him, which could be the case if the wife owns the liquid investments and the husband owns illiquid assets, he can receive the bequest of her estate even though it may cost more in estate taxes to the children at his subsequent death. If this is not the case, he can disclaim the bequest and the disclaimed assets will pass into the trust in Article VI of her will. Because the trust is for his lifetime benefit, the disclaimer will still allow him the benefits from the wife's estate during his lifetime, but the trust will not be subject to estate tax in his estate at his subsequent death. This is an obvious estate tax savings to the children at little inconvenience to the husband.

ARTICLE VI

Trust for Husband's Life

I direct that, after satisfying all the bequests and devises hereinabove made, and after the payment of all administration expenses and death taxes as hereinabove provided, my Executor shall deliver and convey all the disclaimed assets of my estate to the Trustee hereinafter named (herein called Trustee). The Trustee shall hold, manage, and control all of the aforesaid property and all other property received by the Trustee on account of my death as a trust estate, with all of the rights and powers, and subject to the limitations, hereinafter enumerated, for the following uses and purposes:

> **Comment:** The trust gives the husband the lifetime benefit from the property placed in the trust. He can even act as trustee, provided his discretion is limited to an ascertainable standard as is done in this trust. See Chapter 6, at 6.32. The trust estate will pass to the children at the husband's death; however, none of the trust assets will be includable in the husband's own estate for estate tax purposes.

A. Until the death of my Husband, the Trustee shall pay the entire net amount of the Trust to my Husband or apply it for his benefit in quarterly or more frequent installments.

B. The Trustee shall distribute to my Husband or apply to my Husband's benefit from the principal of the Trust, such amounts as the Trustee deems proper to provide for his health, maintenance, and support. In determining the amounts of principal to be so disbursed, the Trustee shall take into consideration any other income that my Husband may have from any other source, and my Husband's capital resources other than household goods, residence, and personal effects.

C. Upon the death of my Husband, the Trustee shall distribute the trustee estate in equal shares among my children. If any child shall be deceased at the time of distribution, then such child's share shall be distributed per stirpes and absolutely to such child's then-living issue, if any, and if none, then in like manner unto my other children and their issue, per stirpes.

ARTICLE VII

Appointment of Executor and Trustee

I appoint my Husband to be Executor and Trustee of this Will, to serve without surety on his bond. Should a successor fiduciary be needed in either capacity, I name XYZ Bank and Trust Company, Madisonville, Kentucky, to serve in that capacity.

ARTICLE VIII

Powers of Executor and Trustee

I hereby grant to my Executor and also to the Trustee of the trust established hereunder (including any substitute or successor executor or Trustee) the continuing, absolute, discretionary power to deal with any property, real or personal, held in my estate or in any trust, as freely as I might in the handling of my own affairs. Such power may be exercised independently and without the prior or subsequent approval of any court or judicial authority, and no person dealing with the Executor or Trustee shall be required to inquire into the propriety of any of their actions. Without in any way limiting the generality of the foregoing, I hereby grant to my Executor and also to any Trustee hereunder, the following specific powers and authority in addition to and not in substitution of powers conferred by law:

A. To keep in the trust any original property received from the estate, or from any other source even though the property may not be the type of property prescribed by law for the investment of trust funds.

B. To sell publicly or privately any property of the estate or trust without a court order and upon such terms as he deems proper.

C. To invest and reinvest any part or all of the principal of the estate or trust in stocks, bonds, mortgages, mutual funds, shares in common trust funds, or other securities, as well as any other real or personal property.

D. To exercise discretion as to diversification of estate or trust property and shall not be required to reduce any concentrated holdings merely because of such concentration. The Executor and Trustee are also relieved from any requirements there may be as to the percentage of the estate or trust to be invested in fixed income securities and may invest wholly in common stocks.

E. To sell, exchange, lease, mortgage, repair, and improve and take any prudent steps with regard to any real estate that may be a part of the estate or trust. Any contract on real estate in the estate or trust that is made by the Executor or Trustee shall be binding for the full period of the contract even if the period extends beyond the termination of the estate or trust.

F. To vote shares of stock held in the estate or trust, either in person or by proxy and with or without the power of substitution.

G. To participate in the liquidation, reorganization, incorporation, or any financial readjustment of any corporation or business in which the estate or trust is financially interested.

H. To borrow money from any source, including the Executor or Trustee in his individual capacity, for any purpose connected with the estate or trust property and to mortgage or pledge as security any property of the estate or trust upon such conditions as the Executor or Trustee deems proper.

I. To hold any security in bearer form, in the Executor's or Trustee's own name, or in the name of a duly appointed nominee.

J. At any time the Executor or Trustee is required to divide the principal of the trust, the Executor or Trustee may make such division in cash or in kind, or both, and the judgment of the Executor or Trustee concerning the proper way to make such a division and to value the property being divided shall be binding on all parties.

K. In general, the Executor or Trustee shall have the same powers, authorities, and discretions in the management of the trust property as the Testatrix would have in the management and control of her own property.

ARTICLE IX

Simultaneous Death

If my Husband and I die under circumstances creating any doubt as to which of us survived the other, then it shall be presumed that I survived my Husband.

> **Comment:** A simultaneous death clause must be used in both the husband's and the wife's wills because the estates are unequal between them and the better estate tax result occurs when the spouse with the larger estate is presumed to predecease the other spouse in the event of simultaneous death. It is wise to compute the expected estate tax costs in the event of simultaneous death, to be certain such a clause is needed. The discussion in Chapter 7, at 7.21, should be reviewed.

IN TESTIMONY WHEREOF, I have hereunto set my hand on this the _____ day of _____, 20___.

_____
Testatrix

We, whose names are hereto signed as subscribing witnesses, have, at the request of the Testatrix, Mary Jane Roe, witnessed the execution of this Last Will and Testament consisting of this page and _____ ( ) preceding pages, and each has signed as subscribing witnesses in the presence of the Testatrix and in the presence of each other, on this the ____ day of _____, 20___.

_____ _____
Witness   Address

_____ _____
Witness   Address

[ADD SELF-PROVING NOTARIZATION AS PROVIDED BY STATE LAW]

15.5 Minor's or Educational Trust

A parent desires to establish a college fund for his or her children who are presently ages 4 and 6. The fund will be used for the children's education when each reaches college age and will continue thereafter if the funds are not entirely used for education. For a discussion of the federal gift tax considerations, see Chapter 3, at 3.5, and Chapter 5, at 5.29. Two helpful ABA publications are N. Shurtz, *Education Planning: Taxes, Trusts and Techniques*, (ABA, 2007) and C. D'Aversa, *Tax, Estate and Lifetime Planning for Minors* (ABA, 2006).

TRUST AGREEMENT

THIS TRUST AGREEMENT is entered into between the Settlor, RICHARD HENRY ROE, Madisonville, Kentucky, and the Trustee, MARY JANE ROE, Madisonville, Kentucky.

▶ **Comment:** The settlor should not act as trustee, because this could result in the trust being included in his or her estate if he or she dies before termination of the trust. If the property transferred to the trust is the settlor's property and the settlor's spouse joins in the transfer only for purposes of gift-splitting, she or he should still be able to serve as trustee without the trust estate being taxed to her or his estate in the event she or he dies before termination of the trust. However, if the settlor's spouse dies while the child is under age 18, it is possible the trust will be treated as an asset of the spouse's estate, because she or he will have the ability to discharge his or her parental duty of support from the trust, which could be considered to be tantamount to a general power of appointment. Treas. Reg. § 20.2041-1(c). After the child reaches age 18, there is no further problem. The other alternative is to name a trusted friend or relative, or a financial institution, to serve as trustee.

WITNESSETH

The Settlor has delivered or will deliver to the Trustee the property described in Schedule A. Upon receipt of this property, the Trustee agrees to hold it in trust and to manage and dispose of it according to the provisions of this Trust Agreement.

ARTICLE I

A. The Trustee shall divide the trust property into three equal trusts, one for the benefit of each of the Settlor's children, Delores Lynn Roe, Carol Rae Roe, and Kent Allen Roe. Each of the Settlor's children will be referred to in this Trust Agreement as a "beneficiary."

> ▶ **Comment:** The trust must be separated into separate trust funds for each child rather than one "pot" trust for all the children. This can be accomplished with one trust instrument. In the administration of the trust, separate taxpayer identification numbers are necessary for each child's trust, and separate fiduciary income tax returns are required. If preferred, a separate trust can be created for each child.

B. Until the beneficiary reaches twenty-one years of age, the Trustee may pay to the beneficiary, or pay for the benefit of the beneficiary, as much of the net income and principal of the beneficiary's trust as the Trustee determines to be proper. If any net income remains at the end of each trust year, the Trustee shall add it to the principal of the trust.

> ▶ **Comment:** To qualify for the annual gift tax exclusion, the trust must permit income and principal to be paid to the child before age 21, although it is permissible for none to be paid to the child during this time. Treas. Reg. § 25.2503-4(a).

C. If the beneficiary dies before reaching twenty-one years of age, the beneficiary's trust shall terminate. The beneficiary shall have a general power of appointment over this trust and the Trustee shall pay the entire principal, plus all accumulated income in whatever manner the beneficiary appoints by will, provided the will must specifically refer to this general power of appointment in order for the power to be validly exercised. If the beneficiary does not validly exercise this general power of appointment, the trust property shall be paid to the beneficiary's surviving descendants. If the beneficiary has no surviving descendants, the trust property shall be paid to the Settlor's living descendants. If the Settlor has no living descendants, the trust properties shall be paid to the Settlor's heirs-at-law.

> ▶ **Comment:** Another requirement for the annual gift tax exclusion is that the trust must be payable to the child's estate or pursuant to a general power of appointment if the child dies before age 21.

D. For six months beginning on the beneficiary's twenty-first birthday, the beneficiary may demand in writing payment from the Trustee of the entire principal and all accumulated income of the trust. If the beneficiary makes a timely written demand, the beneficiary's trust shall terminate and the entire principal and all accumulated income shall be paid to the beneficiary. If the beneficiary does not make a timely written demand, this right shall terminate and the trust shall continue on the following terms.

▶ **Comment:** The third requirement for the annual gift tax exclusion is that the trust must terminate at age 21 and be distributed to the child. However, this requirement is met if the child is given a right at age 21 to withdraw the entire trust and elects not to do so. Written notice should be given the child at age 21 of the right to withdraw the trust in its entirety. The trust can then continue for whatever length of time the settlor specifies in the trust. Treas. Reg. § 25.2503-4(b)(2).

1. The Trustee shall pay to the beneficiary, or pay for the beneficiary's benefit, the entire net income in quarterly or other frequent installments.

2. Also, the Trustee shall pay to the beneficiary, or pay for the beneficiary's benefit, so much or all of the principal of the beneficiary's trust as the Trustee determines is needed to provide for the education, support, and general welfare of the beneficiary. Without limiting the discretion of the Trustee, proper usages may include educational or medical needs, the cost of acquiring a home, and the cost of starting or continuing a business.

3. When the beneficiary reaches thirty-five years of age, the trust shall terminate and the entire remaining principal, plus all accumulated income, shall be paid to the beneficiary.

4. If the beneficiary dies before reaching thirty-five years of age, the beneficiary's trust shall terminate and the Trustee shall pay the remaining principal, plus all accumulated income in whatever manner the beneficiary appoints by will, provided the will must specifically refer to this power of appointment in order for the power to be validly exercised. If the beneficiary does not validly exercise this power of appointment, the trust property shall be paid to the beneficiary's surviving descendants. If the beneficiary has no surviving descendants, the trust property shall be distributed to the Settlor's living descendants. If the Settlor has no living descendants, the trust properties shall be paid to the Settlor's heirs-at-laws.

ARTICLE II

The Settlor or any other person may at any time add property to the principal of the trust with consent of the Trustee. Any additions to the trust shall be administered according to the provisions of this trust agreement.

ARTICLE III

The Trustee shall have all powers expressly or implied granted to Trustees by law, as well as the following, specific powers:

▶ **Comment:** The recital of trustee powers is rather standard; however, care should be taken throughout the trust not to limit the powers of discretion of the trustee. The requirement for the annual gift tax exclusion that the trustee may spend income and principal before the beneficiary reaches age 21 is violated when the trustee's discretion is limited, such as to only being spent for "education, health care, or other extraordinary needs." This should be avoided.

A. The Trustee may keep in the trust any original property received from the Settlor, or from any other source even though the property may not be the type of property prescribed by law for the investment of trust funds.

B. The Trustee may sell publicly or privately any property of the trust without a court order and upon such terms as it deems proper.

C. The Trustee may invest and reinvest any part or all of the principal of the trust in stocks, bonds, mortgages, mutual funds, shares in common trust fund, or other securities, as well as any other real or personal property.

D. The Trustee may exercise discretion as to diversification of trust property and shall not be required to reduce any concentrated holdings merely because of such concentration. The Trustee is also relieved from any requirements there may be as to the percentage of the trust to be invested in fixed income securities and may invest wholly in common stocks.

E. The Trustee shall have full power to sell, exchange, lease, mortgage, repair, and improve and take any prudent steps with regard to any real estate that may be a part of the trust. Any contract on real estate in the trust which is made by the Trustee shall be binding for the full period of the contract even if the period extends beyond the termination of the trust.

F. The Trustee shall have the power to vote shares of stock held in the trust, either in person or by proxy and with or without the power of substitution.

G. The Trustee may participate in the liquidation, reorganization, incorporation, or any other financial readjustment of any corporation or business in which the trust is financially interested.

H. The Trustee shall have full power to borrow money from any source, including the Trustee in its individual capacity, for any purpose connected with the trust property and to mortgage or pledge as security any property of the trust upon such conditions as it deems proper.

I. The Trustee shall have the right to hold any security in bearer form, in its own name, or in the name of a duly appointed nominee.

J. Any time the Trustee is required to divide the principal of the trust, it may make such division in cash or in kind, or both, and the judgment of the Trustee concerning the proper way to make such a division and to value the property being divided shall be binding on all parties.

K. During the minority or incapacity of any beneficiary for whom income or principal may be spent, the Trustee may pay the income and principal in any one or more of the following ways: (1) directly to the beneficiary; (2) to the legal guardian of the beneficiary; (3) to a relative of the beneficiary to be spent by the relative for the support, maintenance, and education of the beneficiary; and (4) by making payments directly for the support, maintenance, and education of the beneficiary. The Trustee shall not be required to see the application of any money paid and the receipt from the person to whom the monies are paid shall be full acquittance to the Trustee.

L. In general, the Trustee shall have the same powers, authorities, and discretions in the management of the trust property as the Settlor would have in the management and control of the Settlor's own property.

ARTICLE IV

This trust and the benefits hereunder, both income and principal, which are payable to any beneficiary shall not be subject to assignment, alienation, pledge, attachment, or the claims of creditors.

▶ **Comment:** This spendthrift provision is optional but can be used if desired.

ARTICLE V

The Trustee may at any time designate another individual or financial institution possessing trust powers to act as either a Co-trustee or as a successor Trustee. The instrument designating the Co-trustee or successor Trustee shall be in writing, signed and acknowledged. In the event the present Trustee for any reason ceases to act as Trustee and has not named a successor, XYZ Bank and Trust Company, Madisonville, Kentucky, shall serve as successor Trustee.

▶ **Comment:** This article is used if the trustee is the settlor's wife because it allows her to choose a successor trustee, and if she fails to do so, a corporate trustee is named in the document. If the initial trustee is not the wife or some third party to whom the settlor is willing to give such broad discretion in appointing a cotrustee or successor trustee, the article should be modified accordingly.

ARTICLE VI

Any corporate Trustee shall receive compensation according to its regular schedule of fees in effect at the time the services are rendered.

ARTICLE VII

The Settlor declares this Trust Agreement to be irrevocable and the Settlor has no right to alter, amend, or revoke this trust in any way.

▶ **Comment:** This type of trust must be irrevocable; thus, a provision to this effect must be inserted in the trust.

ARTICLE VIII

This Trust Agreement has been accepted by the Trustee in the Commonwealth of Kentucky and it shall be construed and regulated by the laws of Kentucky.

IN WITNESS WHEREOF, the Settlor and the Trustee have signed their names to this Trust Agreement consisting of this and _____ (___) preceding pages on the _____ day of _____, 20___.

_____
Richard Henry Roe, Settlor

_____
Mary Jane Roe, Trustee

SCHEDULE A

ASSETS   DATE TRANSFERRED

15.6 Irrevocable Life Insurance Trust

If a client has an estate that may reach or exceed the maximum estate exclusion amount, life insurance may create an estate tax problem. Once estate taxes are owed, the tax rate is a flat 40%. The death benefit of life insurance is taxable the same as other estate assets, but the life insurance can be excluded if owned by a third party, such as, a trust.

The trustee must apply for the life insurance on the life of the husband. The trustee will then both own and be the beneficiary of the life insurance proceeds. The premiums also will be paid by the trustee. Normally, income-producing property is not transferred to the trust because the transfer constitutes a taxable gift; thus, the trustee has no funds with which to pay the premiums. The husband can make annual gifts to the trust with which the trustee can pay the premiums. If the trust is structured as a Crummey trust, the gift of the premiums qualifies for the annual gift tax exclusion. Thus, no gift tax will be owed for the gift, which otherwise would be a future-interest gift for which the annual exclusion would not be available. On the death of the husband, the life insurance proceeds will be paid to the trustee, and no estate tax will be owed on the proceeds. For a further discussion, see Chapter 5, at 5.25, and Chapter 8, at 8.42. Two helpful ABA publications are L. Brody et al., *The Irrevocable Life Insurance Trust Forms and Drafting* (3d ed.; ABA, 2011) and L. Mezullo, *An Estate Planner's Guide to Life Insurance* (2d ed.; ABA, 2009).

IRREVOCABLE TRUST AGREEMENT FOR WIFE AND CHILDREN

This Agreement is made the _____ day of _____, 20__, by _____, hereinafter called the Settlor, and XYZ BANK AND TRUST COMPANY, of Madisonville, Kentucky, hereinafter called the Trustee.

> ▶ **Comment:** An insured who holds power in a fiduciary capacity and acts as a trustee of this type of trust may be deemed to possess incidents of ownership in the life insurance policies, thus causing the proceeds to be included in his or her estate. To avoid any possibility of this disastrous result, it is wiser to use a corporate trustee for this type of trust. If not possible, the spouse or a third party can act as trustee. In no event can each spouse serve as trustee for the other spouse's life insurance trust. The IRS considers such an arrangement reciprocal trusts and includes the insurance in the insured spouse's estate, thus defeating the tax savings.

ARTICLE I

Trust Property

The Settlor hereby assigns, transfers, and delivers to the Trustee, its successor and assigns, the property set forth in Schedule A to be held and administered in trust, for the following uses and purposes:

ARTICLE II

Rights in Policies of Insurance

The Trustee is hereby vested with all right, title, and interest in and to any policy or policies of insurance transferred to the Trustee, and is authorized and empowered to exercise, for the purposes of the trust herein created, and as absolute owner of such policy or policies of insurance, all the options, benefits, rights, and privileges under such policy or policies, including the right to borrow upon such policy or policies and to pledge such policy or policies for loan or loans. The Settlor hereby relinquishes all rights and powers in such policy or policies of insurance and will, at the request of the trustee, execute instruments reasonably required to effectuate this relinquishment.

> ▶ **Comment:** This paragraph merely clarifies—with some redundancy—that the settlor-insured possesses no incidents of ownership in the life insurance policies that are owned by the trustee. This paragraph is more important in situations in which existing policies are transferred by the settlor-insured to the trustee, rather than when a new policy is purchased by the trustee on the life of the settlor-insured. If existing policies are given to the trustee, the value of those policies must be obtained from the various insurance companies because the value is a taxable gift to the extent it exceeds any annual exclusions that are available.

ARTICLE III

Payment of Premiums

The Trustee may apply for and purchase insurance policies on the life of the Settlor and shall pay the premiums on such policies first from trust income, if any, and if none, from trust principal, and to allow any such policies to lapse. If the trust assets are insufficient to pay such premiums, the Trustee shall be under no obligation to pay any premiums which may be due. Further, the Trustee shall have no obligation to notify any person of the nonpayment for such premiums or seek to have any other person pay such premiums.

> ▶ **Comment:** This paragraph clarifies the premium payment obligations of the trustee, as well as the action to be taken if the policy premiums are not paid.

ARTICLE IV

Withdrawal Rights During Insured's Lifetime

During the insured's lifetime and immediately following any contribution to the trust, each of the Settlor's then-surviving children shall have the unrestricted right to withdraw (in cash or in kind) an amount equal to such child's proportionate share of any such contribution. A child's proportionate share shall be the amount of such contribution divided by the number of the Settlor's children surviving at the time of the contribution. Each child's right of withdrawal shall not exceed in any one calendar year <u>five thousand dollars or five percent of the value of the principal of the trust as of the end of such calendar year, whichever shall be the greater</u>.

This right of withdrawal is noncumulative and shall lapse thirty calendar days following the date of the contribution, but no later than the last day of the calendar year in which the contribution is made. If any child predeceases the insured, such child's descendants shall succeed to his or her right of annual withdrawal. The right of withdrawal for a child or descendent either under the age of eighteen, or under any other legal disability, shall be exercised by the legal guardian of such person, if any, and if none, the Trustee shall designate an appropriate adult individual who may make the demand on behalf of such person; provided, however, in no event shall the Settlor be entitled to make any such demand.

To assure that the right of withdrawal referred to above is completely effective, the Trustee agrees to notify the Settlor's children or their descendants, legal guardians, or appropriate adults as the case may be, at the last address known to the Trustee, of any deposit made for the purpose of paying premiums, and to allow thirty days after any such notice before applying such deposit toward the payment of premiums on life insurance policies held in the trust.

> **Comment:** This is the provision that qualifies this trust as a Crummey trust and permits the annual gift tax exclusion to apply to the annual gifts to the trust from which the trustee will pay the premiums. The beneficiaries must have the right to withdraw the gift. This right is limited to 30 days and is noncumulative. It should not be limited any further. Notice also must be sent to all beneficiaries advising them of the gift and their right to withdraw the gift. The trustee should send a letter to each beneficiary so advising them upon receipt of the gift. Due to recent private letter rulings, the alternative of sending one letter advising the beneficiaries of the current gift, explaining to the beneficiaries that the same gift will be given at the same time each year thereafter, and advising them of their right to withdraw each annual gift should not be used. Do a letter every time a gift is made.
>
> A problem exists because the annual exclusion ($15,000 per donee, or $30,000 with gift-splitting) exceeds the $5,000 or 5% of the value of the trust assets requirement under the power of appointment rules in IRC Section 2514(e). The problem arises because the demand power is a general power of appointment, and to the extent the gift exceeds $5,000 or 5% of the trust assets, the failure to exercise the power (which should not be exercised) by a beneficiary results in a taxable gift. The trust, as drafted, limits the withdrawal to the 5 or 5 requirement, thus avoiding the gift tax problem. This solution is satisfactory if each beneficiary's proportionate part of the premiums is less than $5,000.
>
> If the settlor desires to make maximum use of the Crummey trust ($15,000 or $30,000 with gift-splitting per beneficiary per year), the general power of appointment rule prevents it. A solution exists if the beneficiaries have testamentary control of their trust. Thus, if the trust vests in the beneficiary and the beneficiary has a general power of appointment over the trust, the gift can exceed the 5 or 5 requirement (Priv. Ltr. Rul. 8229097). If this approach is needed, the underlined portion of the form in the first paragraph of Article IV should be deleted and in lieu thereof the following should be inserted: "the amount of the annual per donee gift tax exclusion, including the amount

of the gift tax exclusion if gift-splitting is elected by the donor." In no event should the spouse be given a right of withdrawal greater than permitted by the 5 or 5 exception to the general power-of-appointment rules, because to do so could cause inclusion of some or all of the trust assets in his or her estate. The trust, as drafted, gives no right of withdrawal to the spouse. A third approach involves what is referred to as a *hanging power*. For an excellent discussion of hanging powers and irrevocable life insurance trusts, see *The Unfunded Irrevocable Life Insurance Trust* (Northwestern Mutual Life Insurance Company, 1998).

ARTICLE V

Rights and Duties Relating to Insurance Policies

After the death of the insured when the policies hereunder shall become payable, the Trustee shall promptly furnish proof of loss to the insurance companies, and shall collect and receive the proceeds of the policies. The Trustee shall have power to execute and deliver receipts and other instruments and to take such action as is appropriate for the collection thereof. If the Trustee deems it necessary to institute legal action for the collection of any policies, it shall be indemnified for all costs, including lawyer's fees.

No insurance company under any policy of insurance deposited with the Trustee hereunder shall be responsible for the application or disposition of the proceeds of such policy by the Trustee. Payment to and receipt by the Trustee of such proceeds shall be a full discharge of the liability of such insurance company under such policy.

The Trustee may accept any of the optional modes of payment provided in any of such policies where such modes of payment are permitted to the Trustee by the insurance company.

ARTICLE VI

Benefits for Wife and Children

The Trustee shall hold all remaining assets of the trust in a single fund until the death of the Settlor's wife. During that time, the Trustee shall pay to, or apply the net income to the use of, such one or more of Settlor's wife, children, and grandchildren, in such amounts and proportions as the Trustee shall deem advisable from time to time, without regard to equality of distribution. The Trustee is also authorized and empowered, at any time and from time to time, to disburse from the principal of the trust such amounts as the Trustee may deem advisable to provide adequately and properly for the support or education of any of such beneficiaries. In determining the amounts of principal to be so disbursed, the Trustee shall take into consideration any other income or property which such permissible distributee of income may have from any other source; and the Trustee's discretion shall be conclusive as to the advisability of any such disbursement and the same shall not be questioned by anyone. For all sums so disbursed, the Trustee shall have full acquittance.

Upon the death of the Settlor's wife, the Trustee shall divide the trust assets into equal funds, one for each child of the Settlor then living, and one for the then-living descendants, collectively, of each deceased child of the Settlor then deceased. Subject to the provisions of paragraph B of this Article, the Trustee shall distribute outright each share set aside for the descendants of a deceased child of the Settlor to such descendants, per stirpes. The shares set aside for the Settlor's living children shall be held in trust as follows:

    A.   Each share set aside for a living child of the Settlor shall be disposed of as follows:

1. The Trustee shall pay all the net income of each child's trust to such child in convenient installments at least as often as quarter-annually until the termination of the trust.
2. After any child has reached the age of twenty-five years, the Trustee shall distribute one-third of the trust fund to such child absolutely. The remainder of such fund shall be retained in trust until age thirty, at which time the Trustee shall distribute one-half of the remainder of the trust fund to such child absolutely. When such child attains the age of thirty-five, the trust shall terminate and the Trustee shall distribute the balance of such child's trust fund to such child, absolutely. If any child shall have attained any of such respective ages at the time when such trust fund is directed to be set apart for such child, such part or parts or all, as the case may be, of such child's trust fund shall be distributed (instead of holding same in trust) as is directed to be distributed to such child upon attaining such respective ages.
3. The Trustee is authorized and empowered, at any time and from time to time, to disburse from the principal of the trust estate created for the Settlor's child (even to the point of completely exhausting same) such amounts as the Trustee deems needed to provide adequately and properly for the support and maintenance of the Settlor's child, such child's spouse, and the child's own children, including but not by way of limitation, expenses incurred by reason of illness, disability, and education; and to enable the Settlor's child to enter into a trade, business or profession, or to make a down-payment on a home. In determining the amounts of principal to be so disbursed, the Trustee shall take into consideration any other income or property which such child may have from any other source.
4. Upon the death of any child of the Settlor, after a separate trust fund has been set apart for such child's benefit under this Section of this Article and before the entire principal of the fund has been distributed, the Trustee shall distribute the trust fund, as then constituted, in such proportions and in such manner, outright or in trust or otherwise, to or for the benefit of any one or more persons or corporations as such child may appoint by specific reference thereto in such child's last will admitted to probate; including the power to appoint the principal of the trust or any part thereof, to such child, or to such child's estate, or creditors, or to the creditors of such child's estate. If such child shall not validly and effectually exercise the foregoing power of appointment with respect to the entire principal of the fund then held in such child's trust, then such part of the principal as such child shall not effectually appoint shall be distributed by representation and absolutely to such child's then-living issue, if any, and if none, then in like manner unto the Settlor's then-living issue, per stirpes.

    ▶ **Comment:** See the discussion following Article IV.

    B.   If any beneficiary to whom the Trustee is directed under this Article to distribute any share of trust principal is under the age of twenty-one years when the distribution is to be made, and if no other trust is then to be held under this instrument, such beneficiary's share shall vest in interest in such beneficiary indefeasibly, but the Trustee may, in the Trustee's sole discretion, withhold possession of it under the provisions of this instrument for such beneficiary's benefit until such beneficiary attains the age of twenty-one years (or dies prior thereto), at which time such beneficiary's portion shall be distributed to such beneficiary (or to such beneficiary's personal representative as the case may be). In the meantime, the Trustee shall disburse so much of the net income and principal of such beneficiary's portion as, in the Trustee's sole discretion, may be necessary to provide for the support, comfort, and education of such beneficiary. For all sums so disbursed the Trustee shall have full acquittance. Any net income not so disbursed shall be annually accumulated by the Trustee and added to the portion from which it was derived.

> **Comment:** These are merely sample dispositive provisions. These provisions can be modified as needed to provide for the beneficiaries. If generation-skipping provisions are contemplated, see Chapter 4.

ARTICLE VII

Withdrawal Right of Wife

In the event any of the life insurance proceeds payable to the Trustee upon the death of the Settlor shall be includible in the gross estate of the Settlor due to the three-year rule under Internal Revenue Code Section 2035, or otherwise, the Settlor's wife shall have the power to demand distribution of any and all amounts of income and principal as she may desire. No beneficiary other than the Settlor's wife shall have any rights to the income or principal from such life insurance proceeds during her entire lifetime.

> **Comment:** This provision is necessary because life insurance transferred to the trust by the settlor within three years of his death will be included in his estate. The life insurance proceeds would not qualify for the marital deduction, because of the provisions of Article VI; thus, this provision is essential.

ARTICLE VIII

Power of Trustee

With reference to the trust estate created herein and every part thereof, the Trustee shall have the following rights and powers without limitation and in addition to power conferred by law:

A. The Trustee may retain or buy from the Settlor's estate, without liability for loss or depreciation resulting from such retention or purchase, original property, real or personal, received or purchased from the Settlor or the Settlor's estate or any other source, although such property may not be income-producing or may not be of the character prescribed by law for the investment of trust funds, and although said property represents a large percentage of the total property of the trust estates or even the entirety thereof.

▶ **Comment:** This provision is needed because the settlor's estate may lack sufficient liquidity to pay estate settlement costs; if this is the case, the insurance can be used to purchase estate assets to provide liquidity. The trust cannot give the estate money, nor may it pay these expenses itself without causing inclusion of at least part of the trust in the settlor's estate.

B. The Trustee may sell publicly or privately, for cash or on time, without an order of court, upon such terms and conditions as to it shall seem best, any property of the trust estates; and no person dealing with the Trustee shall have any obligation to look at the application of the purchase money therefor.

C. The Trustee may invest and reinvest all or any part of the principal of the trust estates in any stocks, bonds, mortgages, mutual funds, shares, or interests in common trust funds, or other securities or property, real, personal, or mixed, and of any kind or nature whatsoever, as it may deem advisable, and without diversification if it deems it advisable, irrespective of whether or not such securities or property are eligible for trust investment under state or any other law, and may change any investment received or made by the Trustee, and may hold cash if it deems it advisable.

D. The Trustee may exercise broad discretion as to diversification of trust property, and shall not be required to reduce any concentrated holdings merely because of such concentration, and shall have full discretion as to the percentage to be invested in fixed income securities, and is specifically relieved from any requirements, legal or otherwise, as to the percentage of the trust estate to be invested in fixed income securities, and may invest and retain invested any trust estate wholly in common stocks.

E. The Trustee shall have full power to sell, convey, lease, or mortgage, repair and improve, and take any and all other steps with regard to any real estate that may at any time be a part of the principal of the trust estates; and any lease of such real property or contract with regard thereto made by the Trustee shall be binding for the full period of the lease or contract, though said period shall extend beyond the termination of the trust.

F. The Trustee shall have the power to vote shares of stock held in the trust estate at stockholders' meetings in person or by special, limited, or general proxy, with or without power of substitution, as to the Trustee shall seem best.

G. The Trustee shall have the power to participate in the liquidation, reorganization, consolidation, incorporation and reincorporation, or any other financial readjustment of any corporation or business in which the trust estate is or shall be financially interested.

H. The Trustee shall have full power to borrow money from any source, for any purpose connected with the protection, preservation, improvement, or development of the trust estate hereunder, whenever in its judgment it deems it advisable, and as security to mortgage or pledge any real estate or personal property forming a part of the trust estate upon such terms and conditions as it may deem advisable.

I. The Trustee shall have authority to hold any and all securities in bearer form, in its own name, or the name of some other person, partnership, or corporation, or in the name of a duly appointed nominee, with or without disclosing the fiduciary ownership thereof.

J. Whenever the Trustee is required, pursuant to a provision hereof, to divide the principal of a trust estate into parts or shares and to distribute or allot same, the Trustee is authorized to make such division in cash or in kind or both; and for the purpose of such division or allotment, the judgment of the Trustee concerning the propriety thereof and relative value of property so distributed or allotted shall be binding and conclusive with respect to all persons interested herein.

K. During the minority or incapacity of any beneficiary to whom income is herein directed to be paid, or for whose benefit income and principal may be expended, the Trustee may pay such income and principal in any one or more of the following ways: (1) directly to said beneficiary; (2) to the legal guardian or committee of said beneficiary; (3) to a relative of said beneficiary to be expended by such relative for the maintenance, health, and education of said beneficiary; (4) by expending the same directly for the maintenance, health, and education of said beneficiary. The Trustee shall not be obliged to see to the application of the funds so paid, but the receipt of such person shall be full acquittance to the Trustee.

L. The Trustee may pay to the Personal Representative of the estate of the Settlor, from the principal of Trust B, such sum or sums as the Personal Representative may certify to be due and payable as the proportionate share of any trust estate herein created of all inheritance and estate taxes (including interest and penalties thereon, if any) due from or assessed against the estate of the Settlor. The certificate of the Personal Representative of the Settlor's estate as to the amount of such proportionate share shall be sufficient authority to the Trustee to pay the same and shall be binding and conclusive upon all persons.

M. In determining whether or not the Settlor is incapacitated, the Trustee may rely upon the findings of the Settlor's personal physician, if any, and if none, the Trustee may rely upon the findings of the physician or physicians the Trustee may employ, and the Trustee shall not be liable to anyone for so acting.

N. The Trustee may, in its discretion, use the principal of the trust estate, or as much thereof as may be necessary, for the purpose of buying at private sale, any securities or other property belonging to the general estate of the Settlor, although such property may not be income producing or may not be of the character prescribed by law for the investment of trust funds and regardless of the diversification or nondiversification thereof. Such purchase is to be at the prevailing market price or fair and reasonable market value at the time of such purchase; provided, however, the Trustee shall not purchase for Trust A any asset which does not qualify for the federal estate tax marital deduction.

O. To continue and operate any business owned by the Settlor at the Settlor's death and to do any and all things deemed appropriate by the Trustee, including the power to incorporate the business and to put additional capital into the business, for such time as it shall deem advisable, without liability for loss resulting from the continuance or operation of the business except for its own negligence; and to close out, liquidate, or sell the business at such time and upon such terms as it shall deem proper.

P. In general, the Trustee shall have the same powers, authorities, and discretions in the management of the trust estate as the Settlor would have in the management and control of the Settlor's own personal estate. The Trustee may continue to exercise any powers and discretions hereunder for a reasonable period after the termination of any trust estate or estates, but only for so long as no rule of law relating to perpetuities would be violated.

ARTICLE IX

Compensation of Trustee

As compensation for the Trustee's services hereunder, any corporate Trustee shall receive the fees set forth in the Trustee's then current Schedule of Trust fees.

ARTICLE X

Trust Irrevocable

This Trust Agreement is hereby declared to be irrevocable and the Settlor shall have no power to alter, modify, amend, or terminate it or the trusts created hereunder in any manner or respect.

> **Comment:** A provision should be inserted to specify that the trust is irrevocable, to ensure the exclusion of the trust from the settlor's estate.

ARTICLE XI

Law Applicable

This Agreement shall be construed and regulated in all respects by the laws of the State of Kentucky.

ARTICLE XII

Spendthrift Provision

Except as otherwise herein specifically provided, no beneficiary of any trust created hereunder shall have any right or power to anticipate, pledge, assign, sell, transfer, alienate, or encumber his or her interest in the trust, in any way; nor shall any such interest in any manner be liable for or subject to the debts, liabilities, or obligations of such beneficiary or claims of any sort against such beneficiary.

ARTICLE XIII

Acceptance of Trust

The Trustee hereby accepts the trust herein created.

IN WITNESS WHEREOF, the parties hereto have executed this instrument in duplicate the day and year first above written.

SETTLOR: _____

TRUSTEE:

XYZ BANK AND TRUST COMPANY

BY: _____

Trust Officer

SCHEDULE A

The Settlor has transferred the following property to the Trustee under the above-described Agreement:

The Trustee accepts the above-listed property in trust under the above-described Agreement.

SETTLOR: _____

TRUSTEE:

XYZ BANK AND TRUST COMPANY

BY _____

Trust Officer

15.7 Will, Trust, and Premarital Agreement

This planning approach is easily illustrated in the example of a young widow who has two children ages 6 and 9. She has recently inherited an estate from her husband that includes the proceeds from a large life insurance policy, in addition to the residence, automobiles, and various items of personal property. The widow has normal concerns of providing for the children's needs, should she die while they are still young. She is also aware of the rights of inheritance of a second spouse, should she remarry and predecease her second spouse. She wants to be protected from that potential problem.

The forms that follow include a will in which the widow can name a guardian for her children, should she predecease them while they are under the age of 18. She has established for the children an inter vivos trust from which their financial needs can be provided. The trust also will enable the inheritance to be held, managed, and used for the children until they are more mature, such as at age 25 or 30. The trustee will normally be a corporate trustee, but an individual trustee can be used. Any insurance or retirement benefits should be made payable to the trust by filling out beneficiary designation forms for each policy as follows: "The proceeds shall be paid to the insured's Trustee, _____, pursuant to a trust entered into by and between the insured and the Trustee on the _____ day of _____, 20___, and including any amendments thereto." If the widow does not die prematurely, she can later change the beneficiary designations to the children equally. The trust should then be amended or revoked.

The widow's concern over the rights of inheritance of a new spouse can be solved with a premarital agreement entered into by the couple before their marriage. (A sample agreement follows the will and trust.) Because the widow may find a premarital agreement a difficult matter to discuss with a prospective new spouse, another approach is for the widow to transfer her property into the inter vivos trust at the present time. The forms that follow are drafted with this approach in mind. A helpful ABA publication is L. Ravdin, *Premarital Agreements: Drafting and Negotiation* (2d ed.; ABA, 2017).

The widow can transfer her property into the trust during her lifetime, act as trustee, and be succeeded by a corporate trustee on her death or resignation. The trust will be for the benefit of her and her children. The trust should be protected from the claims of a new spouse because the trust is not a probate asset. Any claims of fraud by the new husband, such as that the trust was an improper device used to defeat his rights of inheritance, should not be successful if the trust is established and funded well before the marriage. However, the law among the states is not uniform on this issue. The lawyer must be certain of the law in his or her own state.

LAST WILL AND TESTAMENT OF MARY JANE DOE

I, Mary Jane Doe, a resident of Madisonville, Hopkins County, Kentucky, make this my Last Will and Testament, hereby revoking all prior wills and codicils.

ARTICLE I

I direct that my just debts, funeral expenses, costs of administration, and all estate, inheritance, or other transfer taxes that become payable by reason of my death, be paid out of my residuary estate as soon as practicable after my death.

ARTICLE II

I bequeath and devise all the rest, residue, and remainder of the property, real or personal, and wheresoever situated, which I own or in which I may have an interest at my death to the Trustee under a Trust Agreement executed by me on _____ day of _____, 20___, and in full force and effect on the date of the execution of this Will.

► **Comment:** A pour-over will is normally a permissible testamentary instrument; however, the trust must be in existence before the execution of the will. This simply requires that the trust be executed first and then the will. The practitioner must be certain of the effect of a pour-over will under state law.

ARTICLE III

I nominate and appoint _____ as guardian of any of my children during their minority. In the event this guardian ceases to act for any reason, then I nominate and appoint _____ as successor guardian. I direct no bond or surety shall be required of these guardians.

ARTICLE IV

I nominate and appoint _____ as Executor of this my Last Will and Testament. I grant my Executor full power and authority to compromise or otherwise settle or adjust any and all claims, charges, debts, or demands against or in favor of my estate, as fully as I could do if living, and with full power, without order of court, to sell, transfer, or convey any of my property, real or personal, for the purpose of administration, division, or distribution in carrying out the terms of this Will.

I also expressly empower my Executor to sell to the Trustee under the Trust Agreement referred to hereinabove, for cash, any assets in my estate which in the sole discretion of my Executor may be necessary or expedient in order to produce cash for the payment of taxes or costs of administration, such sale to be at the prevailing market price or fair and reasonable market value at the time of said sale. My Executor may determine, without regard to any rule of law, what assets shall be sold in order to produce cash for the purposes hereinabove set out.

I nominate and appoint _____ to be the successor Executor. Either my Executor or my successor Executor shall be allowed to serve without surety on their bond and without performing any formalities in the settlement of my estate as are not mandatory under the law.

IN TESTIMONY WHEREOF, I have hereunto set my hand on this the _____ day of _____, 20___.

_____
Mary Jane Doe

We, whose names are hereto signed as subscribing witnesses, have at the request of the Testatrix, _____, witnessed the execution of this Will, consisting of this page and _____ (___) preceding pages, and each has signed as subscribing witness in the presence of the Testatrix and in the presence of each other on the _____ day of _____, 20___.

_____   _____
Witness   Address

_____   _____
Witness   Address

[ADD SELF-PROVING NOTARIZATION AS PROVIDED BY STATE LAW]

TRUST

THIS TRUST AGREEMENT entered into by Mary Jane Doe, of Madisonville, Kentucky, as Settlor and Trustee.

WITNESSETH

I will hold and administer all assets transferred to this trust in accordance with the following terms and provisions.

ARTICLE I

Identification of Beneficiaries

1.1 The term "children" shall be understood to mean my children, whose names are _____, _____, and _____.

ARTICLE II

Right during Lifetime

2.1 During my life, all or such part of the net income and principal of the trust as I may direct shall be paid to me or to such person or persons as I may designate from time to time. Net income not so distributed shall be accumulated and added to the principal of the trust.

2.2 Should I become incapacitated, then the Trustee shall use or expend so much of the income and principal of the trust for my benefit, and for the benefit of my children, as the Trustee may deem advisable from time to time for the health, maintenance, support, and education, including vocational, college, graduate, and professional schooling of my children.

2.3 During my lifetime, the Trustee shall follow my written directions, if they are given, with regard to the management and control of the trust estate. If I give no instructions as to the management and control of the trust estate, the Trustee may act in accordance with the powers granted herein in Article VI.

2.4 When acting at the Trustee's discretion, or with my consent, the Trustee shall be relieved from any liability arising out of such action except such liability as may arise from the Trustee's own gross negligence or intentional misconduct.

ARTICLE III

Rights after My Death

3.1 After my death, all assets transferred to the Trustee by my personal representative shall be added to the other property which was transferred to the trust during my lifetime.

> ▶ **Comment:** This trust establishes separate shares for each child, rather than one pot trust for all the children. The generation-skipping transfer tax forces the use of separate shares in many situations. The discussion in Chapter 4, at 4.31 should be helpful. If a pot trust is appropriate, the alternate Article III that is provided can be used.

3.2 The Trustee shall divide and partition the trust property into trusts of equal value, one trust for each of my children then living, and one trust for the issue, if any, taken collectively and on a per stirpes basis, of each child of mine who shall have died. Each such trust above provided for shall be designated by the name of the particular child of mine living at my death or who shall have died leaving issue surviving. Each of said trusts shall be held and administered for the benefit of the child whose name designates that particular trust and for the surviving issue of any deceased child all as hereinafter more particularized. Each of the trusts shall be held and administered by the Trustee as a separate and distinct trust.

> **Comment:** As can be seen, this paragraph establishes a separate trust for each child of the settlor and a pot trust for the children of any deceased child.

3.3 The Trustee shall pay to or for the benefit of each living child whose name designates each particular trust, and for any child not living, unto the issue of such child so much of the income and principal of the particular trust as the Trustee deems necessary and appropriate to provide for such child's health, maintenance, support, and education, including vocational, college, graduate, and professional schooling. Any income of any particular trust not distributed shall be added to the principal of the child's trust. Any distributions made to the issue of a deceased child whose name designates a particular trust need not be equal among such issue and shall not be charged against their respective share of the particular trust.

3.4 Upon a child attaining the age of _____ (___) years, _____ percent (___%) of his or her trust shall be distributed to such child outright and free of any further trust; and upon such child attaining the age of _____ (___) years, the entire balance of his or her trust shall be distributed to such child outright and free of any further trust. The trust for the issue of a deceased child shall terminate upon the youngest issue reaching age twenty-one (21) and shall be distributed outright and per stirpes among the deceased child's issue.

> **Comment:** This paragraph provides for the termination of each child's trust, but with distribution of the trust principal at two separate times, typically one-half at one age and the remaining one-half three to five years later. Modification can easily be made if the desire is for more or less frequent distribution of trust principal. The trust for the issue of a deceased child terminates when the youngest issue reaches a minimum age, such as 21.

ALTERNATE ARTICLE III

Rights after My Death

3.1 After my death, all assets transferred to the Trustee by my personal representative shall be added to the other property which was transferred to the trust during my lifetime.

3.2 Until the _____ (_____) birthday of the youngest of my children, the Trustee shall collect the income from the property comprising the trust estate, and shall pay or use all, part, or none of the net income and principal of the trust, without regard to equality of distribution, to or for the benefit of my children, to be used for the support, maintenance, health, and education of such children, or for their benefit in the event of illness, emergency, or extraordinary or unusual circumstances, as the

Trustee, in its sole discretion, may deem necessary after taking into consideration any other funds readily available for such purposes. Any net income not currently distributed shall be annually added to the principal of the trust. Further, disbursements of income and principal shall not be taken into account in the final distribution of the trust estate.

    3.3   After each of my children reaches the age of _____ (_____) years, the Trustee, in its sole discretion, may advance to such child an amount to enable this child to enter into a trade, business or profession, or to buy a home, and (regardless of other provisions to the contrary) such amount shall be charged as an advancement without interest to this child upon the final distribution of the trust. The Trustee, however, shall not be liable if, for any reason, such advancement exceeds the child's share upon the final distribution of the trust.

    3.4   Upon the youngest of my children attaining the age of _____ (_____) years, the trust shall terminate and the Trustee shall distribute the trust estate to, or for, the benefit of each of my children, in equal shares. In the event any of my children should die prior to receiving his or her complete distribution from the trust estate, then the share to which that deceased child would have been entitled had that child been living at the time of distribution, shall be distributed per stirpes to the issue of that deceased child. If the deceased child should have no issue surviving at the time of distribution from the trust estate, then that child's share shall be distributed equally by the Trustee to my then surviving children.

ARTICLE IV

Restriction on Beneficiaries' Rights

    4.1   No beneficiary of the trusts created herein shall have the right or power to anticipate, by assignment or otherwise, any income or principal given to such beneficiary by this instrument or any portion thereof; nor in advance of actually receiving same shall have the right or power to sell, transfer, encumber, or in any way charge same, nor shall such income or principal or any portion of same be subject to any execution, levy, sale, garnishment, attachment, insolvency, bankruptcy, or other legal proceeding of any character, or in any manner or event be subject to the payment of such beneficiary's debts.

> ▶ **Comment:** This spendthrift clause should protect the trust from the claims of the children's creditors, but normally it would not be successful against claims of the settlor's creditors.

ARTICLE V

Maximum Duration of Trust

    5.1   Notwithstanding anything herein to the contrary, the trusts under this instrument shall terminate not later than twenty-one years after the death of the last survivor of me and my issue living on the date of my death, at the end of which period the Trustee shall distribute each remaining portion of the trust property to the beneficiary or beneficiaries, at that time, of the current income thereof, and if there is more than one beneficiary, in the proportions in which they are beneficiaries.

ARTICLE VI

Powers of Trustee

6.1 With reference to the trust estate created herein and every part thereof, the Trustee shall have the following rights and powers without limitation and in addition to power conferred by law:

6.2 The Trustee may sell publicly or privately, for cash or on time, without an order of court, upon such terms and conditions as to it shall seem best, any property of the trust estates; and no person dealing with the Trustee shall have any obligation to look to the application of the purchase money therefor.

6.3 The Trustee may invest and reinvest all or any part of the principal of the trust estates in any stocks, bonds, mortgages, shares, or interests in common trust funds, or other securities or property, real, personal, or mixed, and of any kind or nature whatsoever, as it may deem advisable, and without diversification if it deems it advisable, irrespective of whether or not such securities or property are eligible for trust investment under state or any other law, and may change any investment received or made by the Trustee, and may hold cash if it deems it advisable.

6.4 The Trustee may exercise broad discretion as to diversification of trust property, and shall not be required to reduce any concentrated holdings merely because of such concentration, and shall have full discretion as to the percentage to be invested in fixed income securities, and is specifically relieved from any requirements, legal or otherwise, as to the percentage of the trust estate to be invested in fixed income securities, and may invest and retain invested any trust estate wholly in common stocks.

6.5 The Trustee shall have full power to sell, convey, lease, or mortgage, repair and improve, and take any and all other steps with regard to any real estate that may at any time be a part of the principal of the trust estates; and any lease of such real property or contract with regard thereto made by the Trustee shall be binding for the full period of the lease or contract, though said period shall extend beyond the termination of the trust.

6.6 The Trustee shall have the power to vote shares of stock held in the trust estates at stockholders' meetings in person or by special, limited, or general proxy, with or without power of substitution, as to the Trustee shall seem best.

6.7 The Trustee shall have the power to participate in the liquidation, reorganization, consolidation, incorporation and reincorporation, or any other financial readjustment of any corporation or business in which the trust estates are or shall be financially interested.

6.8 The Trustee shall have full power to borrow money from any source, for any purpose connected with the protection, preservation, improvement, or development of the trust estate hereunder, whenever in its judgment it deems it advisable, and as security to mortgage or pledge any real estate or personal property forming a part of the trust estate upon such terms and conditions as it may deem advisable.

6.9 The Trustee shall have authority to hold any and all securities in bearer form, in its own name, or the name of some other person, partnership, or corporation, or in the name of a duly appointed nominee, with or without disclosing the fiduciary ownership thereof.

6.10 Whenever the Trustee is required, pursuant to a provision hereof, to divide the principal of a trust estate into parts or shares and to distribute or allot same, the Trustee is authorized to make such division in cash or in kind or both; and for the purpose of such division or allotment, the judgment of the Trustee concerning the propriety thereof and relative value of property so distributed or allotted shall be binding and conclusive with respect to all persons interested herein.

6.11 During the minority or incapacity of any beneficiary to whom income is herein directed to be paid, or for whose benefit income and principal may be expended, the Trustee may pay such income and principal in any one or more of the following ways: (1) directly to said beneficiary; (2) to the legal guardian or committee of said beneficiary; (3) to a relative of said beneficiary to be expended by such relative for the maintenance, health, and education of said beneficiary; (4) by expending the same directly for the maintenance, health, and education of said beneficiary. The Trustee shall not be obliged to see to the application of the funds so paid, but the receipt of such person shall be full acquittance to the Trustee.

6.12 The Trustee may pay to the Personal Representative of my estate from the principal of the Trust, such sum or sums as the Personal Representative may certify to be due and payable as inheritance and estate taxes (including interest and penalties thereon, if any) due from or assessed against my estate. The certificate of the Personal Representative of my estate as to the amount owed shall be sufficient authority to the Trustee to pay the same and shall be binding and conclusive upon all persons.

6.13 In determining whether or not I am incapacitated, the Trustee may rely upon the findings of my personal physician, if any, and if none, the Trustee may rely upon the findings of the physician or physicians the Trustee may employ, and the Trustee shall not be liable to anyone for so acting.

6.14 To continue and operate any business owned by me at my death and to do any and all things deemed appropriate by the Trustee, including the power to incorporate the business and to put additional capital into the business, for such time as it shall deem advisable, without liability for loss resulting from the continuance or operation of the business except for its own negligence; and to close out, liquidate, or sell the business at such time and upon such terms as it shall deem proper.

6.15 In general, the Trustee shall have the same powers, authorities, and discretions in the management of the trust estate as I would have in the management and control of my own personal estate. The Trustee may continue to exercise any powers and discretions hereunder for a reasonable period after the termination of any trust estate or estates, but only for so long as no rule of law relating to perpetuities would be violated.

ARTICLE VII

Provision Relating to Trustees

7.1 Upon the death, resignation, or incapacity of the present Trustee, XYZ Bank and Trust Company, Madisonville, Kentucky, shall be the successor Trustee. In determining whether or not the present Trustee is incapacitated, the successor Trustee may rely upon the findings of such individual Trustee's personal physician, if any, and if none, the successor Trustee may rely upon the findings of the physician or physicians the successor Trustee may employ.

7.2 Any successor Trustee shall have all the title, powers, and discretion of the Trustee succeeded, without the necessity of any conveyance or transfer.

7.3 After the death of the Settlor and during the existence of the trust, a majority of the adult beneficiaries age twenty-one or older shall have the right to remove any acting Trustee and appoint a successor Trustee; provided, however, that such successor Trustee must be a trust company or bank organized under the laws of the United States or one of the states thereof possessing trust powers and having trust assets under administration of not less than $10,000,000. Such right of removal shall be continuing and shall be exercised by serving the acting Trustee with written notice of its removal, which notice shall specify the successor Trustee and certify its willingness to serve as such. Within sixty days thereafter, the Trustee so removed shall institute proceedings for the settlement of its accounts and deliver all assets then held to its successor, whereupon it shall have full acquittance for all assets so delivered (subject to judicial settlement of its account, if required) and shall have no further duties hereunder.

7.4 Each Trustee hereunder shall have the right to resign at any time by giving thirty days written notice to that effect to the current income beneficiary or beneficiaries of the trust. Thereafter, such beneficiary or beneficiaries shall have the right within such thirty-day period to appoint a successor Trustee and shall notify the Trustee of such appointment. Such successor Trustee must be a trust company or bank possessing the qualifications hereinabove set out. In the event the current income beneficiary or beneficiaries shall fail to designate a successor Trustee within the time specified, then the acting Trustee may petition a court of competent jurisdiction for the appointment of a successor and the judicial settlement of its accounts.

> ▶ **Comment:** This article is drafted pursuant to the assumption that the settlor acts as trustee, with a corporate trustee acting as successor trustee following the death of the settlor. This article permits a majority of the children age 21 or older to remove the corporate trustee and appoint another corporate trustee. This is normally a good idea; however, if the children are in need of the protection of a spendthrift trust, it may be better to omit this right. It allows a "spendthrift" child to shop around for a corporate trustee who will be overly liberal in spending principal.

ARTICLE VIII

Audit

8.1 The Trustee shall be under no duty to examine, verify, question, or audit the books, records, or accounts or transactions of any Executor, Administrator, Personal Representative, or prior Trustee of mine, nor shall the Trustee have any responsibility for any act or omission of any such Executor, Administrator, Personal Representative, or prior Trustee.

ARTICLE IX

Law Applicable

9.1 This Agreement shall be construed and regulated in all respects by the laws of the State of Kentucky.

ARTICLE X

Right to Amend or Revoke

10.1 I reserve the right and power to alter, amend, or revoke this Agreement, at any time and from time to time, either in whole or in part, without the consent of the Trustee or any beneficiary hereunder, by written notice to the Trustee to that effect, provided, however, that the duties, responsibilities, and compensation of the Trustee shall not be altered or modified without the Trustee's written consent.

ARTICLE XI

Acceptance of Trust

11.1 The Trustee hereby accepts the trust herein created.

IN WITNESS WHEREOF, the parties hereto have executed this instrument on this the _____ day of _____, 20_____.

SETTLOR AND TRUSTEE:

_____

SUCCESSOR TRUSTEE:

_____

SCHEDULE A

ASSETS   DATE TRANSFERRED

Premarital Agreement

THIS PREMARITAL AGREEMENT entered into by and between _____ (wife), herein referred to as the First Party, and _____ (husband), herein referred to as the Second Party:

> ▶ **Comment:** The form as drafted contemplates the Second Party having a large estate and the First Party's having a much smaller estate. The Second Party waives any claim to the First Party's estate, but provides for the First Party through the use of the personal residence and life insurance that will fund a trust for the First Party's unmarried lifetime. The Second Party's will and a trust to carry out the intent of this agreement are not provided but can be adapted from those provided for the First Party. This agreement is simple but to the point. By avoiding excessive over-precision, it is believed there is less chance to argue about ambiguity at a later date. Full disclosure on Schedules A and B is critical.

Witnesseth

WHEREAS, the First and Second Parties plan to marry and have entered into an agreement as to how the property that each of them owned prior to their marriage should be disposed of upon the death of each of them,

WHEREAS, the First and Second Parties now desire to perfect such agreement in writing, and

WHEREAS, the First and Second Parties each understand that pursuant to this agreement they are forgoing their statutory interest in the estate of the other party;

NOW THEREFORE, in consideration of the mutual promises of the parties that are being made by each of them in consideration of their marriage, it is mutually agreed as follows:

1. The First Party shall keep and retain sole ownership and control of all property that was owned by her at the time of her marriage to the Second Party and shall have the right to dispose of such property either during lifetime or at her death by her Last Will and Testament without interference by the Second Party, his heirs, personal representatives, and assigns, as if she had remained unmarried.

2. The Second Party shall keep and retain sole ownership and control of all property that was owned by him at the time of his marriage to the First Party and shall have the right to dispose of such property either during lifetime or at his death by his Last Will and Testament without interference by the First Party, her heirs, personal representatives, and assigns, as if he had remained unmarried.

3. The First and Second Parties further agree that any property that either should inherit from any source whatsoever other than from each other shall be treated as the sole property of the party who inherited such property and shall be disposed of by the party inheriting such property without interference from the other party in just the same manner as set forth above in paragraphs 1 and 2.

4. In the event the First Party survives the Second Party, the Second Party agrees to provide the First Party with the use, throughout her unmarried lifetime, of the residence that he and she are living in at the time of his death, or the Second Party at his election may provide the First Party with a similar residence for her unmarried lifetime. Further, the Second Party shall cause all his life insurance, which consists of those policies set forth in Schedule B, to be made payable to a trust that shall pay income only for the benefit of the First Party during her unmarried lifetime; however, the First Party shall have no right to make any lifetime disposition of the insurance proceeds, nor the right to direct how such proceeds should pass at her death. The Second Party shall keep such policies in force and effect or may substitute other property of equal or greater value.

> ▶ **Comment:** This provision will have to be modified based on the agreement of the parties. It is offered merely for illustrative purposes.

5. In an effort to provide full disclosure by each party to the other, Schedule A attached hereto sets forth the assets that were owned by the First Party at the time of the parties' marriage, and Schedule B sets forth the assets that were owned by the Second Party at the time of the parties' marriage. Each party recognizes that the description of the assets owned by each of the parties is intended only as a general description and the values inserted therein are intended only as good faith approximations. Each party further covenants to the other that there has been a complete and full disclosure made to the other of the parties' assets prior to their marriage.

6. The First Party and the Second Party each hereby expressly waive and release the right to take against any Last Will and Testament of the other party, pursuant to the provisions of any statute or rule of law granting dower, courtesy, marital portion, homestead, or other rights, of, in, and to the estate of the other, and further agree that in no event and under no circumstances shall they have any right of election to take against any Last Will and Testament of the other party; provided, however, such right does not exist as to assets acquired by the First Party and Second Party after the date of their marriage.

> **Comment:** This last phrase should be carefully considered. As drafted, it preserves each spouse's statutory rights to property acquired during the marriage. If not desired, then it should be deleted.

7. The Second Party has not been represented by independent counsel, but has been fully advised of his right to seek counsel and does waive such right.

> **Comment:** The practitioner has an unresolvable conflict of interest when attempting to represent both parties to this type of agreement. Therefore, only one party can be represented. The other party should be encouraged to seek independent counsel. If the party chooses not to do so, then this paragraph should be inserted in the agreement.

8. All of the terms, covenants, and conditions of this Agreement shall be binding upon the parties hereto, their heirs, personal representatives, and assigns.

IN WITNESS WHEREOF, the parties have hereunto set their hands on this the _____ day of _____, 20__.

WITNESS:

_____

WITNESS:

_____

FIRST PARTY:

_____

SECOND PARTY:

_____

(STATE OF KENTUCKY)

(COUNTY OF HOPKINS)

Subscribed and sworn to before me by _____ and _____ on this the _____ day of _____, 20____.

_____

Notary Public, Hopkins County, KY

My Commission Expires: _____

SCHEDULE A

FIRST PARTY'S ASSETS

ASSET   APPROXIMATE VALUE

SCHEDULE B

SECOND PARTY'S ASSETS

ASSET   APPROXIMATE VALUE

15.8 Special Needs Trust for Handicapped Child

A widow has two adult children, who are the only heirs to whom she plans to devise her estate. One of the children is handicapped and has little prospect of improving to the point of being self-sufficient. The handicapped child is in good health and thus may live much of her life in institutional care. The child presently qualifies for federal and state public assistance payments owing to her handicap.

The widow does not want the child's inheritance to cause her to be disqualified from receiving her present public assistance payments. She also does not want the child's inheritance to be received in a manner that will require it to be expended as a condition of receiving public assistance payments. Further, she does not want the inheritance to be subject to attachment by the government as reimbursement for the public assistance payments. Her desire is that the child's inheritance be available if needed for the child's benefit, but that any portion not needed should be allowed to accumulate until the child's death. The principal can then be paid to the widow's other child or to such other beneficiaries as she may desire. The will that follows carries out this intention.

This will is based on a form from the Foundation for Lifetime Advocacy, Seattle, Washington, and is used with permission. A helpful ABA publication is C. Kruse, *Third Party and Self Created Trusts: Planning for the Elderly and Disabled Client* (3d ed.; ABA, 2002).

LAST WILL AND TESTAMENT OF MARY JANE ROE

I, Mary Jane Roe, presently residing in Madisonville, Hopkins County, Kentucky, make this my last will and testament, hereby revoking all prior wills and codicils.

ARTICLE I

I direct that my just debts, funeral expenses, costs of administration of my estate, and all estate, inheritance, or other transfer taxes imposed due to my death, be paid as soon as practicable after my death.

> ▶ **Comment:** This is a rather standard clause, but before using it, a determination must be made that the clause is appropriate. For example, should all taxes be charged against the residue? In the hypothetical situation presented this would appear appropriate, but that may not be the case if the will contains specific bequests or the estate contains life insurance or other nonprobate property that is paid outside the estate and yet is subject to estate tax. Also, the estate may have indebtedness that the testator would not want paid during administration, such as a mortgage on real estate. If so, the will should specify that a devise of real estate that is subject to a mortgage is not to be paid, but rather that the devisee should receive the real estate subject to the mortgage.

ARTICLE II

I have two children whose names are Mary Ellen Roe and Jane Elizabeth Roe. My child Jane Elizabeth Roe is handicapped to such a degree as to require special care.

> ▶ **Comment:** This will is written for a widow. If it is written for a married couple, the normal dispositive provisions for the surviving spouse should be included. The disposition that follows in Article III would then be an alternate disposition if the spouse were to predecease the testator. If the estate being planned is for a couple and it is large enough to involve federal estate taxes, consideration must be given to the marital deduction and the A-B trust estate planning approach. If the A-B Trust approach is desired, the wording of this will can be modified for that purpose rather easily. Much of the wording that follows in Articles III, IV, and VI can be inserted in lieu of the normal dispositive provisions for the children. (Also, see the discussion in Chapter 5, at 5.24; and if marital deduction planning is necessary, the Will and Trust at 15.3.)

ARTICLE III

I bequeath and devise all the rest, residue, and remainder of my estate, both real and personal, and wheresoever situated, including all property that I may acquire after the execution of this will, one-half to my daughter Mary Ellen Roe, and the remaining one-half to the XYZ Bank and Trust Company, Madisonville, Kentucky, as Trustee, to be held and administered as a trust estate pursuant to the provisions of the testamentary trust set forth herein. In the event Mary Ellen Roe should predecease me, I direct her share shall be distributed to _____. In the event Jane Elizabeth Roe should predecease me, I direct the share which would otherwise be distributed to the aforesaid Trustee shall instead be distributed to _____. I specifically make no provisions for my daughter Jane Elizabeth Roe, as I know she will be adequately provided for otherwise.

> ▶ **Comment:** This provision clarifies that the handicapped child receives no inheritance. Although the use of a family member as trustee may be satisfactory, the better approach is to name a corporate trustee. This should place the trust in the strongest position to argue that the trust estate cannot be expended for basic support, which is otherwise provided by government subsidies.

ARTICLE IV

The aforesaid Trustee shall hold, manage, and control all of the property that shall pass to it under this will, or otherwise, as a trust estate for the following uses and purposes:

A. Throughout the lifetime of my daughter Jane Elizabeth Roe, unless this trust is sooner terminated, the Trustee shall collect the income from the property comprising the trust estate, and shall pay or use all, part, or none of the net income and principal of the trust to or for the benefit of my said daughter to provide for her extra and supplemental care, maintenance, support, and education in addition to the benefits my said daughter otherwise receives as a result of her handicap or disability from any local, state, or federal government, or from any public or private agencies, any of which provide services or benefits to persons who are handicapped.

B. It is the express purpose of this trust to supplement other benefits that my said daughter is entitled to receive. This trust is not intended to provide basic support, but rather is to be a discretionary trust to provide for supplemental needs of the beneficiary that are not otherwise provided for by various public and private assistance. To this end, the Trustee may provide such resources and experiences as will contribute to making the beneficiary's life as pleasant, comfortable, and happy as possible. The Trustee in its sole discretion may purchase such services or items as it deems appropriate in order to carry out this intent, including, by way of illustration, vacation, entertainment, and recreational trips and the expenses of a traveling companion to accompany the beneficiary on such trips.

> **Comment:** This provision clarifies that the purpose of the trust is only to provide for the "extras" and not for basic support, which is provided by governmental or other assistance programs. This should be sufficient to prevent the trust from being considered an asset of the beneficiary that would be required to be spent as a condition of receiving government assistance.

C. Any payments from the trust for services or for the benefit of the beneficiary shall be paid directly to the person or business that supplies such services or benefits for the beneficiary. Nonetheless, the Trustee may exercise its discretion in allowing the beneficiary such periodic allowances for personal spending as the Trustee deems to be appropriate.

D. The Trustee shall have absolute discretion in making the determinations required of it herein. Its decisions shall be final and binding and shall not be subject to any question by any one or any court.

E. This trust shall terminate upon the death of the beneficiary, Jane Elizabeth Roe, and shall be distributed to _____. However, in the event of a determination by a court or agency of competent jurisdiction that the income or principal of the trust is liable for the basic maintenance, support, and medical care of the beneficiary that would otherwise be provided for the beneficiary by local, state, or federal government agencies or programs, or from any public or private agencies, then and in such event, the trust shall terminate and the then remaining trust estate shall be distributed as if the beneficiary is deceased as set forth above in Article III.

▶ **Comment:** This provision is designed to ensure that the trust cannot keep the beneficiary from qualifying for government or other assistance. If the trust does disqualify the beneficiary from receiving such assistance, the trust simply terminates, in which event the beneficiary then owns no assets and should then qualify for government assistance.

ARTICLE V

With reference to the trust estate created herein and every part thereof, the Trustee shall have the following rights and powers without limitation and in addition to powers conferred by law:

A. The Trustee may keep in the trust any original property received from the Settlor, or from any other source even though the property may not be the type of property prescribed by law for the investment of trust funds.

B. The Trustee may sell publicly or privately any property of the trust without a court order and upon such terms as it deems proper.

C. The Trustee may invest and reinvest any part or all of the principal of the trust in stocks, bonds, mortgages, mutual funds, shares in common trust fund or other securities, as well as any other real or personal property.

D. The Trustee may exercise discretion as to diversification of trust property and shall not be required to reduce any concentrated holdings merely because of such concentration. The Trustee is also relieved from any requirements there may be as to the percentage of the trust to be invested in fixed income securities and may invest wholly in common stocks.

E. The Trustee shall have full power to sell, exchange, lease, mortgage, repair and improve and take any prudent steps with regard to any real estate that may be a part of the trust. Any contract on real estate in the trust that is made by the Trustee shall be binding for the full period of the contract even if the period extends beyond the termination of the trust.

F. The Trustee shall have the power to vote shares of stock held in the trust, either in person or by proxy and with or without the power of substitution.

G. The Trustee may participate in the liquidation, reorganization, incorporation, or any financial readjustment of any corporation or business in which the trust is financially interested.

H. The Trustee shall have full power to borrow money from any source, including the Trustee in its individual capacity, for any purpose connected with the trust property and to mortgage or pledge as security any property of the trust upon such conditions as the Trustee deems proper.

I. The Trustee shall have the right to hold any security in bearer form, in its own name, or in the name of a duly appointed nominee.

J. At any time the Trustee is required to divide the principal of the trust, it may make such division in cash or in kind, or both, and the judgment of the Trustee concerning the proper way to make such a division and to value the property being divided shall be binding on all parties.

K. During the minority or incapacity of any beneficiary to whom income or principal may be distributed, the Trustee may pay the income and principal in any one or more of the following ways: (1) directly to the beneficiary; (2) to the legal guardian of the beneficiary; (3) to a relative of the beneficiary to be spent by the relative for the support, maintenance, and education of the beneficiary; and (4) by making payments directly for the support, maintenance, and education of the beneficiary. The Trustee shall not be required to see to the application of any money paid, and the receipt from the person to whom the money is paid shall be a full acquittance to the Trustee.

L. In general, the Trustee shall have the same powers, authorities, and discretions in the management of the trust property as the Settlor would have in the management and control of the Settlor's own property.

ARTICLE VI

The beneficiary shall have no interest in either the income or principal of this trust. The assets of this trust shall not be subject to assignment or alienation by anyone or through any process. Further, the trust shall not be subject to garnishment, attachment, levy, or any other legal process of any court or creditor, nor shall the trust assets be an asset in any bankruptcy proceedings.

▶ **Comment:** The spendthrift provision is designed to ensure that the trust cannot be attached by any government agency that seeks reimbursement for monies it has paid on behalf of the beneficiary.

ARTICLE VII

Appointment of Executor

I nominate and appoint XYZ Bank and Trust Company, Madisonville, Kentucky, to be Executor of this my Last Will and Testament. My Executor shall possess all power granted by law and in addition shall possess all those powers granted to the Trustee in Article V.

IN TESTIMONY WHEREOF, I have hereunto set my hand on this the _____ day of _____, 20___.

_____

Mary Jane Roe

We, whose names are hereto signed as subscribing witnesses, have, at the request of the Testatrix, witnessed the execution of this Will, consisting of this page and _____ (____) preceding pages, and each has signed as subscribing witness in the presence of the Testatrix and in the presence of each other, on this the _____ day of _____, 20___.

_____   _____
Witness   Address

_____   _____
Witness   Address

[ADD SELF-PROVING NOTARIZATION AS PROVIDED BY STATE LAW]

15.9 Income-Only Trust

This trust is of limited usage, as it is irrevocable and also limits the beneficiary to income only from the trust. Principal cannot be distributed to the beneficiary. Most clients will not be comfortable with these restrictions. Its usage is further limited due to the 60-month "look-back" period for transfers without consideration. The reader will recall that transfers without consideration within 60 months of applying for Medicaid creates a disqualification from those benefits. In those limited situations where these restrictions are not deemed to be a serious disadvantage, then the use of this trust may be appropriate. In the right situations (after the 60 months), only income is required to be spent for long-term care expenses, with the state paying the balance of those expenses, as the trust principal is not deemed to be a resource for purposes of Medicaid eligibility. Further, the trust principal is not subject to estate recovery following the death of the trust beneficiary.

TRUST AGREEMENT

We, Richard Henry Roe and Mary Jane Roe, currently of _____, acting as grantors hereby transfer to Richard Henry Roe and Mary Jane Roe, currently of _____, acting as co-trustees (referred to in the singular as trustee), the sum of Ten Dollars ($10.00). This amount and all investments, reinvestments, and additions that may sometimes be referred to in this instrument as the "trust property" or "trust assets" are to be held subject to the following provisions:

1. Name of Trust. This instrument and the initial trust hereby established may be named the "Richard and Mary Roe Income Only Trust."

2. Family Information. Our children are _____, and all references in this trust to "our children" are only to them.

3. Provisions during Our Lifetime. During the lifetime of both of us and during the lifetime of the survivor of us, the trustee shall pay to us, or to the survivor of us, all of the net trust income in quarterly or more frequent installments. The principal of this trust shall not be available under any circumstances for payment to either of us or to any future spouse of either of us. Under no circumstances may our trustee at any time make any such distribution of principal to either of us or to any future spouse. The term "principal" as defined in this instrument shall mean any real estate, money, or other asset except for interest, dividends, rental income, or other ordinary income that does not qualify for capital gains treatment. Finally, the trustee shall make distributions of income only and shall not distribute principal, adjust between principal and income, convert principal to income, or convert principal or income to a new trust amount.

4. Payment of Debts and Funeral Expenses. No portion of the assets of this trust shall be used for the payment of our debts or funeral expenses, as the payment of those expenses is provided for in each of our Last Wills and Testament.

5. Allocations at Our Deaths. Following the death of the last of us to die, the trust shall terminate and the trust property shall be distributed in equal shares to our children. If a child is deceased, that deceased child's share shall be distributed to his or her then living descendants per stirpes.

6. Special Provisions. In addition to the other provisions of this trust agreement:

a. Reliance on Will. The trustee may rely on a will admitted to probate in any jurisdiction as the last will and testament of such person, or may assume (absent actual knowledge to the contrary) that the person had no will if a will has not been admitted to probate within three (3) months after such person's death.

b. Method of Payment. If a person entitled to receive income or principal distributions is unable to manage his or her financial affairs due to any type of mental or physical incapacity, then distributions may be made to or for such person's benefit, including making distributions to such person's guardian, conservator, or committee.

7. Protection from Creditors. No trust beneficiary shall have the right to sell, transfer, assign, alienate, pledge, or in any way encumber trust assets, including income and principal, nor shall trust assets be subject to execution, levy, sale, garnishment, attachment, bankruptcy, or other legal proceedings. Any such actions by a trust beneficiary or a third party seeking to enforce a claim against the trust assets shall not be recognized under any circumstances by the trustee.

8. Definitions. For all purposes of this instrument, the following shall apply:

a. The words "child," "children," "descendant," or "descendants" shall exclude adopted persons unless they are adopted prior to eighteen (18) years; and shall include only persons legitimately born unless a decree of adoption terminates the parental rights of the natural mother during her lifetime, or the natural father signs a written notarized instrument during his lifetime in which he irrevocably states that the child is to be considered legitimately born for purposes of inheriting under this trust.

b. Whenever assets are to be divided and allocated "per stirpes," the assets to be divided or allocated shall be divided into as many equal shares as are necessary to divide or allocate one share to each then living child of such person and to provide one share collectively for the then living descendants of each child of such person who then is deceased leaving one or more descendants then living. Any collective share shall be divided and allocated per stirpes among the descendants of such deceased person in accordance with the preceding sentence.

9. Trustee Powers. In the administration of the trusts, the trustee shall have the following powers and rights and all others granted by law:

a. To sell publicly or privately any trust property, for cash or on time, without an order of court and upon such terms and conditions as our trustee deems proper;

and no person dealing with our trustee shall have any obligation to look to the application of the purchase money.

b. To invest and reinvest all or any part of the principal of the trust in any stocks, bonds, mortgages, shares, or interests in common trust funds, mutual funds, or other securities or property, real, personal, or mixed, and of any kind or nature whatsoever, as the trustee deems proper, and without diversification if the trustee deems it advisable, irrespective of whether or not such securities or property are eligible for trust investment under state or any other law, and may change any investment received or made by the trustee, and may hold cash if the trustee deems it advisable.

c. To exercise broad discretion as to diversification of trust property, and shall not be required to reduce any concentrated holdings merely because of such concentration, and shall have full discretion as to the percentage to be invested in fixed income securities, and is specifically relieved from any requirements, legal or otherwise, as to the percentage of the trust assets to be invested in fixed income securities, and may invest or retain invested any trust estates wholly in common stocks.

d. To sell, convey, lease, or mortgage, repair and improve, and take any and all other steps with regard to any real estate that may at any time be a part of the principal of the trust; and any lease of such real property or contract with regard thereto made by the trustee shall be binding for the full period of the lease or contract, even though the period shall extend beyond the termination of the trust.

e. To vote shares of stock held in the trust at stockholders' meetings in person or by special, limited, or general proxy, with or without power of substitution, as seems best to the trustee.

f. To participate in the liquidation, reorganization, consolidation, incorporation and reincorporation, or any other financial readjustment of any corporation, limited liability company, or business in which the trust is or shall be financially interested.

g. To borrow money from any source for any purpose connected with the protection, preservation, improvement, or development of the trust hereunder, whenever in the trustee's judgment the trustee deems it advisable, and as security to mortgage or pledge any real estate or personal property forming a part of the trust upon such terms and conditions as the trustee may deem advisable.

h. To hold any and all securities in bearer form, in the trustee's own name, or the name of some other person, partnership, or corporation, or in the name of a duly appointed nominee, with or without disclosing the fiduciary ownership.

i. To pay such income and principal during the minority or incapacity of any beneficiary for whose benefit income and principal may be expended, in any one or more of the following ways: (1) directly to the beneficiary; (2) to the legal guardian, conservator, committee, or a custodian under a Uniform Gift or Transfer to Minors Act of the beneficiary; (3) to a relative of the beneficiary to be expended by the relative for the maintenance, health, and education of the beneficiary; or (4) by expending the same directly for the maintenance, health, and education of the beneficiary. The trustee shall not be obliged to see to the application of the funds so expended, but the receipt of such person shall be full acquittance to the trustee.

j. To have the same powers, authorities, and discretions in the management of the trust as we would have in the management and control of our own personal assets. The trustee may continue to exercise any powers and discretions granted in this instrument for a reasonable period after the termination of any trust under this instrument.

10. Trustee Resignation. Our trustee may resign at any time by giving written notice to our successor trustee named below, if any, and if none, then written notice shall be given to each current adult income beneficiary who is then living.

11. Trustee Succession and Appointment. If one of the initial trustees dies, becomes incompetent, resigns, or ceases to serve for any reason, then the other of them shall serve as sole trustee. If both Richard Henry Roe and Mary Jane Roe cease to act as co-trustees due to death, incompetency, resignation, or cease to serve for any reason, then _____ shall serve as successor trustee. _____ shall have the right to name a successor trustee who may be an individual or a financial institution possessing trust powers under state or federal law.

12. Powers of Successor Trustee. Each successor trustee shall have the same rights, titles, powers, duties, discretions, and immunities and otherwise be in the same position as if originally named trustee. No successor trustee shall be personally liable for any act or failure to act of a predecessor trustee. Further, a successor trustee may accept the account furnished and the property delivered by or for a predecessor trustee without liability for so doing, and such acceptance shall be a full and complete discharge to the predecessor trustee.

13. Compensation of Trustee. An individual trustee shall not be paid any compensation, but shall be reimbursed for out-of-pocket expenses.

14. Court Accountings. To the extent such requirements can be waived, the trustee shall not be required (a) to file any inventory of trust property or accounts or reports of the administration of the trusts, or to register the trusts, in any court; (b) to furnish any bond or other security for the proper performance of the trustee's duties; or (c) to obtain authority from a court for the exercise of any power conferred on the trustee by this instrument. This waiver does not preclude the trustee from registering any trust created in this instrument and petitioning a court having jurisdiction over registered trusts for a judicial ruling on any matter relating to administration of any trust created in this instrument.

15. Severability. If any provisions of this trust shall be unenforceable, the remaining provisions shall nevertheless be carried into effect.

16. Certification of Incompetency. Any person acting or named to act as a trustee in this instrument is considered to be unable to serve or to continue serving when a physician whom such person has consulted within the prior three (3) years has certified as to such consultation and the certification states that the person is incapable of managing the affairs of the trusts we have established in this instrument, regardless of cause and regardless of whether there is an adjudication of incompetency. No person shall be liable to anyone for actions taken in reliance on the physician's certification or for dealing with a trustee other than the one removed for incompetency based on such certification.

17. Titles and References. The underscored titles of paragraphs in this instrument are for information purposes only and shall be given no legal effect.

18. Governing Law. The laws of the State of Kentucky shall govern the interpretation and validity of the provisions of this instrument and all questions relating to the management, administration, investment, and distribution of the trusts hereby created.

Notwithstanding the foregoing, our trustee shall have the power, exercisable in the trustee's sole and absolute discretion, to declare by written instrument that the forum for this trust and all trusts established herein shall be another state, in which event the laws of that state shall govern the interpretation and validity of the provisions of this instrument and all questions relating to the management, administration, investment, and distribution of the trusts hereby created.

19. Irrevocability. We declare that this trust is irrevocable and may not be altered, amended, revoked, or in any way modified, in whole or in part. It is our expressed intent by this trust instrument to preclude any right to modify this instrument upon execution by both of us.

The undersigned have signed this instrument and have established the foregoing trusts on this the _____ day of _____, 20____.

Grantors:

_____
Richard Henry Roe

_____
Mary Jane Roe

Trustees:

_____
Richard Henry Roe

_____
Mary Jane Roe

SCHEDULE A

Richard and Mary Roe Income Only Trust

Cash	$ 10.00

15.10 Charitable Remainder Trusts

There are two types of charitable remainder trusts: the charitable remainder annuity trust and the charitable remainder unitrust. There are many variations. Fortunately, the IRS has made drafting easy. It has provided charitable remainder trust forms that it will accept as meeting all IRS drafting requirements. The charitable remainder unitrust inter vivos forms include those with (1) one measuring life; (2) a term of years; (3) two measuring lives, payable concurrently; (4) two measuring lives, payable concurrently and consecutively; and the same four options for testamentary documents. *See* Rev. Proc. 2005-52 through 2005-59. The same eight options with charitable remainder annuity trusts are at Rev. Proc. 2003-53 through 2003-60. All forms are available at irs.gov, at Internal Revenue Bulletin 2005-34 for the unitrust forms and at Internal Revenue Bulletin 2003-31 for the annuity forms.

15.11 Standby Trust

An older couple have none of their children living near them. Because of this, they are concerned about the handling of their financial affairs in the event of the disability of one or both of them. They are not prepared to transfer their estate to a trust at the present time, but they recognize that this may be needed in the future if required due to disability.

The trust that follows is designed to respond to this need. It permits the trustee to provide for the financial needs of both spouses and, on the death of the second spouse, for the trust estate to be distributed to the couple's children. A pour-over will should be used by each spouse that will transfer into the trust any property that has not earlier been transferred into the trust. Sample pour-over wills have not been provided, but can easily be adapted from the pour-over will at 15.3. A power of attorney also should be granted to an individual or to the trustee, which will permit the couple's property to be transferred into the trust at such time as disability or other appropriate circumstances require. A general power of attorney can be used, or, if preferred, a limited power of attorney can be drafted for use only in this event. A sample general power of attorney is provided.

If the couple so desires, they can transfer their property into the trust during their lifetime. This creates the so-called living trust, which often will simplify the probate process. If the settlor desires to act as trustee with a corporate trustee acting as successor, an article similar to Article V in the trust at 15.5 should be inserted.

AGREEMENT

THIS TRUST AGREEMENT is entered into between the Settlor, _____, _____, Kentucky, and the Trustee, XYZ Bank and Trust Company, Madisonville, Kentucky.

> **Comment:** This trust does not make use of marital deduction and portability planning. If the couple's estate approaches the combined federal estate tax exclusion amount exemption, it is more appropriate to use the A-B Trust approach to lessen federal estate taxes. The A-B trust can be drafted to permit early funding because of disability. The trust at 15.3 permits this in Article VI. Thus, in larger estates the will and trust provided at 15.3 can be used, coupled with a power of attorney to fund the trust during the settlor's lifetime.

WITNESSETH:

The Settlor has delivered or will deliver to the Trustee the property described in Schedule A. Upon receipt of this property, the Trustee agrees to hold it in trust and to manage and dispose of it according to the provisions of this Trust Agreement.

ARTICLE I

A. During the Settlor's lifetime, the Trustee shall pay to the Settlor and the Settlor's wife, or pay for their benefit, as much of the net income and principal from the trust as the Settlor shall request. If the Settlor makes no request, due to disability or otherwise, the Trustee in its sole and absolute discretion may distribute to, or for the benefit of, the Settlor and the Settlor's wife, such amounts of income and principal as needed for their reasonable health, maintenance, and support. If any net income remains at the end of each trust year, the Trustee shall add it to the principal of the trust.

B. Upon the Settlor's death, the Trustee shall pay all expenses and indebtedness of the Settlor's estate, including the expenses of his last illness and funeral, unless other provisions have been made for their payment. Also, the Trustee shall pay any administrative expenses and any estate, inheritance, or other death taxes that are owed by the Settlor's estate.

C. If the Settlor's wife, _____, survives him, the trust shall continue and the Trustee shall manage and dispose of the Trust as follows:

1. The Trustee shall pay as much of the net income and principal as it believes in its sole discretion to be proper to be provided for the health, support, and maintenance of the Settlor's wife, _____. If any net income remains at the end of the trust year, the Trustee shall add it to the principal of the trust.

2. Upon the death of the Settlor's wife, the Trustee shall pay all expenses and indebtedness of the estate of the Settlor's wife, including expenses for her last illness and funeral, as well as any administrative expenses and any real estate, inheritance, or other death taxes that are owed by the estate or the Settlor's wife.

D. After the death of the Settlor's wife or after the Settlor's death, if the Settlor's wife dies before him, the trust shall terminate and the Trustee shall divide the trust property into two equal shares, one for the benefit of each of the Settlor's children, _____ and _____, and distribute each share outright to each child. In the event either of the Settlor's children should die prior to receiving his or her complete distribution from the trust estate, then the share to which that deceased child would have been entitled had that child been living at the time of distribution shall be distributed outright and per stirpes to the issue of that deceased child. If the deceased child should have no issue surviving at the time of distribution from the trust estate, then that child's share shall be distributed by the Trustee to the Settlor's other then surviving child.

ARTICLE II

The Settlor or any other person may at any time add property to the principal of the trust with the consent of the Trustee. Any additions to the trust shall be administered according to the provisions of this trust agreement.

ARTICLE III

The Settlor grants the Trustee all powers generally conferred upon a Trustee by law. The Trustee shall have the following powers in addition to any other powers given to it in this trust or by law.

A. The Trustee may keep in the trust any original property received from the Settlor, or from any other source, even though the property may not be the type of property prescribed by law for the investment of trust funds.

B. The Trustee may sell publicly or privately any property of the trust without a court order and upon such terms as it deems proper.

C. The Trustee may invest and reinvest any part or all of the principal of the trust in stocks, bonds, mortgages, shares in common trust funds, or other securities, as well as any other real or personal property.

D. The Trustee may exercise discretion as to diversification of trust property and shall not be required to reduce any concentrated holdings merely because of such concentration. The Trustee is also relieved from any requirements there may be as to the percentage of the trust to be invested in fixed income securities and may invest wholly in common stocks.

E. The Trustee shall have the full power to sell, exchange, lease, mortgage, repair and improve and take any prudent steps with regard to any real estate that may be a part of the trust. Any contract on real estate in the trust that is made by the Trustee shall be binding for the full period of the contract if the period extends beyond the termination of the trust.

F. The Trustee shall have the power to vote shares of stock held in the trust, either in person or by proxy and with or without the power of substitution.

G. The Trustee may participate in the liquidation, reorganization, incorporation, or any other financial readjustment of any corporation or business in which the trust is financially interested.

H. The Trustee shall have full power to borrow money from any source, including the Trustee in its individual capacity, for any purpose connected with the trust property, and to mortgage or pledge as security any property of the trust upon such conditions as it deems proper.

I. The Trustee shall have the right to hold any security in bearer form, in its own name, or in the name of a duly appointed nominee.

J. Any time the Trustee is required to divide the principal of the trust, it may make such division in cash, or in kind, or both, and the judgment of the Trustee concerning the proper way to make such a division and to value the property being divided shall be binding on all parties.

K. During the incapacity of any beneficiary to whom income or principal may be spent, the Trustee may pay the income and principal in any one or more of the following ways: (1) to the legal guardian of the beneficiary; (2) to a relative to the beneficiary to be spent by the relative for the support, maintenance, and health care of the beneficiary; and (3) by making payments directly for the support, maintenance, and health care of the beneficiary. The Trustee shall not be required to see to the application of any money paid and the receipt from the person to whom the monies are paid shall be full acquittance to the Trustee.

L. In general, the Trustee shall have the same powers, authorities, and discretions in the management of the trust property as the Settlor would have in the management and control of his own property.

ARTICLE IV

The Trustee shall receive compensation according to its regular schedule of fees in effect at the time the services are rendered, and if the Trustee has no regular schedule of fees then the compensation shall be in an amount not to exceed the compensation permitted for fiduciaries under Kentucky law.

ARTICLE V

The Settlor declares this Trust Agreement to be revocable and the Settlor may alter, amend, or revoke this trust at any time and in any way.

ARTICLE VI

This Trust Agreement shall be construed and regulated by the laws of Kentucky.

IN TESTIMONY WHEREOF, the Settlor and the Trustee have signed their names to this Trust Agreement consisting of this and _____ (___) preceding pages on the _____ day of _____, 20___.

SETTLOR:

_____

TRUSTEE:

_____

SCHEDULE A

ASSETS   DATE TRANSFERRED

 I, _____, _____ (Street), _____ (City), Kentucky, being of full age, hereby make, constitute, and appoint my trusted friend, _____, _____ (Street), _____ (City), Kentucky, my true and lawful attorney in fact, for me and in my name and on my behalf with full and general power to transact any kind of business, whether the same pertains to my personal property or real property, and to act for me in my place and stead in any way that I myself could do, including but not limited to the power to sign, seal, execute, deliver, and acknowledge any deed, lease, covenant, indenture, agreement, mortgage, note, receipt, or release, and to sell and dispose of any proceeds thereof; to sign my name to any check or draft on any bank account of mine (whether held solely by me or jointly by me and another) and to endorse or sign any check or draft or other instrument payable to me or to my order; to ask, demand, sue for recovery, collect, and receive all sums of money, debts, accounts, interest, and dividends whatsoever, whether now or hereafter to become due, owing, or payable, and to execute and deliver any and all other papers for me.

 Further, I expressly direct that upon my becoming disabled or otherwise incapacitated, as determined in the discretion of my said attorney in fact, that he shall transfer and convey any or all property held in my name solely or held in my name jointly with another, including but not limited to stocks, bonds, mutual funds, certificates of deposit, and savings certificates or accounts, to the XYZ Bank and Trust Company, Madisonville, Kentucky, as Trustee under a trust agreement executed between me and the XYZ Bank and Trust Company, Madisonville, Kentucky, on the ___ day of _____, 20__, and in full force and effect on the date of execution of this power of attorney.

 Giving and granting unto my said attorney in fact full power and authority to do and perform any and every act and thing whatsoever requisite and necessary to be done in and about the premises, I hereby ratify and confirm all that my said attorney in fact shall lawfully do or cause to be done by virtue of these present.

 This power of attorney shall not be affected by the disability of the principal, as it is my intent that the authority hereby conferred shall be exercisable notwithstanding my disability or incapacity, and that among all other purposes authorized by this power of attorney that it be utilized upon my disability or incapacity to fund the above referred to trust agreement.

 In the event my attorney in fact is himself disabled, unable to serve, or ceases to act, I appoint _____, _____ (Street), _____ (City), _____ (State), to act as my alternate or successor attorney in fact with the same authority and power granted herein.

IN TESTIMONY WHEREOF, witness my signature on this the _____ day of _____, 20___.

_____
WITNESS

_____
WITNESS

[ADD SELF-PROVING NOTARIZATION AS PROVIDED BY STATE LAW]

I, _____, a Notary Public within and for the state and county aforesaid, do hereby certify that the foregoing Power of Attorney was on this day produced to me in my county by _____, who executed and acknowledged the same before me to be his act and deed in due form of law and by _____ and _____ acting as witnesses.

Given under my hand and notarial seal on this the _____ day, of _____, 20___.

_____
Notary Public, Hopkins County, KY

My Commission Expires: _____

15.12 Living Trust

Much is written about living trusts. Their advantage may be overestimated, but in many cases they are appropriate. The primary advantages of a living trust are privacy, avoidance of probate, and simplifying estate settlement, particularly when the estate consists of numerous stocks, bonds, mutual funds, and other similar investments. The form that follows is a simple living trust designed for estates under the applicable exemption amount. Because some assets will still pass by will, a simple pour-over will should be used. The wills at 15.3 and 15.7 can be used for this purpose. For larger estates—those that require the A-B or disclaimer planning approach because the estate exceeds the combined exclusion amount—the form at 15.3 or 15.4 should be used. By transferring assets into the trust during one's lifetime, the advantages of a living trust are obtained.

LIVING TRUST

THIS TRUST AGREEMENT is entered into by JOHN A. ROE, of Madisonville, Kentucky, as both Settlor and Trustee.

▶ **Comment:** This trust does not make use of marital deduction or portability planning. If the couple's estate approaches the combined federal estate tax exclusion amount, it is more appropriate to use the A-B trust or disclaimer trust approach to lessen federal estate taxes. See the trust at 15.3 and 15.4.

WITNESSETH:

I have delivered or will deliver to the Trustee the property described in Schedule A. Upon receipt of this property, the Trustee agrees to hold it in trust and to manage and dispose of it according to the provisions of this Trust Agreement.

ARTICLE I

A. During my lifetime, the Trustee shall pay to me and my wife, Jane D. Roe, or pay for our benefit, as much of the net income and principal from the trust as I shall request. If I make no request, due to disability or otherwise, the Trustee may distribute to, or for the benefit of, my wife and me such amounts of income and principal as needed for our reasonable health, maintenance, and support. If any net income remains at the end of each trust year, the Trustee shall add it to the principal of the trust.

B. Upon my death, the Trustee shall pay all expenses and indebtedness of my estate, including the expenses of my last illness and funeral, unless other provisions have been made for their payment. Also, the Trustee shall pay any administrative expenses and any estate, inheritance, or other death taxes that are owed by my estate.

C. If my wife, Jane D. Roe, survives me, the trust shall continue and the Trustee shall manage and dispose of the Trust as follows:

1. The Trustee shall pay as much of the net income and principal as necessary to provide for the health, support, and maintenance of my wife, Jane D. Roe. If any net income remains at the end of the trust year, the Trustee shall add it to the principal of the trust.
2. Upon the death of my wife, the Trustee shall pay all expenses and indebtedness of the estate of my wife, including expenses for her last illness and funeral, as well as any administrative expenses and any real estate, inheritance, or other death taxes that are owed by the estate or my wife.

D. After the death of both my wife and me, the trust shall terminate and the Trustee shall divide the trust property into two equal shares, one for the benefit of each of our children, _____ and _____, and distribute each share outright to each child. In the event either of our children should die prior to receiving his or her complete distribution from the trust estate, then the share to which that deceased child would have been entitled had that child been living at the time of distribution shall be distributed outright and per stirpes to the issue of that deceased child. If the deceased child should have no issue surviving at the time of distribution from the trust estate, then that child's share shall be distributed by the Trustee to our other then surviving child, if living, and if not, to that child's issue, per stirpes.

ARTICLE II

I, or any other person, may at any time add property to the principal of the trust with the consent of the Trustee. Any additions to the trust shall be administered according to the provisions of this trust agreement.

ARTICLE III

I grant the Trustee all powers generally conferred upon a Trustee by law. The Trustee shall have the following powers in addition to any other powers given to the Trustee in this trust or by law.

A. The Trustee may keep in the trust any original property received from me, or from any other source, even though the property may not be the type of property prescribed by law for the investment of trust funds.

B. The Trustee may sell, publicly or privately, any property of the trust without a court order and upon such terms as it deems proper.

C. The Trustee may invest and reinvest any part or all of the principal of the trust in stocks, bonds, mortgages, shares in common trust funds, or other securities, as well as any other real or personal property.

D. The Trustee may exercise discretion as to diversification of trust property and shall not be required to reduce any concentrated holdings merely because of such concentration. The Trustee is also relieved from any requirements there may be as to the percentage of the trust to be invested in fixed income securities and may invest wholly in common stocks.

E. The Trustee shall have the full power to sell, exchange, lease, mortgage, repair, and improve and take any prudent steps with regard to any real estate that may be a part of the trust. Any contract on real estate in the trust that is made by the Trustee shall be binding for the full period of the contract if the period extends beyond the termination of the trust.

F. The Trustee shall have the power to vote shares of stock held in the trust, either in person or by proxy, and with or without the power of substitution.

G. The Trustee may participate in the liquidation, reorganization, incorporation, or any other financial readjustment of any corporation or business in which the trust is financially interested.

H. The Trustee shall have full power to borrow money from any source, including the Trustee in the Trustee's individual capacity, for any purpose connected with the trust property and to mortgage or pledge as security any property of the trust upon such conditions as the Trustee deems proper.

I. The Trustee shall have the right to hold any security in bearer form, in the Trustee's own name, or in the name of a duly appointed nominee.

J. Any time the Trustee is required to divide the principal of the trust, the Trustee may make such division in cash, or in kind, or both, and the judgment of the Trustee concerning the proper way to make such a division and to value the property being divided shall be binding on all parties.

K. During the incapacity of any beneficiary to whom income or principal may be spent, the Trustee may pay the income and principal in any one or more of the following ways: (1) to the legal guardian of the beneficiary; (2) to a relative of the beneficiary to be spent by the relative for the support, maintenance, and health care of the beneficiary; and (3) by making payments directly for the support, maintenance, and health care of the beneficiary. The Trustee shall not be required to see to the application of any money paid and the receipt from the person to whom the monies are paid shall be full acquittance to the Trustee.

L. In general, the Trustee shall have the same powers, authorities, and discretions in the management of the trust property as I would have in the management and control of my own property.

ARTICLE IV

If I cease to act as Trustee, or if I am incompetent, then my wife, Jane D. Roe, shall act as Trustee. If my wife fails or ceases to act as Trustee, then my children, _____ and _____, shall act as Co-Trustees. No bond or court reporting shall be required of my Trustees.

ARTICLE V

I declare this Trust Agreement to be revocable and I may alter, amend, or revoke this trust at any time and in any way.

ARTICLE VI

This Trust Agreement shall be construed and regulated by the laws of Kentucky.

IN TESTIMONY WHEREOF, the undersigned have signed their names to this Trust Agreement consisting of this and _____ (___) preceding pages on the _____ day of _____, 20____.

SETTLOR & TRUSTEE:

_____

SUCCESSOR TRUSTEE:

_____

SCHEDULE A

ASSETS	DATE TRANSFERRED
Ten Dollars ($10.00)	January 1, 20___

Index

A

A-B Trust Planning Approach
  acceptance of trust, 224
  audit, 222
  establishing trust funds, 208–9
  identification of beneficiaries, 208
  insurance policies, 209, 220–21
  introduction, 207
  last will and testament, 205–7
  law in, 222
  maximum duration of trust, 217–18
  presumption of survivorship, 222
  right during lifetime to fund trust, 217
  right to amend or revoke, 221
  second marriages and, 204
  spendthrift restriction, 221–22
  technical directions and definitions, 209–11
  Trust A, marital trust, 211–14
  Trust B, residuary, 213–16
  trustee compensation, 221
  trustee powers, 218–20
  trustee removal and resignation, 222–23
A-B trusts, 74–76, 81, 102, 204, 255
"Added-back" gifts, 41
Adjusted gross estate, 38–39, 174
Adjusted income tax basis, 52–53
"Adjusted taxable gift," 40–41
Administrative costs, 38–39, 179, 187
Advisors, 9
Alternate valuation date, 172–73
Alternative minimum tax (AMT), 142
Annual exclusion, 50–51, 229, 235
Annual gift tax exclusion, 49–51, 80, 170, 233
  Crummey v. Commissioner on, 56–57
  minor's or educational trust, 229
Annuities, 33–34, 108, 124, 126
Annuity trusts, 77–78, 126–27, 264
Applicable exclusion amount, 41–42
Appreciated property, 121, 128
Appreciation, 127

income tax basis in gift property and, 51–53
  taxes and, 31, 47, 210
Ascertainable standard limit, 89–90, 191
Asset questionnaire
  bonds in, 11
  business in, 12
  cash equivalents in, 11
  liabilities in, 14
  life insurance in, 13
  mutual funds in, 12
  personal property in, 13
  real estate in, 12
  retirement benefits in, 12
  stocks in, 11
Asset valuation
  background, 159–60
  book-value, 165–66
  buy-sell agreements, 167–68
  capitalization-of-income, 166
  closely held stock, 164–68
  cost method, 160
  discounts, 167
  gross valuation misstatement in, 160
  income approach, 161
  intangible personal property, 163–64
  market data approach, 160–61, 163
  real estate, 160–62
  special-use, 161–62, 174–75
  tangible personal property, 163
Assets, 185, 268
  division of, 245–46
Assignment of income, 49
Attribution rules, 140–42
Audit, 222, 250
Authorization, 21
Average annual after-tax profits, 166

B

B Trust, 75–76, 103
  See also A-B trusts
Beneficiaries, 57, 223, 247
  death of, 229–30
  designation of, 113, 207–8
  distribution to, 214–15

273

Beneficiaries (*Continued*)
  incapacity of, 171–72, 267
  income tax bracket and, 213
  principal and, 216, 219, 230–31, 237, 249, 257–58, 261–62
  as trustees, 190, 192–93, 233
Bequests, 29–30, 68, 205, 225
Billing, 5, 28
Bonds, 11, 55, 164, 177–78
Book-value, 135, 165–66
Borrowing, 239, 248, 257, 261, 267
Business, 12, 168, 249, 268
  trustees and, 220, 240
  See also closely held business
Buy-sell agreements, 202
  asset valuation, 167–68
  attribution rules and, 140–42
  background, 133–34
  Corporate Redemption Agreement, 195–99
  cross-purchase agreements in, 134–37
  income tax basis, 139
  life insurance and, 136–39
  partnerships, 142–43
  redemption and cross-purchase agreements, 134–36
  sales price, 135–36
  specific considerations, 136–43
By-pass. *See* A-B trusts

C

Capital gains, 121, 167
  B Trust and, 76
  principal and, 191
Capitalization rate, 166
Capitalization-of-income, 166
Cash, 120
Cash equivalents, 11
  life insurance and, 37–38
Charge tax to bequest (will form), 68
Charge Tax to Property (trust form), 68–69
Charitable deduction, 54
Charitable giving
  background, 119–20
  cash and ordinary income property, 120
  charitable lead trust (CLT), 129–30
  charitable remainder trusts, 78, 125–30, 264
  estate and gift tax requirements, 120
  future-interest property, 122
  gift annuities, 124
  gift of undivided interest, 125
  income tax and, 120
  IRA distribution, 130
  long-term capital gain property, 121
  pooled income fund, 125
  qualified conservation contributions, 123–24
  remainder interest in farm or personal residence, 123
  special types of, 123–25
  tangible personal property, 121
  tax-exempt organizations, 122–23
Charitable lead trust (CLT), 129–30
Charitable remainder annuity trust (CRAT), 77–78, 126–27, 264
Charitable remainder trusts
  charitable lead trust (CLT) compared to, 129–30
  without income tax, 127–28
  life insurance with, 78, 128–29
  sample form, 264
  splitting of, 125–26
  types of, 126–27
Charitable remainder unitrust (CRUT), 77–78, 126–27, 264
Charitable unitrust trust, 129
Checklist, 5
  See also dispositive checklist
Children, 3, 26, 224
  advances for, 247
  death of, 215–16, 236–37, 246–47
  definitions of, 208, 260
  as executor, 183
  grandchildren, 7–8, 26, 65
  inheritance for, 112
  "kiddie tax," 47, 54–55
  living will and, 270
  net unearned income and, 55
  pot trusts and, 82–83
  principal for, 216, 219, 237–38
  from prior marriage, 102
  qualified terminable interest property (QTIP) trust and, 77
  withdrawal rights of, 234–35
  See also minor children
Client employment additional terms and conditions, 20–21
Clients, 20–21
  dispositive checklist, 24–27
  engagement letters, 3, 15–18
  estate tax worksheet, 23

family questionnaire, 6–10
initial client contact, 1–2
initial conference, 2–4
privacy notice, 22
"Cliff" vesting, 153
Closely held business, 31, 174
   estate taxes deferred payment, 175–76
   retirement plans in, 146
   special-use valuation of, 162
Closely held stock, 164–68
CLT. *See* charitable lead trust
Common-law states, 95–96
   terminable interest rule in, 99–100
Community property states, 95–96
   terminable interest rule in, 99–100
Compensation
   of trustees, 189, 221, 232, 241, 267
   See also fees
Conference. *See* initial conference
Conflicts, potential, 15–16, 18
Conservation easements, 123–24
Constructive ownership, 140
Corporate executors, 183–84, 218
Corporate Redemption Agreement
   amendments and termination, 198
   binding effect, 198
   buy-sell agreements, 195–99
   insurance policies, 197–98
   interpretation, 198
   law in, 198
   manner of payment, 197
   purchase of decedent's stock, 196–97
   purchase price, 197
   restrictions and endorsement in, 198
   sale during lifetime, 196
   sample form, 196–99
   stock in, 196–97
Corporate trustees, 188–90, 192–93
   compensation of, 232
   for irrevocable life insurance trusts, 233
Corporation
   control of, 32–33
   self-employed persons and, 149–50
   "transfer for value" rule and, 109
Cost method, 160
Cost-of-living increases, 41
Court accountings, 262
Court records, probate, 74
CRAT. *See* charitable remainder annuity trust
Creating a Power Limited to Ascertainable Standard (trust form), 90

Credit shelter. *See* A-B trusts
Creditors, 36, 232, 260
Cross-purchase agreements
   in buy-sell agreements, 134–37
   estate taxes in, 137
   income tax basis and, 139, 201
   life insurance and, 200
   redemption agreements compared to, 134, 200
   "transfer for value" rule in, 138–39
   See also stockholder cross-purchase agreement
Crummey trusts, 80, 233–35
Crummey v. Commissioner, 56–57, 80, 113–14
CRUT. *See* charitable remainder unitrust

D

Data, 1, 3
Death benefits, 157
Death tax, 5, 41
Deaths, 5, 41
   of beneficiaries, 229–30
   in buy-sell agreements, 137
   of children, 215–16, 236–37, 246–47
   distributions at, 156–57, 158 n.55
   intestate, 215
   rights after, 245–47
   simultaneous, 98, 206, 227
Deductions, 5, 54
   in taxable estate, 39–40
   See also marital deduction
Deed, 50
Defined benefit plan, 146
Defined contribution plans, 147
Delivery of gift, 49–50
Direct skip, 66–68, 71 n.25
Disabilities, 79, 84, 254–58
Disclaimer trusts, 80–81, 171
   marital deduction planning with, 224–28
Disclaimers, 49, 69, 170–71
Discounts, 167
Discretionary trust, 51, 215, 256
Disinheritance, 10
Dispositive checklist
   children in, 26
   concluding provisions in, 25
   disposition of residue, 24
   executor in, 25
   grandchildren in, 26
   guardian in, 25
   residence in, 24
   specific gifts in, 24

Dispositive checklist (*Continued*)
  tangible personal property, 24
  tax clause in, 25
  trust provisions in, 25–27
  trustees in, 26–27
Distributions, 65, 70 n.15, 191
  to beneficiaries, 214–15
  at death, 156–57, 158 n.55
  in lifetime, 155–56
  minimum, 154–55
Diversification, 171, 231, 239, 248, 257, 261, 266
Dividends, 140–42
  in asset valuation, 163–64
Divorce, 6–7
  irrevocable trusts and, 115
  marital deduction and, 54
  premature distributions and, 154, 158 n.41
  testamentary power of appointment and, 87
Donor, "strings" retention of, 32–33
Double taxation, 69
Drafting, of powers of appointment, 91–92

E

Earned income, 149–50
Education, 4
Educational funds, 54–55
Educational trusts. *See* Minor's or Educational Trust
"Eligible employer," for simple 401(k) plan, 149
Engagement letter for couple
  additional standard terms in, 18
  fees in, 18
  joint representation in, 17–18
  potential conflicts in, 18
  scope of representation in, 17
Engagement letter for individuals
  additional standard terms in, 16
  potential conflicts in, 15–16
  representation scope in, 15
Engagement letters, 3, 15–18
"Entity" attribution, 141–42
Estate
  freeze, 164
  litigation, 171–72
  tax year selection, 178
  termination, 179–80
Estate and gift tax
  provisions, 87–88
  requirements, 120

Estate of Anthony J. Frank, 167
Estate of Ford v. Commissioner, 167
Estate of Joseph H. Lauder, 167
Estate planning, 5
  See also postmortem estate planning
Estate tax overview
  adjusted gross estate, 38–39
  filing and payment, 41–42
  gross estate, 30–38
  introduction to, 29–30
  net estate tax, 40–41
  taxable estate in, 39–40
  Unified Transfer Tax Rate Schedule, 44
Estate tax worksheet, 23
Estate tax(es), 128, 186–87, 210, 227, 233, 265
  adjusted gross estate, 38–39
  alternate valuation date and, 173
  amendments to, 101–2
  in cross-purchase agreements, 137
  death benefits and, 157
  deferred payment, 175–76
  estate litigation and, 172
  exclusions from, 34
  gift tax related to, 29–31
  in postmortem estate planning, 172–76
  power of appointment and, 88–89
  taxable estate, 39–40
  See also gross estate
Excise tax, 29–30
Exclusions, 34, 41–42, 46–49, 236
  annual, 50–51, 229, 235
Executors, 25
  appointment of, 226, 244, 258
  children as, 183
  corporate, 183–84, 218
  duties, 183–87
  fee waiver and, 180
  powers of, 226–27
  surviving spouse as, 184
Expenses, 20, 179
  living will and, 270
  medical, 54, 177
  standby trusts, 265–66
Extensions, of payment, 41–42

F

Facade easement, 123–24
Fair market value, 126, 165
  definition of, 159
  family businesses and, 168

"Family" attribution, 141–42
Family businesses, 168
Family questionnaire
  advisors in, 9
  children/grandchildren in, 7–8
  divorce in, 6–7
  parents in, 9
  premarital or postnuptial agreement in, 6–7
  spouse/partner facts in, 6–7, 9–10
Family trusts. *See* A-B trusts
Farms, 31, 123
  estate taxes deferred payment, 175–76
  payment extensions on, 42
  special-use valuation for, 162
Federal estate tax, 5, 29–30, 187
  standby trusts, 265
Federal estate tax law amendments (1981), 101–2
Federal estate tax return, 40, 139, 174, 210
  alternate valuation date and, 172–73
  direct skip and, 66
  IRS Form 706, 41–42
  marital deduction on, 97
  portability and, 75
  pot trusts and, 67
Fees, 15, 18, 180
Fiduciary income tax, 180
Filing and payment, 41–42
Filing joint returns, 178
Filing limit, estate tax, 210
First-time home buyer, 151
5 or 5 Power of Appointment (trust form), 191
Flat tax, 64
Flexible Trusts and Estates for Uncertain Times, 5th ed. (Horn), 204
Foreign death tax, 41
Foundations, private, 122–23
401(k) plans, 148–49
Full disclosure, 252
Future-interest property, 122

G

General power of appointment, 36, 114, 228
  A-B trust and, 75, 204
  A-B Trust Planning Approach and, 204
  definition of, 87–88
  marital trusts and, 211–12
  in minor's or educational trust, 228–29
  principal and, 190–91
  terminable interest rule and, 101
  trustees and, 37, 190–91
General power of attorney, 264–65
General Utilities doctrine, 167
Generation assignment, 64
Generation-skipping transfer tax, 245
  background, 63–64
  direct skip, 66–67, 71 n.25
  disclaimers, 69, 171
  double taxation, 69
  overview, 64–67
  portability, 69–70
  pot trusts, 67
  skip person, 64
  tax apportionment clauses, 67–69
  taxable distribution, 65, 70 n.15
  taxable termination, 66–67
  transferor, 64–65
Generation-skipping trusts, 81
Gift annuities, 124
Gift tax, 87, 120
  annual exclusion of, 49–51, 56–57, 80, 170, 229, 233
  estate taxes related to, 29–31
  general powers of appointment and, 88
  life insurance and, 32, 38
  limited powers of appointment and, 89
  marital deduction, 103 n.1
  testamentary power of appointment and, 235–36
Gift tax overview
  annual exclusion, 50–51
  background, 46–50
  general requirements, 47–48
  gift-giving advantages, 46–47
  gifts for benefit of children, 54–55
  gift-splitting, 47–48, 51
  income tax basis, 51–53
  special situations, 56–58
  transfers not subject to gift tax, 53–54
Gift tax special considerations
  assignment of income, 49
  delivery of gift, 49–50
  disclaimers, 49
  services in, 48
Gift-giving advantages, 46–47
Gifts, 56
  adjusted income tax basis and, 52–53
  for children, 54–55
  in estate tax worksheet, 23
  gross estate and, 30–32
  income tax bracket and, 47

Gifts (*Continued*)
  indebtedness and, 58
  joint bank account transfer of, 50
  life insurance and, 57, 109–10
  net estate tax and, 40–41
  of services, 48
  undivided interest, 125
Good faith approximations, 252
"Graded" vesting, 153
Grandchildren, 7–8, 26
  as skip persons, 65
Granting Inter Vivos and Testamentary Power of Appointment (trust form), 86–87
Granting Limited Power of Appointment (trust form), 89
Granting Power of Appointment (trust form), 91–92
Grantor, 73
Gross estate, 39, 99, 174
  administrative expenses from, 179
  annuities and retirement benefits, 33–34
  distributions at death and, 156–57
  in estate tax overview, 30–32
  in estate tax worksheet, 23
  general power of appointment and, 36
  gifts and, 30–32
  joint interests, 35–36
  life insurance, 37–38
  powers of appointment, 36–37
  transfers with control retained by decedent, 32–33
Gross valuation misstatement, 160
Group life insurance, 111
Growth stocks, 55
Guardians, 25, 111–12
  for minor children, 206, 242–43

H

Hanging power, 115, 236
Horn, J., 204

I

Incapacity, 245
  of attorney, 268
  of beneficiaries, 171–72, 267
  of trustees, 249–50
Incidents of ownership, 37, 114
Income, sprinkling of, 191–92
Income approach, in asset valuation, 161

Income tax, 60–62, 140, 180
  alternate valuation date and, 173
  buy-sell agreements and, 142–43
  charitable giving and, 120
  charitable remainder trust without, 127–28
  of decedent, 186–87
  distributions during lifetime and, 155–56
  postmortem estate planning and, 177–80
  premature distributions and, 154
  on taxable gain, 35–36
Income tax basis, 201
  appreciation and, 51–53
  in buy-sell agreements, 139
  gift tax overview, 51–53
  loss and, 52
Income tax bracket
  beneficiaries and, 213
  in buy-sell agreements, 137
  gifts and, 47
  income sprinkling and, 191
Income-only trusts, 79–80
  allocations in, 260
  creditors in, 260
  definitions of, 260
  lifetime provisions in, 259
  sample form, 259–64
  special provisions, 260
  trustee powers, 260–62
Indebtedness, 255
  gifts and, 58
Independent counsel, 253
Individual, engagement letter for, 15–16
Individual retirement account (IRA), 130, 150–51, 155
Individual trustees, 189
  life insurance on, 192–93
  powers over principal, 190–91
  powers to sprinkle income, 192
  principal and, 191–92
Inheritance, 10, 255
  for children, 112
  in premarital agreement, 252
  See also trusts
Initial client contact, 1–2
Initial conference
  children related to, 3
  client at, 2–3
  data at, 3

education in, 4
engagement letters and, 3
estate plan formulation after, 5
lawyer at, 3–4
marriage stability and, 2–3
mental capacity at, 3–4
probate process in, 4
secrets at, 2–3
sensitivity at, 2–3
undue influence at, 4
validity at, 3–4
Installment sale, 101
Instructions letter, 28
Insurance, 109, 234, 236
  in A-B Trust Planning Approach, 209, 220–21
  in Corporate Redemption Agreement, 197–98
  See also specific insurance
Intangible personal property, 163–64
Inter vivos trust, 73, 112, 243–44, 264
  powers of appointment and, 86–87
  trustees and, 74
Interest, 46, 122, 125, 167, 197, 211
  in estate taxes deferred payment, 176
  joint, 35–36
  for life, 96–97
  remainder, 123, 175
  in stockholder cross-purchase agreement, 199–201
  terminable interest rule, 99–102
  universal life insurance and, 107
  See also qualified terminable interest property
Internal Revenue Service (IRS), 159, 164, 172–73, 209, 264
  annuities and, 33, 108
  Crummey v. Commissioner and, 80
  disclaimers and, 49
  Form 706, 41–42
  Form 709, Gift-Splitting, 51
  Form 712, Life Insurance Statement, 57
  gifts and, 122
  joint interests, 35
  life insurance and, 38, 107
  Revenue Procedure 64-19, 210
  stock redemption and, 47
  Tax Rate Schedules, Estate and Nongrantor Trusts, 62
  Tax Rate Schedules, Individual Income, 60–61

  taxable estate and, 39
  valuation tables, 34
Interpretation, of powers of appointment, 91–92
Intestate death, 215
Inventories, 185
  book-value and, 165
Investments, 188–89, 206, 218, 223, 239, 248
IRA. *See* individual retirement account
Irrevocable life insurance trust
  benefits for wife and children, 236–38
  ownership, 233–34
  premiums payment, 234
  rights and duties related to insurance policies, 236
  rights in policies of insurance, 234
  sample form, 233–42
  spendthrift restriction, 241
  trustee compensation, 241
  trustee power in, 234, 238–41
  withdrawal right of wife, 238
  withdrawal rights during insured's lifetime, 234–36
  witnesses, 242
Irrevocable life insurance trusts, 113–15, 233
Irrevocable proxy, 135
Irrevocable trusts, 57
  divorce and, 115
  educational trusts as, 232
  See also income-only trusts; irrevocable life insurance trusts
IRS. *See* Internal Revenue Service
IRS Form 706, Estate Tax Return, 41–42
IRS Form 709, Gift-Splitting, 51
IRS Form 712, Life Insurance Statement, 57
IRS Revenue Procedure 64-19, 210

J

Joint bank account transfer, of gifts, 50
Joint holder, in general power of appointment, 88
Joint income tax returns, 178
Joint interests, 35–36
Joint representation, 17–18

K

Key employee, 153
Key-man insurance, 110–11
"Kiddie tax," 47, 54–55

L

Last Will and Testament, 205–7, 214–15
  drafting, 5
  location and Letter of Instructions and, 28
  See also marital deduction planning with disclaimer trust
Last Will and Testament forms
  charge tax to bequest, 68
  donee exercising power of appointment, 92
  donee not exercising power, 92
  executor's discretion on tax decisions, 179
  exonerate bequest from tax, 68
  sample form, 242–44
  simultaneous death clause, 98
  time clause, 100
Law, 101–2, 198, 222, 263
Lawyers, 2–4, 22, 253, 268
Letter of instructions, 28
Liabilities, 5, 14, 186–87, 217
Life insurance, 13, 111, 117, 198–99, 202–3
  of another, 38
  buy-sell agreements and, 136–39
  charitable remainder trust with, 78, 128–29
  cross-purchase agreement and, 200
  gift tax and, 32, 38
  gifts and, 57, 109–10
  gross estate, 37–38
  on individual trustees, 192–93
  marital deduction and, 137–38
  stockholder cross-purchase agreement and, 200, 202–3
  third-party beneficiary of, 57
  trustees and, 207
  trusts and, 192–93
Life insurance planning, 117
  basic types in, 105–7
  benefits received during lifetime in, 108
  benefits received following death in, 108–10
  group insurance in, 111
  irrevocable life insurance trusts in, 113–15
  key-man insurance in, 110–11
  revocable life insurance trusts in, 111–13
  special types in, 110–11
  split-dollar insurance in, 110
  taxation and, 107–10
  term life insurance in, 106
  trusts in, 111–15
  universal life insurance in, 106–7
  variable life insurance in, 107
  whole life insurance in, 106
Life insurance trusts, 192–93, 220
  irrevocable, 113–15, 233–42
  revocable, 111–13
  sample forms, 233–42
Lifetime, 196
  distributions in, 108, 155–56, 234–36, 245, 259
  principal in, 217
Lifetime gift, 29–30
Limited powers of appointment, 88–89
  irrevocable trusts and, 115
  revocable trusts and, 112–13
  of wife, 215
Limiting Individual Trustee's Power Over Distributions for Support (trust form), 191
Limiting Trustee's Power over Insurance (trust form), 193
Liquidation, 165
Liquidity, 238–39
Litigation, estate, 171–72
Living trusts, 81–82
  pour-over will for, 269
  sample form, 269–72
  standby trusts compared to, 84
Living will
  principal and, 270–71
  trustee powers, 271–72
Lump-sum payment, 34

M

Marital deduction, 103 n.1
  A-B trust and, 75
  in A-B Trust Planning Approach, 209–10
  adjusted gross estate and, 38
  administrative costs and, 38
  charitable remainder trust and, 128
  definition of, 95
  divorce and, 54
  life insurance and, 137–38
  living will and, 270
  portability and, 102–3
  under qualified terminable interest property (QTIP), 40

qualified terminable interest property (QTIP) trust and, 76–77
standby trusts, 265
as transfer not subject to gift tax, 53–54
Marital deduction planning
background, 95–96
basic requirements, 96–97
includable in gross estate, 99
marital deduction and portability, 102–3
powers of appointment and, 99
property must pass to survivor, 98–99
qualified terminable interest property (QTIP) and, 97
survived by spouse, 97–98
terminable interest rule, 99–102
testamentary power of appointment and, 96–97
Marital deduction planning with disclaimer trust, 228
bequest to husband, 225
executor and trustee appointment, 226
executor and trustee powers, 226–27
identification of spouse and children, 224
sample form, 224–28
tangible personal property disposition, 225
tax payment, 225
trust for husband's life, 225–26
trustee powers in, 226–27
Marital trusts. *See* A-B trusts
Market data approach, 160–61, 163
Marketability lack, 167
Marriage stability, 2–3
See also divorce
Medicaid, 78–79, 259
Medical expenses, 54, 177
Mental capacity, 3–4
Mini-Mental State Examination (MMSE), 4
Minor children
guardians for, 206, 242–43
principal and, 219
trustees and, 214
Minority interest, 167
Minor's or Educational Trust, 51, 82
annual gift tax exclusion, 229
sample form, 228–33
separation in, 229
settlor as trustee, 230
trustee powers, 230–32

trustee powers in, 230–32
written demand of, 229–30
MMSE. *See* Mini-Mental State Examination
Money-purchase plans, 148
Monthly statements, 20
Multiple of earnings, 135
Mutual funds, 12, 55

N
Net estate tax, 40–41
Net gifts, 56–57
Net income, 211
living will and, 270
residuary Trust B, 213
standby trusts, 265
trustees and, 215
Net unearned income, 55
Nondiscrimination rules, 148–49, 153
Nongeneral power of appointment. *See* limited powers of appointment
Nonpublic personal information, 22
Nontax services, 5

O
Ordinary income property, 120
Outright gift, 103
Ownership, 2, 37, 114, 140
irrevocable life insurance trust, 233–34

P
Parents, 9
Partners, in family, 6–7, 9–10
Partnerships
buy-sell agreements, 142–43
"transfer for value" rule and, 138
Payments, 175–76, 197, 225, 234
extensions of, 41–42
lump-sum, 34
public assistance, 254–57
voluntary, 34, 157
Pecuniary share formula clause, 208–9
Penalty taxes, 154–55
Pension plans, 146–47, 150
Periodic reviews, 28
Personal property, 13
intangible, 163–64
tangible, 24, 121, 163, 225
Personal representative, 205–6, 210–11
Pooled income fund, 125

Portability, 41, 102–3
  A-B trust and, 75–76
  generation-skipping transfer tax, 69–70
  living will and, 270
  standby trusts, 265
Post-engagement services, 21
Postmortem estate planning
  administrative costs, 179
  alternate valuation date, 172–73
  background, 169
  estate taxes deferred payment, 175–76
  estate taxes in, 172–76
  estate termination, 179–80
  estate's tax year selection, 178
  executor's fee waiver, 180
  filing joint returns, 178
  income tax and, 177–80
  medical expenses, 177
  qualified disclaimers, 170–71
  Section 303 stock redemption, 173–74
  Series E and EE U.S. Savings Bonds, 177–78
  special-use valuation, 174–75
  will and estate litigation, 171–72
Postnuptial agreement, 6–7
Pot trusts, 67, 82–83, 246
Pour-over will, 243–44, 264
  for living trusts, 269
Power Limited to Ascertainable Standard (trust form), 191
Power of attorney, 268
  general, 264–65
Powers of appointment
  5 or 5 power, 90–91, 191
  annual exclusion and, 235
  ascertainable standard limit, 89–90
  background, 85–87
  definition of, 85
  effective uses of, 88–91
  estate and gift tax provisions, 87–88
  gross estate, 36–37
  inter vivos trust and, 86–87
  interpretation and drafting, 91–92
  limited, 88–89, 112–13, 115, 215
  marital deduction planning and, 99
  miscellaneous forms, 92–93
  uses of, 85–87
  See also general power of appointment; testamentary power of appointment
Premarital agreement, 6–7, 77, 243, 251–54
Premarital trusts, 77, 251
Premature distributions, 154, 158 n.41

Premiums, 117, 234
  as benefits received during lifetime, 108
  in universal life insurance, 107
Prenuptial agreement. *See* premarital agreement
Present-interest gift, 46
Presumption of survivorship, 222
Principal
  beneficiaries and, 216, 219, 230–31, 237, 249, 257–58, 261–62
  capital gains and, 191
  for children, 216, 219, 237–38
  division of, 240, 249, 257
  general power of appointment and, 190–91
  individual trustees and, 191–92
  in lifetime, 217
  living will and, 270–71
  marital trusts and, 211–14
  minor children and, 219
  securities and, 219
  standards related to, 191
  standby trusts and, 265–66
Prior estates, 41
Prior marriage, children from, 102
Privacy, 74
Privacy notice, 22
Private foundations, 122–23
Probate, 4, 112
  court records, 74
  gift giving and, 46
Profits, average annual after-tax, 166
Profit-sharing plans, 147
Protective election, 176
Public assistance payments, 254–57

Q

QTIP. *See* qualified terminable interest property
Qualified conservation contributions, 123–24
Qualified disclaimers, 170–71
Qualified terminable interest property (QTIP), 39–40
  A-B Trust Planning Approach and, 204
  federal estate tax law amendment (1981) and, 101
  marital deduction planning and, 97
  transferor and, 65
Qualified terminable interest property (QTIP) trusts, 76–77, 211–13

Qualified tuition program, 55
Questionnaire
  asset, 11–14
  family, 6–10

R
Real estate, 12, 205–6, 271
  trustees and, 231, 239
  valuation, 160–62
Reasonable cause, 175
Redemption agreements, 139
  in buy-sell agreements, 134–36
  cross-purchase agreements compared to, 134, 200
  dividend problems with, 140–42
  See also Corporate Redemption Agreement
Remainder interest, 123, 175
Removal of trustee (sample form), 189–90
Renunciation, 170
Representation, 15, 17–18
Residence, 24, 123
Residuary property, 205
Residue, 24, 255
Retire plan types, 146–52
Retirement plans and benefits, 12
  annuities, 33–34, 108, 124, 126
  background, 146
  distributions at death, 156–57, 158 n.55
  distributions during lifetime, 155–56
  401(k) plans, 148–49
  IRA, 130, 150–51, 155
  minimum distributions, 154–55
  money-purchase plans, 148
  nondiscrimination rules, 153
  participation, 152–53
  penalty taxes, 154–55
  pension plans, 146–47
  premature distributions, 154
  profit-sharing plans, 147
  retire plan types, 146–52
  Roth 401(k) plans, 149
  Roth IRA, 151
  self-employed persons, 149–50
  SEP, 150
  SIMPLE IRA, 151–52
  social security integration, 153–54
  top-heavy plans, 153
  vesting, 152
Revocable life insurance trusts, 111–13
  See also A-B Trust Planning Approach
Right of survivorship, 35

Right(s), 217, 234–36, 253
  to amend or revoke, 221, 251
  after death, 245–47
Roth 401(k) plans, 149
Roth IRA, 151
Rule against perpetuities, 216–18

S
Sample forms
  A-B Trust Planning Approach, 204–24
  Charitable Remainder Trusts, 264
  Corporate Redemption Agreement, 195–99
  Income-Only Trust, 259–64
  Irrevocable Life Insurance Trust, 233–42
  Living Trusts, 269–72
  Marital Deduction Planning with Disclaimer Trust, 224–28
  Minor's or Educational Trust, 228–33
  Premarital Agreement, 251–54
  Removal of Trustee, 189–90
  Standby Trusts, 264–69
  State Law and, 195
  Stockholder Cross-Purchase Agreement, 199–203
  will forms, 242–44
Savings clause, 210
Savings Incentive Match Plan for Employees (SIMPLE), 151–52
Second marriages, 102, 242–43
  A-B Trust Planning Approach and, 204
Secrets, 2–3
Section 303 stock redemption, 173–74
Securities, 219
Self-employed persons, 149–50
SEP. *See* simplified employee pension plan
Series E and EE U.S. Savings Bonds, 55, 177–78
Services, 5, 21, 48
SIMPLE. *See* Savings Incentive Match Plan for Employees
SIMPLE IRA, 151–52
Simplified employee pension plan (SEP), 150
Simultaneous deaths, 98, 206, 227
60-month "look-back" period, 259
Skip person, 64–65
  See also generation-skipping transfer tax
Social security integration, 153–54

Special needs trusts, 78–79
   for handicapped child, 258
   public assistance payments and, 254–57
Special-use valuation, 161–62, 174–75
Spendthrift restriction, 221–22, 241, 247, 250
Spendthrift trusts, 83
Split gifts, 47–48, 51
Split-dollar insurance, 110
Splitting, of charitable remainder trusts, 125–26
Spouse, 6–7, 9–10, 184, 224
   distributions during lifetime and, 156
   principal and, 191
   qualified disclaimers and, 171
   survival of, 97–98, 100
   voluntary payments to, 157
   See also widows; wife
Sprinkle income, 191–92
SSI. *See* Supplemental Security Income
Standby trusts
   assets of, 268
   expenses and, 265–66
   federal estate tax, 265
   living trusts compared to, 84
   net income and, 265
   portability, 265
   principal and, 265–66
   sample form, 264–69
   termination of, 266
   trustee compensation and, 267
   trustee powers in, 266–67
State death tax, 5
State law, 100, 195
Statutory rights, 253
Stepped-up income tax basis, 53
Stock, 11, 50, 55, 121, 248, 261, 271
   attribution rules and, 140–42
   closely held, 164–68
   in Corporate Redemption Agreement, 196–97
Stock certificates, 135
Stock redemption, 47, 196–97
   Section 303, 173–74
Stockholder cross-purchase agreement
   buy-sell agreement and, 202
   income tax basis of, 201
   interest in, 199–201
   life insurance and, 200, 202–3
   sales price in, 201
   sample form, 199–203
   termination of, 202–3

   transfer-for-value rule, 200
   valuation in, 199, 201, 203
   withdrawal in, 202
"Strings" retention, of donor, 32–33
Successor personal representative, 205–6
Successor trustees, 188–90, 222–23, 232, 262
Supplemental Security Income (SSI), 78–79
Survivorship, 35, 98–99, 222

T

Tangible personal property, 24, 121, 163, 225
Tax apportionment clauses
   direct skip and, 67–68
   property and, 68–69
Tax clause, 25
Tax services, 5
Taxable distribution, 65, 70 n.15
Taxable estate, 39–40
Taxable gain, 35–36
Taxable termination, 66–67
Taxation, 69
   life insurance planning and, 107–10
Taxes, 154–55, 225
   appreciation and, 31, 47, 210
   ascertainable standard limit power of appointment and, 89–90
   estate tax worksheet, 23
   5 or 5 power, 90–91
   marital trusts and, 212–13
   trustees and, 219
   See also estate tax(es)
Tax-exempt organizations, 122–23
Term life insurance, 37–38, 106, 117
Terminable interest, 100
   marital trusts and, 211
   See also qualified terminable interest property
Terminable interest rule, 99–102
Termination, 20, 66–67, 140, 197–98
   of living will, 270
   in postmortem estate planning, 179–80
   of standby trusts, 266
   of stockholder cross-purchase agreement, 202–3
   of trust, 246–47, 256–57
Testamentary power of appointment, 86
   divorce and, 87
   gift tax exclusion and, 235–36
   marital deduction planning and, 96–97

Testamentary trust, 74, 112
  power of appointment and, 86–87
Third-party beneficiary, 57
Third-party contributors, 34
Three-year rule, 37, 48, 238
  life insurance policy and, 109
Title ownership, 2
Top-heavy retirement plans, 153
"Transfer for value" rule, 108–9, 138–39, 200
Transfer tax, 44, 63–70, 70 n.15, 71 n.25, 171, 245
Transferor
  generation-skipping transfer tax, 64–65
  qualified disclaimers and, 170
  qualified terminable interest property (QTIP) and, 65
Transfers
  with control retained by decedent, 32–33
  not subject to gift tax, 53–54
Trust A, marital trust, 211–14
Trust B, residuary, 213–16
Trust forms
  Charge Tax to Property, 68–69
  Creating a Power Limited to Ascertainable Standard, 90
  5 or 5 Power of Appointment, 191
  Granting Inter Vivos and Testamentary Power of Appointment, 86–87
  Granting Limited Power of Appointment, 89
  Granting Power of Appointment, 91–92
  Limiting Individual Trustee's Power Over Distributions for Support, 191
  Limiting Trustee's Power over Insurance, 193
  Power Limited to Ascertainable Standard, 191
  Widow's Trust Agreement, 245–51
Trust funds, 208–9
Trust provisions, 25–27
Trustee powers, 190–93
  in A-B Trust Planning Approach, 218–20
  in income-only trust, 260–62
  in irrevocable life insurance trust, 234, 238–41
  in living will, 271–72
  in marital deduction planning with disclaimer trust, 226–27
  in minor's or educational trust, 230–32
  in standby trusts, 266–67
  in widow's trust, 248–49
Trustees, 26–27
  appointment of, 226, 262
  beneficiaries as, 190, 192–93, 233
  as beneficiary designation, 207
  business and, 220, 240
  choice of, 187–88
  compensation of, 189, 221, 232, 241, 267
  corporate, 188–90, 192–93, 232–33
  general power of appointment and, 37, 190–91
  incapacity of, 249–50
  incompetency of, 263
  individual, 188–93
  insurance and, 220–21
  inter vivos trust and, 74
  investments by, 188–89, 206, 218, 223, 239, 248
  liability of, 217
  life insurance and, 207
  minor children and, 214
  net income and, 215
  in pot trusts, 83
  real estate and, 231, 239
  removal of, 188–90, 222–23, 250
  resignation of, 190, 222–23, 250, 262
  successor, 188–90, 222–23, 232, 262
  taxable termination and, 66
  taxes and, 219
Trustor, 73
Trusts, 224
  A, 74–77, 103
  A-B, 74–76
  B, 75–76, 103
  background on, 73–74
  charitable remainder, 77–78
  charitable lead trust (CLT), 129–30
  CRAT, 77–78, 126–27, 264
  Crummey, 80, 233–35
  Crummey v. Commissioner and, 56–57, 80, 113–14
  CRUT, 77–78, 126–27, 264
  disclaimer, 80–81
  drafting, 5
  duration of, 217–18, 247
  executors' duties related to, 187
  generation-skipping, 81
  in generation-skipping transfers, 64
  gifts to, 50–51
  income-only, 79–80, 259–64

Trusts (*Continued*)
   inter vivos, 73–74, 86–87, 112, 243–44, 264
   irrevocable, 57, 115, 232
   irrevocable life insurance, 113–15, 233
   life insurance and, 192–93
   life insurance planning and, 111–15
   living, 81–82, 84, 269–72
   pot, 67, 82–83, 246
   premarital, 77, 251
   qualified terminable interest property (QTIP), 76–77, 211–13
   situs of, 222
   skip person and, 65
   special needs, 78–79, 254–58
   spendthrift, 83
   standby, 84, 264–69
   testamentary, 74, 86–87, 112
   unfunded life insurance, 220
   See also A-B Trust Planning Approach; Minor's or Educational Trust
Tuition, 54–55
2503(c) trusts. *See* Minor's or Educational Trust

U

Undivided interest, 30, 125
Unfunded life insurance trust, 220
Unified credit
   A-B trust and, 75
   cost-of-living increases and, 41
   in estate tax worksheet, 23
Unified Transfer Tax Rate Schedule, 44
Uniform premiums for $1,000 of group term life insurance protection, 117
Uniform Simultaneous Death Act, 98
Universal life insurance, 106–7
US Savings Bonds, 55, 177–78

V

Valuation, 159, 172–73
   real estate, 160–62
   special-use, 161–62, 174–75
   in stockholder cross-purchase agreement, 199, 201, 203
   See also asset valuation
Variable life insurance, 107
Vesting, 152–53
Voluntary employer payments, 34

W

Whole life insurance, 106
Widows, 77
   power of appointment in, 86
   special needs trust for handicapped child of, 254–58
   will of, 242–44
Widow's trust
   audit, 250
   maximum duration of trust, 247
   restriction on beneficiaries' rights, 247
   right during lifetime, 245
   right to amend or revoke, 251
   rights after my death, 245–47
   trustee powers in, 248–49
   trustee provision, 249–50
Widow's Trust Agreement (trust form), 245–51
Wife
   benefits for, 236–38
   limited powers of appointment of, 215
   See also A-B Trust Planning Approach
Wills. *See* Last Will and Testament
Withdrawal, 114, 202, 234–36, 238
Witnesses, 207, 228, 242, 244